# A SHORT HISTORY OF ANCIENT ROME

# A SHORT HISTORY OF ANCIENT ROME

## PASCAL HUGHES AND DAN SMITH

HANOVER
SQUARE
PRESS

HANOVER
SQUARE
PRESS™

Recycling programs
for this product may
not exist in your area.

ISBN-13: 978-1-335-00132-0

A Short History of Ancient Rome

First published in Great Britain in 2025 by Bantam, an imprint of Transworld Publishers. This edition published in 2025.

Copyright © 2025 by Pascal Hughes

Map bases by Lovell Johns Ltd.

All rights reserved. No part of this book may be used or reproduced in any manner whatsoever without written permission.

Without limiting the exclusive rights of any author, contributor or the publisher of this publication, any unauthorized use of this publication to train generative artificial intelligence (AI) technologies is expressly prohibited. Harlequin also exercises their rights under Article 4(3) of the Digital Single Market Directive 2019/790 and expressly reserves this publication from the text and data mining exception.

This publication contains opinions and ideas of the author. It is intended for informational and educational purposes only. The reader should seek the services of a competent professional for expert assistance or professional advice. Reference to any organization, publication or website does not constitute or imply an endorsement by the author or the publisher. The author and the publisher specifically disclaim any and all liability arising directly or indirectly from the use or application of any information contained in this publication.

TM and ® are trademarks of Harlequin Enterprises ULC.

Hanover Square Press
22 Adelaide St. West, 41st Floor
Toronto, Ontario M5H 4E3, Canada
HanoverSqPress.com

HarperCollins Publishers
Macken House, 39/40 Mayor Street Upper,
Dublin 1, D01 C9W8, Ireland
www.HarperCollins.com

**Printed in U.S.A.**

# CONTENTS

|  | Map: Rome: City of Seven Hills | viii |
|---|---|---|
|  | Map: The Roman Empire | x |
|  | Preface | xiii |
| 1 | Romulus: The Legend Begins | 1 |
| 2 | Lucretia: Roman Womanhood and the Birth of the Roman Republic | 19 |
| 3 | Appius Claudius Caecus: All Roads Lead from Rome | 37 |
| 4 | Fabius Maximus: First Italy, then the World | 53 |
| 5 | Hannibal: The Adversary | 69 |
| 6 | Sulla: A Crumbling Republic | 89 |
| 7 | Spartacus: The Slave Revolt | 109 |
| 8 | All Hail Caesar!: The Emperor Who Wasn't | 127 |
| 9 | Octavian: Birth of the Empire | 153 |
| 10 | Nero: Lust for Power | 173 |
| 11 | Boudica and the Romans in Britain: The Edge of the World | 193 |
| 12 | Julia Felix: A Time Capsule of Life under the Romans | 213 |
| 13 | Trajan: Good Times in the Pax Romana | 229 |
| 14 | The Colosseum: Spirit and Soul of Rome | 247 |
| 15 | Severus: The Battle for Stability | 261 |
| 16 | Zenobia: Roman Division and Decline | 279 |

| | | |
|---|---|---|
| 17 | Empress Helena: The Rise of Christianity | 297 |
| 18 | Attila: Harbinger of Doom | 311 |

*Postscript: That Which Is Left Behind*   331

*Acknowledgements*   335

# MAPS

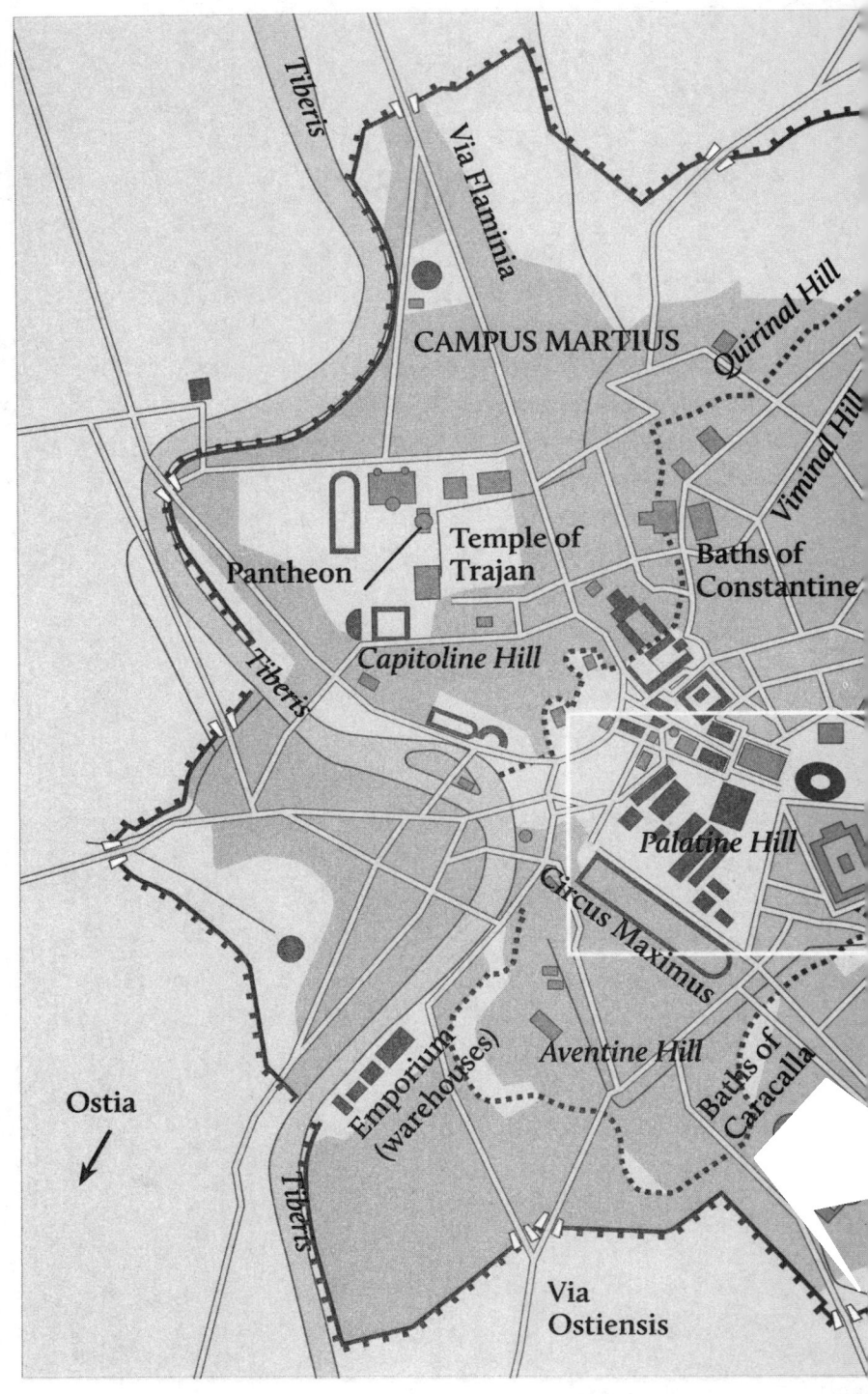

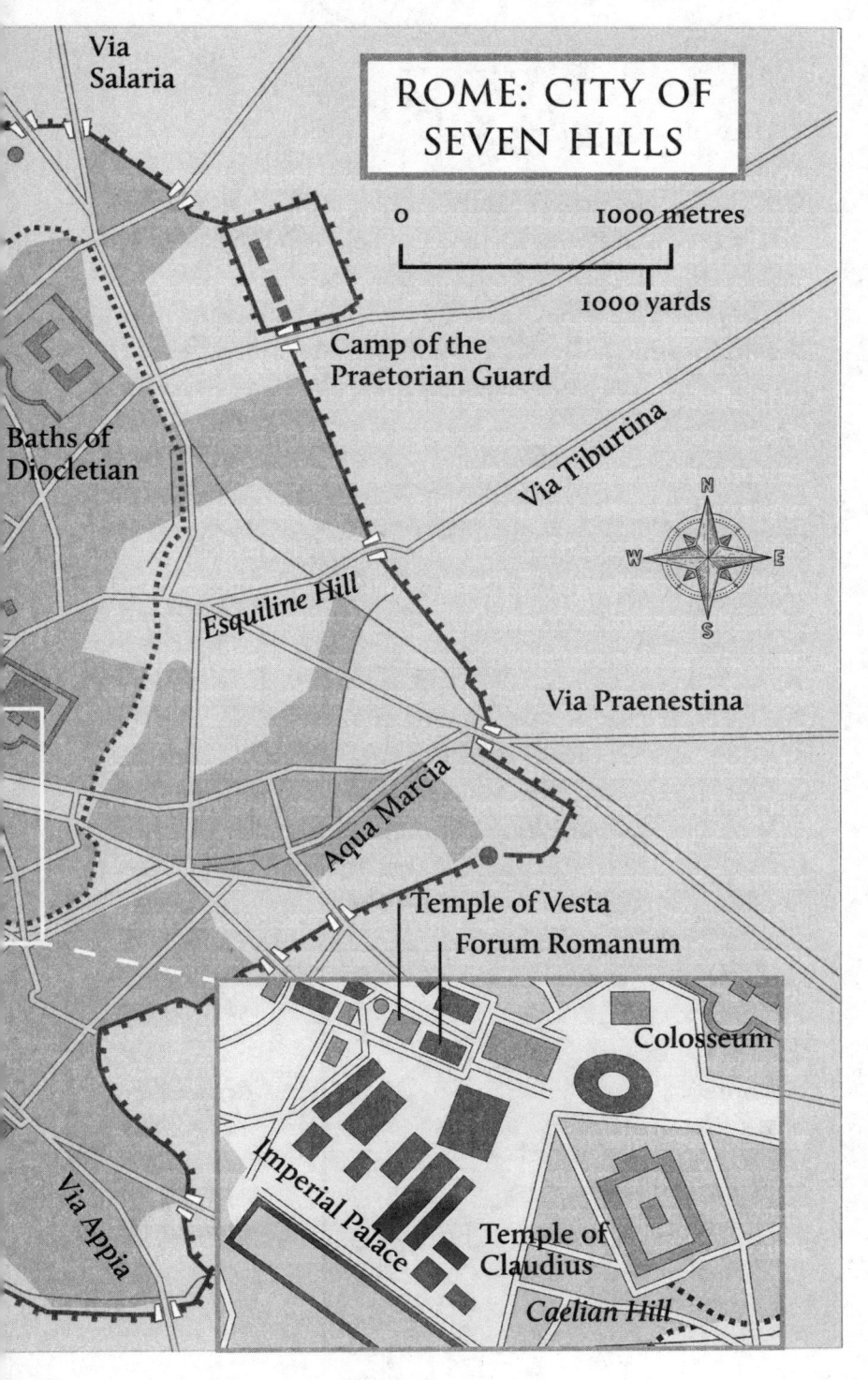

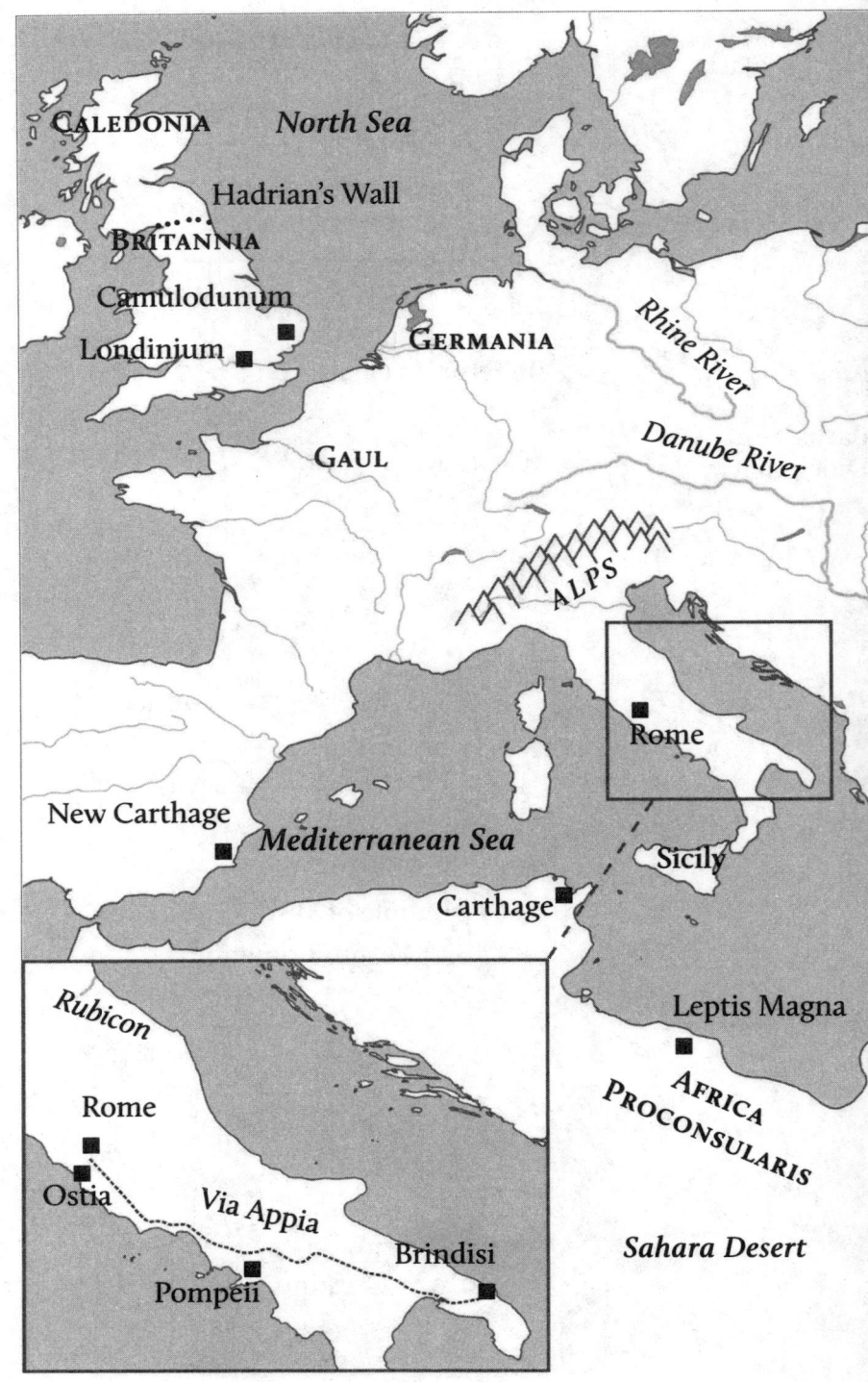

# PREFACE

There is a famous scene in Monty Python's *Life of Brian* in which the question is posed: just what did the Romans ever do for us? Gradually, a long list of that civilization's accomplishments emerges, taking in everything from sanitation and roads to medicine and education . . . but notably not peace!

Beneath the humour lies truth. We in modern times owe so much to the Roman ancients. Virtually every significant aspect of our society traces a path in one way or another back to theirs, which dominated much of the world for a thousand years and more.

In the chapters that follow you will find the story of that civilization, from foundation to collapse. You will be immersed in a world that is both extraordinarily different from but curiously relatable to our own. Building on the blueprint of the Noiser Network's chart-topping *Short History of . . .* podcast, this retelling of Rome's remarkable story will bring its characters and events to life, with dramatized scenes built around the known facts and put into their wider context. I do not claim to cover every twist and turn (if I did, this book would be far too big to pick up), but by focusing on some of the most pivotal and interesting characters and events, I hope to capture the essence of what made Rome so important and why it continues to fascinate us.

But to begin this journey through the history of one of the world's great cultures, we must first enter the realm of myth and legend . . .

# 1
# ROMULUS: THE LEGEND BEGINS

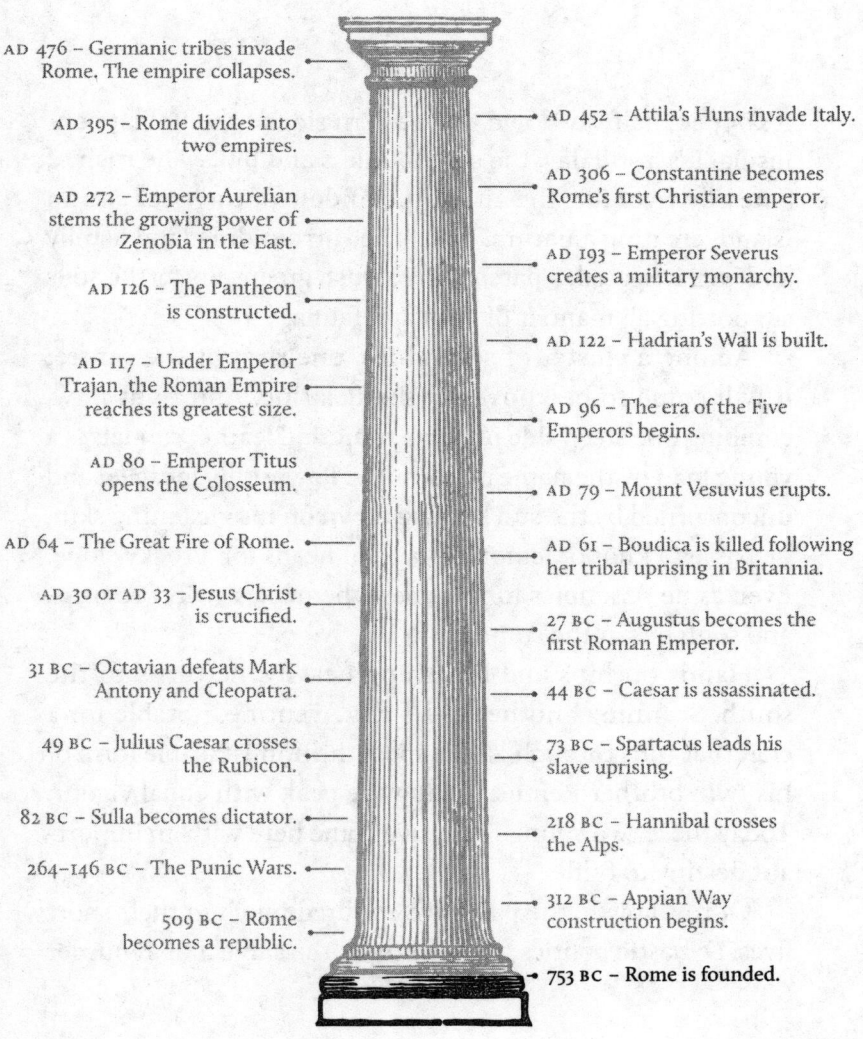

- AD 476 – Germanic tribes invade Rome. The empire collapses.
- AD 452 – Attila's Huns invade Italy.
- AD 395 – Rome divides into two empires.
- AD 306 – Constantine becomes Rome's first Christian emperor.
- AD 272 – Emperor Aurelian stems the growing power of Zenobia in the East.
- AD 193 – Emperor Severus creates a military monarchy.
- AD 126 – The Pantheon is constructed.
- AD 122 – Hadrian's Wall is built.
- AD 117 – Under Emperor Trajan, the Roman Empire reaches its greatest size.
- AD 96 – The era of the Five Emperors begins.
- AD 80 – Emperor Titus opens the Colosseum.
- AD 79 – Mount Vesuvius erupts.
- AD 64 – The Great Fire of Rome.
- AD 61 – Boudica is killed following her tribal uprising in Britannia.
- AD 30 or AD 33 – Jesus Christ is crucified.
- 27 BC – Augustus becomes the first Roman Emperor.
- 31 BC – Octavian defeats Mark Antony and Cleopatra.
- 44 BC – Caesar is assassinated.
- 49 BC – Julius Caesar crosses the Rubicon.
- 73 BC – Spartacus leads his slave uprising.
- 82 BC – Sulla becomes dictator.
- 218 BC – Hannibal crosses the Alps.
- 264–146 BC – The Punic Wars.
- 312 BC – Appian Way construction begins.
- 509 BC – Rome becomes a republic.
- **753 BC – Rome is founded.**

It's 753 BC, halfway down the western side of the Italian peninsula. It's a still day, the sky cloudless and blue. The rush of a nearby river fills the air. In the middle of the river sits an island, creating a natural ford. The surrounding land is hilly and well irrigated, a patchwork of lush greens, its fertile soils supporting all manner of flora and fauna.

Among a cluster of seven hills, one rises at the centre: it will come to be known as the Palatine. And right now, climbing one steep side of it in a tunic and leather sandals is a young man by the name of Romulus. Powerfully muscled and unconcerned by the sun beating down on his glistening skin, he passes a knot of lemon trees then heads for a rocky slope. Even as he scrambles for purchase, he makes swift progress, and soon he's at the summit.

Hands on hips and breathing heavily, he turns to the south. Scanning another hill – the Aventine, notable for a cleft that runs through it – he spots the unmistakable form of his twin brother Remus, scaling the peak with equal vigour. Today these two young men have come here with an important destiny to fulfil.

Of royal birth, the pair have endured much in their short lives. Dynastic politics has seen them the subject of a murder attempt in their childhood, and their claims to power continue to leave them vulnerable. It was around these hills many years ago that they were rescued from almost certain death. Now in early adulthood, they have vowed to found a city here.

Their enterprising plan has, however, driven a wedge between them. Romulus is determined that he should rule the new settlement – but his brother is no less determined. It pains Romulus to be at odds with Remus, having shared many happy times with him and survived so much together. But some things are even more important than blood. Both are fit, healthy and ambitious, and there is no obvious superior candidate. So, they have reached agreement in a bid to bring their feuding to an end. They will leave the decision in the lap of the gods. They have come out here to take the auspices – that is to say, to study the behaviour of the birds in the heavens above in search of omens indicating who will lead the new city.

Romulus now turns his attention to the wide blue sky above him. Squinting against the bright sunlight, he can spot nothing of encouragement; but now comes the sound of enthusiastic shouting from Remus on the Aventine. He can just make out the shape of his brother peering upwards, gesturing to something above him. There, a large, dark bird is gliding on the breeze, great black wings occasionally flapping for uplift. A vulture. Then another, and another, circling above Remus, until there are six in total. Romulus cannot deny that this is a sign of divine will if ever there were one. But now a shadow moves over where Romulus stands on the Palatine too, and he looks up to see birds of his own. Not merely six vultures, but seven, eight, nine . . . he counts a dozen in total. Remus may have distinguished his omen first, but his is only half the magnitude of that of his twin.

A little later, when the sun is going down, Romulus meets with his brother and their bands of followers to discuss the signs. As far as Romulus sees it, it's clear the gods want *him* to take command of the city. But Remus argues back, claiming the kingship as his own and rallying his supporters to his cause. It's unclear who becomes aggressive first, but soon the disagreement turns physical. What begins as jostling among the two factions descends quickly into violence, with punches thrown.

Though the disagreement is far from settled, somehow the brawl is broken up – Romulus, at least, has more important things to do. Soon, he and his men set to work, building walls for the new city that shall be named in his honour: Rome. Remus, though, will not retreat from the confrontation. In a gesture of mockery, he bounds over the walls as they are being constructed. Affronted, Romulus is overcome by a fit of rage. With his supporters in close attendance, he makes for his twin, determined to force him into submission. Amid the ferocious tussle, Remus is struck down and mortally wounded – no one seems to know whether by his brother or one of Romulus's supporters.

Romulus bears down over Remus, a man whose blood he shares and with whom he has overcome so much, but there is sign of neither compassion nor regret. His eyes still ablaze with rage, Romulus addresses his dying brother. Whoever dares scale his city walls, he declares, can expect to perish. Incapacitated, Remus looks back into his twin's furious eyes, takes one final breath, and expires – the very first casualty of the towering pride and ambition of his twin's city.

So, the historians of antiquity will have us believe, begins the story of Rome, destined to become perhaps the most powerful metropolis humanity has yet built. A city that begins with a few walls rising from a hillside, its foundations established on pride and ambition at any cost – even violence, betrayal and fratricide.

## ORIGIN STORY

Tradition has it that Rome was founded in the middle of the eighth century BC, but in truth the historical foundations for such a claim and for the stories about how it emerged are contested and frequently shaky. For the saga of Romulus and Remus and many other details of the city's origin story, we rely on sources written hundreds of years after the events they claim to depict. The most important of these are by the historians Livy and Dionysius of Halicarnassus, who in turn relied in large part on earlier sources that have been lost to time, most notably a history of Rome by the chronicler Quintus Fabius Pictor, who lived in the third century BC, but whose work has survived only in fragments.

These writers left us accounts that were less concerned with the truth of Rome's early days than with telling a powerful story to explain the Rome in which they now lived. Key to the story of Romulus and Remus, for example, is a connection the twins share with the god of war – something that explains and justifies the violence with which the city is founded, but also the enthusiasm with which its later inhabitants pursue territory and power. Romulus's bloody conquest of his own brother lays a foundation for the crucial values of the society in which the historians setting down his story were writing: strength, expansion, domination and personal glory are greater even, in this case, than blood. All history is an act of interpretation, but the chroniclers of Rome's early years gave themselves extravagant room to interpret as they saw fit and embellish wherever they felt it necessary. So, the story of the city's birth and emergence can be understood in the context of mythology as much as history. That is not to devalue the significance of these narratives, but we must recognize them for what they are – windows on how Rome saw itself and wished to project its image into the world.

*But what do we really know about the region where Rome came to be built, in the time before Romulus and after him? According to his own legend, what exactly was his relationship with the gods? And did he ever really exist at all?*

## A CITY ON A HILLSIDE

The story of one of the greatest societies ever to exist on earth begins in a sunny region roughly midway down the boot-shaped Italian peninsula, its toes thrusting out into the Mediterranean. It's a place of well-irrigated plains, flecked with springs and streams and rivers. Drinking water is plentiful and the soil is rich, supporting a varied agriculture. The mighty Tiber river, destined to become famous the world over, is navigable up to the island near where Romulus is said to have built the first city walls, some 15 miles inland. It provides access to the sea, with all the trading and communication advantages that offers. The hilly landscape that supposedly so appealed to Romulus and his brother offers natural defence, whether from armed invaders or the rising waters that result from sporadic flooding. It is as if these undulating slopes were made for the erection of fortresses and, in time, a formidable city.

## THE SEVEN HILLS OF ROME

The Palatine and Aventine Hills are just two of the seven upon which the ancient walled city of Rome eventually sat. Set just to the east of the Tiber river, with the Palatine Hill at their centre, they towered over marshland until the various hitherto distinct communities on each peak came together to drain the land some time around the sixth century BC. The Esquiline was the largest of the hills, originally serving as a burial ground for the new city, while the Capitoline and Palatine were the most politically and religiously important. The other three hills are the Quirinal (historically inhabited by the Sabines, according to legend), the Caelian and the Viminal.

There have been people on the peninsula since the Stone Age, and in the centuries preceding Rome's foundation a complex web of different settled groups inhabits its expanse. Some of the most sophisticated settlements belong to the Etruscans, whose region, Etruria, comes to cover a large expanse north and south of Rome itself. Greek settlers have established impressive urban colonies of their own, such as Neapolis and Taras – coastal metropoles in the south of the peninsula. There are a great many more tribal peoples spread across the land in smaller settlements, including the Latins, prevalent in the area around what will become Rome. Graves here provide macabre evidence of human habitation in the immediate vicinity from at least 1000 BC, with pottery shards indicating human presence dating back perhaps as much as 500 years earlier. Nonetheless, it is not until the eighth century BC – around the time of the legendary Romulus – that there are signs of more concentrated, permanent settlement.

## DIVINE BEGINNINGS

Even as the archaeological record approximately coincides with the account of Romulus's foundation of the city, there is little in the way of evidence to confirm the origin stories presented by Quintus Fabius Pictor, Livy and others. But these foundation myths are the ones that Rome's civilization preserved, the proud tales they chose to base their identity upon and use to justify their position in the world. Stories, then, that we need to hear if we're to understand the progress of the Roman state over the following thousand years.

The city's origins, according to its later historians, can be traced all the way back to a Trojan prince by the name of Aeneas. Many generations before the days of Romulus and Remus, he escapes his burning city and sails to what is now Italy. Eventually integrating with the locals, he founds a city some miles from what will one day be the site of Rome. Power is passed down until eventually one of the ancient prince's descendants, Amulius, overthrows his brother Numitor.

But after Numitor's daughter Rhea Silvia is raped by the god Mars, she gives birth to twin boys, Romulus and Remus. Recognizing them as rivals for his crown, King Amulius has the boys cast into the flowing Tiber, where they are destined – he is sure – to meet a grisly end.

For Rome's later citizens brought up on the stories of Romulus and Remus, this lineage proves a clear pathway back to the gods. Mars, as the god of war and father of the twins, roots the state in a rich divine military heritage, while further back Aeneas is said to have been born of the goddess Venus. With such pedigree, no wonder Romans would come to consider themselves a cut above the mere mortals that inhabited the earth beside them.

## THE BROTHERHOOD

Fate conspires so that Romulus and Remus do not drown as their great-uncle hopes. Instead, as the Tiber's floodwaters subside, the basket in which they have been placed washes up on the slopes of the Capitoline Hill. Still, not far away, apparent danger looms for the two infants unable to fend for themselves. A female wolf is on the prowl, having come down from the mountains in search of food and water. Her ears prick up at the noise of the babies crying. Following the sound, she steals closer, until at last she sees the pair, lying in the basket, vulnerable and helpless.

She approaches stealthily, her paws padding across the soft earth, until she is within striking distance. But she does not launch an attack. Instead, she lays herself down and offers them her mother's milk. The boys eagerly drink. Before long a herdsman, a man named Faustulus, comes across the scene; he finds the she-wolf gently licking the heads of the twins as she suckles them. When she has finished, he scoops up the children and takes them to his homestead, presenting them to his wife, Larentia, to raise them.

Initially unaware that these are the lost grandsons of King Amulius's deposed brother, the couple care for the twins. They grow into youthhood, spending their days chasing round the forests and hunting. They are fine physical specimens and full of spirit too – so much so that their adoptive parents begin to wonder whether there might be something divine about them. When they tire of tracking animals, they go after robbers instead, stalking them and taking their booty, which they share out with the community of shepherds among whom the boys feel so at home. That is until one February day during Lupercalia, a festival of health and fertility. A posse of their bandit-victims has tracked the brothers down, intent on revenge. They lie in wait for Romulus and Remus, preparing their ambush. When they strike, the twins fight back. Romulus is able to escape capture, but Remus is not so lucky. He is taken by the bandits to King Amulius, and accused of raiding the lands of Amulius's brother, the deposed former king, Numitor. Amulius hands Remus over to Numitor for suitable punishment.

Back at his homestead, Faustulus has by now pieced together the truth of his adoptive sons' identities. He reveals to Romulus his belief that the twins are in fact princes. When Numitor learns that his prisoner has a twin, and then when he considers their age and Remus's disposition – entirely devoid of the subservience one might expect from a shepherd's son in the presence of royalty – he too concludes that the youths are likely the grandchildren he had long believed were lost to him. A plan is hatched in which Romulus and a small platoon of his young shepherd friends coordinate an attack on the palace of Amulius, supported by Remus and reinforcements sent by Numitor. Amulius is slain and the crown returned to Numitor. Now celebrated as princes, Romulus and Remus dream up their plan to build a city of their own, precisely on the spot where the she-wolf and the herdsman had come to their rescue.

## THE BIRTH OF ROME

Their fraternal unity is, however, shattered in the face of personal ambition. When the contest of the auguries fails to deliver a clear victor, Romulus resorts to the savagery that sees his brother killed. Romulus rules alone in the city named in his honour. The lesson to the generations of Romans that follow is clear: in the pursuit of personal glory, no sacrifice is too great.

Having made offerings to the god Hercules, Romulus sets about completing the fortification of the Palatine Hill and then commissions building on plots beyond it, anticipating the growth of the city. He also sets out a series of laws for his people to follow, while developing his own regal image so that his citizens – still relatively few in number – might better accept his authority. He clothes himself in finery and appoints twelve lictors, officials whose job is to attend him personally.

But it's no good reigning over a great city if there is nobody there to rule, so next he attends to building a population. He invites refugees from neighbouring tribal groups to settle there, regardless of their social status. Word spreads about the fledgling city, including the fact that it offers asylum to fugitives and bandits, and soon Rome's population swells with those dissatisfied with their prospects elsewhere. In this way, Romulus sets an early precedent for expansion by assimilation – something that will come to define the republic (and, latterly, empire) that will soon radiate from his city.

For the purposes of military service and taxation, he divides the population into three tribes, each administered by an official called a tribune. Each tribe is further subdivided into ten smaller groups called *curiae*, overseen by a *curio*. He demands that every *curia* provides ten cavalry and a hundred foot soldiers (the commander of such a 'century' coming to be known as a centurion). He also establishes a council made up of a hundred senators, drawn from among the most prominent families, to help keep order and provide him with advice.

As the years pass and the city establishes itself under Romulus's rule, Rome comes to surpass many of its tribal neighbours in both military prowess and prestige. It even becomes a serious rival to those old antagonists of his predecessors the Etruscans, and other powerful groups, like the ancient local warrior tribe the Sabines. In the battle for expansion across the Italian peninsula, Rome is holding its own. But Romulus recognizes that a society made up mostly of men, however militarily adept, will get his state only so far. If his city is to thrive for more than a generation, he needs to find women to marry his soldiers and birth their children. And fast.

## THE RAPE OF THE SABINE WOMEN

It's a few years after the founding of Rome, and a black-haired Sabine in his late teens is taking a moment to rest in the shade of an olive grove. As well as his father, he is travelling with his mother and younger sister among a large contingent of his fellow tribespeople. He is weary from the journey they have made from their territory amid the Apennine Mountains many miles east of Rome, but he is keen to see the new city he has heard so much about. It's still a little way away, but even from here he can see the impressive stone buildings, bright and new in the glorious afternoon sunlight. Springing from the hillsides, they are bigger and more imposing than anything they have at home. He catches his father eyeing the scene with admiration too, but knows the older man would never acknowledge the neighbouring territory's achievements. The rivalry between their peoples is too strong for that.

The rest over, the Sabine group now get to their feet, wrapping up the remains of the bread and stowing away leather water pouches in their horses' saddles. Soon they're on the move again, the boy rushing ahead at the front, struggling to keep a lid on his excitement. Because Romulus has invited them and several other groups from the local regions for what promises to be a spectacular new games, all in honour of Neptunus Equester, patron god of chariot racing. Though the boy's father has his suspicions about Romulus's motive, most of the tribespeople think it's just a bid to raise his own prestige. And in any case, the gesture has been well received. Aside from the large crowd of Sabines, the teen can see a mass of people from other tribes descending on the city from all directions.

Over several hours this throng of humanity gathers at the location of the games. Many of the men arriving have come fresh from the battlefield, their bandaged wounds still healing, but few are willing to miss this chance to exercise rivalries in a joyful way, removed from the grit and gore of endless fighting. The boy can hardly wait for the signal that the festivities have begun.

Soon enough he hears a commotion growing around him. This must be it, he thinks. But there is none of the ceremony he has been expecting. Instead, only confusion, then panic – voices are raised, and everyone starts running. Looking up, the boy realizes why. Streaming down from Rome's hills comes a small army of local youths, not much older than himself, with weapons drawn. They set upon the Sabine men, and though his father tries to drag him away, the teen fights back. He throws his fists wildly in the melee, until he feels a hard thump to the back of his head. His knees buckle beneath him and he falls. Dazed on the dusty ground, he looks up to see his father being held by two Roman lads as another picks up his frantic sister and carries her away. She is, he realizes, just one of dozens of the invited young women to suffer this fate.

As suddenly as it began, the raid finishes. The Sabines left behind – grieving parents, brothers and husbands seething with a mixture of shock, heartbreak and incandescent rage – can hardly fathom the deception perpetrated upon them. They came as visitors in good faith, but leave as witnesses to an organized mass kidnapping, unwitting suppliers of brides for Rome's young men. Nor are the maidens who have been seized any less indignant. Yet Romulus tells them the blame lies squarely with their own Sabine guardians, whom he says have rejected the Romans' previously polite suggestions of intermarriage. He begins to appease some of the young women by granting them Roman citizenship and all the rights that brings forth. But among the various peoples of the central Italian peninsula his actions are regarded with fear and abhorrence. Envoys travel to the palace of the Sabine king, Titus Tatius, and plans are made for an attack on Rome.

Romulus relies on his army's strength to repel the enemy on the battlefield, and in celebration of victory he consecrates a temple to Jupiter, the first such building in Rome. Nonetheless, the Sabines remain a force to be reckoned with and make further advances on the city, briefly seizing the citadel. The Roman army takes up a position in the valley between the Palatine and Capitoline Hills, poised for a defining battle.

To the kidnapped young women, this seems the worst of all worlds. By now time has passed and many of the women, willingly or otherwise, have become wives to Roman husbands and mothers to Roman children. If the Sabines win, these new brides of Rome will lose their families. If the Romans win, it will be their fathers and brothers who perish. So, with no consideration for their welfare, they race to where the men are fighting, throwing themselves between the warring parties, weapons flying around them. They plead for an end to the fighting, arguing it would be better that they themselves perish rather than be forced to live either as widows or orphans. An eerie silence falls across the battlefield as the combatants, commoners and leaders alike consider their words. The first tentative steps are made towards not only a peace but a treaty that unites the two powers under Roman sovereignty, with Romulus ruling alongside Titus Tatius. Not for the first time, nor for the last, Rome consolidates its position through a wily mixture of brutality, military heft and peaceable assimilation.

## THE END OF ROMULUS

Romulus and Tatius rule in harmony for a time, until Tatius is slain while away from the city by enemies of his family. Romulus continues to enjoy military success, notably defeating the rival cities of Fidenae and Etruscan-ruled Veii, although the Etruscans remain a formidable opponent to Roman ambitions. Nonetheless, there is also cultural crossover between the two peoples, with the Romans for instance adopting the traditionally Etruscan toga and their love of gladiatorial battle.

Then, in 716 BC, while Romulus is inspecting his troops, the sky turns suddenly grey. A thunderstorm brings in a dense cloud that wraps itself around the king, shielding him from the view of those on the ground. The legendary father of Rome is never seen again. At least this is the story as Livy tells it, although he concedes that it's also possible Romulus has been murdered by a gang of disgruntled senators – a pattern, if true, that will be played out many times in Rome's future.

Whatever the facts surrounding his death, Romulus is succeeded by a Sabine, Numa Pompilius, who develops the city's religious and political institutions, as well as growing a cult around his predecessor. Among the citizenry, it comes to be accepted that Romulus has been raised into heaven by Mars himself – further evidence of the city's military credentials and confirmation of its right to continue its expansion.

So ends the earthly story of Romulus, the purported founder of one of the great powers in history. But apart from the tales set down by Livy and his contemporaries, there's precious little to say that he truly existed. Even so, interest in him is reignited almost three millennia later, in 2020, when a sixth-century BC tomb is discovered in an ancient Roman temple claimed by some to be linked to Romulus. Although the discovery prompts academic debate, the veracity of his story remains a mystery that is unlikely ever to be decisively solved.

Nonetheless, the legend of Rome's creation tells us much about its view of itself: why it believed in its divine right to conquer and colonize, how it came to grow a martial tradition, and how it looked to state-build through a combination of military force and political nous. These are all traits that have been shared by other expansionist political entities across history. Yet there is something distinctly Roman in the celebration of Romulus, a man who kills his own brother. It not only establishes Rome's potential for political violence and assassination, but, perhaps even more fundamentally, it leaves no doubt that the state always comes first, even above family loyalty. For Rome's ancient chroniclers, it mattered less if their story of the city's foundation was fundamentally true than that they produced a tale that could be read as the blueprint upon which the future glory of Rome was built.

# 2

# LUCRETIA: ROMAN WOMANHOOD AND THE BIRTH OF THE ROMAN REPUBLIC

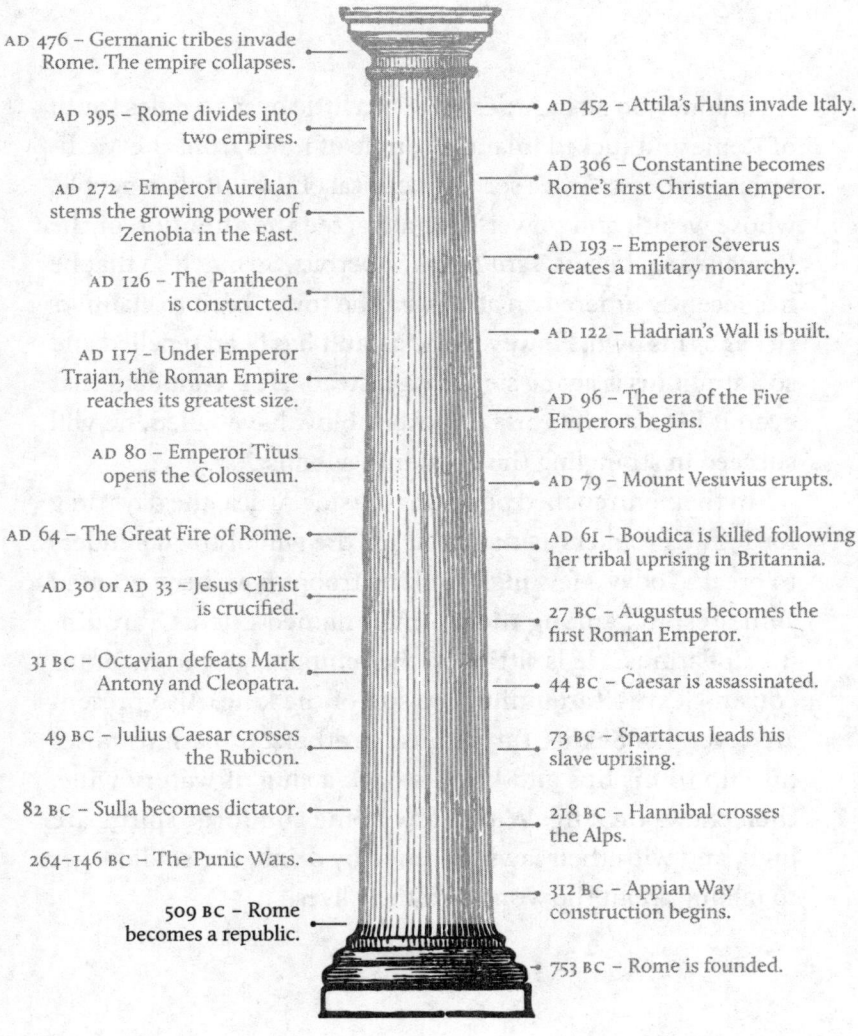

AD 476 – Germanic tribes invade Rome. The empire collapses.

AD 452 – Attila's Huns invade Italy.

AD 395 – Rome divides into two empires.

AD 306 – Constantine becomes Rome's first Christian emperor.

AD 272 – Emperor Aurelian stems the growing power of Zenobia in the East.

AD 193 – Emperor Severus creates a military monarchy.

AD 126 – The Pantheon is constructed.

AD 122 – Hadrian's Wall is built.

AD 117 – Under Emperor Trajan, the Roman Empire reaches its greatest size.

AD 96 – The era of the Five Emperors begins.

AD 80 – Emperor Titus opens the Colosseum.

AD 79 – Mount Vesuvius erupts.

AD 64 – The Great Fire of Rome.

AD 61 – Boudica is killed following her tribal uprising in Britannia.

AD 30 or AD 33 – Jesus Christ is crucified.

27 BC – Augustus becomes the first Roman Emperor.

31 BC – Octavian defeats Mark Antony and Cleopatra.

44 BC – Caesar is assassinated.

49 BC – Julius Caesar crosses the Rubicon.

73 BC – Spartacus leads his slave uprising.

82 BC – Sulla becomes dictator.

218 BC – Hannibal crosses the Alps.

264–146 BC – The Punic Wars.

312 BC – Appian Way construction begins.

509 BC – Rome becomes a republic.

753 BC – Rome is founded.

It's around 509 BC in Ardea, a town a little over 20 miles south of Rome and tucked inland a couple of miles from the Mediterranean coast. Ardea serves as capital of the Rutulian people, whose wealth and power have attracted the attention of the Roman king, Lucius Tarquinius Superbus. So much so that he has recently ordered an attack on the town, keen to claim its riches as his own. However, the assault has been repelled and so Tarquinius is laying siege to it instead. He is confident that even if his attempts at a knockout blow have failed, he will succeed in strangling the town into submission.

In their entrenched positions outside Ardea, the days drag for Rome's soldiers as they wait for the will of the defenders to break. Today a few high-ranking troops have been granted some respite, among them a man named Lucius Tarquinius Collatinus. He is sitting in the temporary quarters of his cousin, Sextus Tarquinius, the son of the king. Also present are several of Sextus Tarquinius's brothers. Collatinus raises his cup to his lips and knocks back a slug of watery wine, then chews on a fig. With a few home comforts, spirits are high, and with their jaws loosened by drink, the soldiers get to talking about the women in their lives.

Collatinus listens to the princes waxing lyrical about their wives in turn. Their chat has quickly become a competition to decide who has married best, but he tires of their bragging. There is no need to trade in boasts, he says. Why don't they prepare their horses and ride back to Rome? Then, taking their spouses off guard, they'll be able to see what their wives get up to in their absence. That way, they'll see for themselves whose wife is most virtuous.

The men enthusiastically agree to his proposal and get to their feet. Throwing open the entrance to the tent, they stride outside into the busy camp, untether their horses and race across the verdant landscape for Rome.

It is dusk by the time they arrive, their horses glistening with perspiration, and the princes go in search of their wives. The first few homes they check are empty, but then, just as the men are beginning to worry, they approach the terrace of one villa and hear a sound that makes them frown. Gathered together at a long table are nearly all of their wives, surrounded by young friends, enjoying what appears to be a banquet. The odour of freshly prepared food drifts over on the breeze as the princes creep closer, hiding behind pillars and bushes and glancing at one another, unsure how to react. This is not the display of restrained duty they have been hoping for, nor evidence of their women struggling on as best they can while their husbands are away in the field. Instead, their animated chatter and sporadic gales of laughter serve as proof that they are rather enjoying themselves.

Collatinus's face is drawn in an expression somewhere between sympathy and smugness. He has high hopes for his own wife, Lucretia, who – he quietly thanks the gods – is not with the other women. He leads the princes off to Collatia, his hometown a few miles north-east, where they bring their horses to a halt still some distance from his villa. Lamplight gently illuminates the scene at this late hour. Collatinus makes out the silhouette of his beloved Lucretia in the atrium, the main room of their home. Keeping his distance at a window, with the other men crowded quietly behind him, he smiles as she turns her face into the light of a lamp, her widely acknowledged beauty evident even from afar. Servants bustle purposefully about her but she is a beacon of calm, huddled over a pile of wool that she is deftly sewing with a bone needle – a study in self-controlled industry. Even in an unguarded moment she is the epitome of the ideal Roman wife – working at home for the good of her family, engaged in, to the Roman mind, that most elevated and admirably modest of female occupations, needlework.

Collatinus need hardly say anything to his companions. In this contest of the wives, there is no doubt who has emerged victorious. He looks on, his heart bulging with pride.

As they walk away, the other princes ruefully pat Collatinus on the back in congratulation, before readying their horses for the ride back to camp. But at the side of the group, one man lingers unnoticed by the window much longer than decency allows. Sextus Tarquinius, the son of the king, remains behind a pillar, his fingers gripping the stone, unable to take his eyes off Lucretia, this peerless embodiment of Roman femininity. His is a base lust fuelled not only by physical attraction but Lucretia's chaste goodness. A lust that will change the path of Rome for ever.

## HISTORY AND MYTH

The history of ancient Rome is dominated by the stories of men, both great and wretched. It is a civilization patriarchal in nature, and documented almost exclusively by men. Save for a few exceptions, where women do appear they are little more than footnotes. Lucretia, however, is one of these exceptions. A woman at once crucial to the historical development of Rome, sparking the transition from monarchy to republic, but also emblematic of what it means to be Roman, and specifically how Rome believes its women should be. An agent of change and a symbol of Roman self-image.

But with the notions of legend playing a vital role in this story, arguably the single most important female figure in early ancient Roman history is still shrouded in mystery. It seems likely that an historical figure by the name of Lucretia did exist but there are no contemporary records to rely upon. Instead, just as with the tales concerning Rome's beginnings, we are left only with sources written later by the likes of Livy and Dionysius of Halicarnassus, who are less concerned with documenting factual truth than mythologizing the image of Rome and its noble values.

*While it is impossible to be certain of the veracity of the events described by these authors, the story of Lucretia has nonetheless been passed down to explain Rome's early political evolution. Even if the accounts involve fabrication and elaboration, they have intrinsic worth for the many insights they provide into the Roman psyche. So, how did this noblewoman and paragon of domestic virtue become the subject of Roman legend? How did the unchecked lust of a prince lead to the collapse of an entire power structure? And what does her legend tell us about the values of the republic that followed?*

## ROME'S MONARCHY

The Rome inhabited by the fabled Lucretia has, according to the accepted narrative, been a monarchy since its founding by Romulus in around 753 BC. In the near two and a half centuries since, there have been just six more kings, including the current incumbent, Lucius Tarquinius Superbus – Tarquin 'the Proud' – who has reigned since 534 BC. Each king before him has held the crown for between twenty-four and forty-four years, which might suggest this has been a period of significant stability. After all, the king has virtually absolute power, his Senate little more than a council to do his bidding. However, the crown is not simply passed from father to son. Instead, a new monarch must be elected by the Curiate Assembly, a body representing the thirty *curiae*, themselves subdivisions of the three tribes of Rome said to have been established by Romulus. The Curiate Assembly is dominated by representatives of the patrician class (made up of long-established families) and gets to choose who will reign. Though in theory the system democratizes the decision to an extent, in practice it also breeds political intrigue.

Romulus's successor, Numa Pompilius, enjoyed a long tenure in which he cultivated many of the institutions that came to define early Rome, including its calendar and its priesthood of Vestal Virgins. Though Pompilius is said to have died of old age after a forty-three-year reign, those who came after him often met more dramatic ends. His immediate successor, the bellicose Tullus Hostilius, was either murdered or died from plague or being struck by lightning, depending on your source.

Years pass, and the city expands. Its civic and religious development sees it rapidly emerge as a leading civilization. Rome gradually dominates over its Latin, Sabine and Etruscan neighbours but also focuses on its own architectural grandeur, building the great sporting arena the Circus Maximus, city walls and temples, as well as a pioneering sewage system. Over time, greater rights are also granted to its commoner citizens, the plebeians.

But as each king comes and goes, he lives in increasingly elevated, rarefied seclusion, often making decisions unilaterally, and the threat of assassination is never far away. When Lucius Tarquinius Superbus takes the throne, he's on shaky ground right from the start thanks to the bloodthirsty nature of his ascent to power: he's only in the top spot thanks to being responsible for the assassination of his father-in-law – an assault that is said to have concluded with his wife, Tullia, running over her own father's body in a carriage. Once in power, the couple forge a reputation for the ruthless treatment of their enemies, killing political rivals suspected of maintaining loyalty to the previous king and refusing to consult with the Senate on political and legal matters.

The final straw comes in the form of a personal tragedy that is now unfolding as a result of Lucretia's triumph in the 'contest of the wives'. Soon, Superbus and the Tarquinius family from which he hails will become so unpopular that the people of Rome have had enough not just of his dynasty but of the concept of monarchy altogether.

## THE RAPE OF LUCRETIA

It is a few days after the contest, and Collatinus and his comrades are back in camp. Lucretia is at home in Collatia, busying herself with domestic duties once more. With night drawing in, a slave interrupts her as she spins more yarn. Two gentlemen have just arrived on horses, the slave tells her. And they're not just any guests: it is the king's son, Lucretia's husband's cousin Sextus Tarquinius, and one of his attendants. Frowning, Lucretia puts away her work and requests that dinner is prepared for the unexpected guests. As the slave hurries off, she readies herself to welcome them.

She does not quite know what to make of the prince's arrival while her husband is absent, and though she keeps her feelings well concealed beneath a thick layer of practised politeness, she doesn't much care for the way he looks at her either. By the time they have eaten supper, it is thick with darkness outside. Lucretia calls her servants and arranges for the guest bedrooms to be readied. Then she excuses herself and heads to her own bed. Her eyelids heavy from the day's toils, she drifts off to sleep. Around her, the villa is quiet, its occupants at rest. All is peaceful.

Peaceful, at least, save for delicate footsteps on the tiled corridor outside her room, too quiet for her to hear. But then her eyes are wide open as she is shocked from her slumber by a weight on her chest. In the confusion of her instant wakefulness, she makes out the figure of Sextus Tarquinius looming over her, his left hand pressing her down. In his right hand, his sword is drawn. She opens her mouth to scream but Tarquinius is ahead of her. Utter a sound, he tells her, and she will die. She stares into his face, etched with a mix of controlled violence and uncontrollable lust. Having just coolly threatened her life, she listens now as he proclaims his love, pleads with her to submit to him, then threatens her again. But she refuses to cede. If death is her only alternative, then rather that, she tells him.

The prince, however, is not to be deterred. Her heart thumping, Lucretia receives a terrible ultimatum. If she chooses death rather than submission, he will ensure her disgrace regardless. He will arrange the scene so that whoever discovers her corpse will find the body of a naked slave beside her; it will appear that the pair were engaged in an affair. Her husband and family will be forced to deal not just with the tragic loss of her life but with the deep shame that comes with adultery according to Rome's moral codebook.

With whatever meagre agency she thought she may have had in this awful situation now stolen from her, she recognizes that fighting back is futile.

So it is that Lucretia is raped by Sextus Tarquinius.

## REVELATION

It's the following morning, and Lucretia is sitting in her room, staring at her bed. Her attacker left some time ago, unapologetic and jubilant. Her body aches as she thinks her way through what to do next. Summoning a slave, she gives instructions that a messenger be sent to find her husband and father. Each is to be told to find a trusted friend and come straight to the villa.

Time drags as she awaits their arrival and a sadness like grief overtakes her. At last, her father comes with a friend, followed by Collatinus, who is accompanied by a man named

Lucius Junius Brutus. Even before they are all seated, tears start to roll down Lucretia's cheeks. Her husband asks if all is well, as if he does not already know the answer. As calmly as she can, she lays out the details of the crime committed against her. There is the print of a strange man in his marital bed, she tells Collatinus. Her honour has been ripped from her, she explains, even though she is guiltless.

When she has finished recounting her attack, she asks the four men to make a pledge: to ensure that her attacker does not go unpunished. Each in turn takes the oath, while also attempting to reassure her that the sin is entirely that of Sextus Tarquinius. Though such behaviour from any man is reprehensible, it's that much worse that Sextus is a prince, and this act of grotesque entitlement is just another demonstration of the sneering disregard in which the royal family seem to hold their subjects. With their promise, the men tell her, they will show the Tarquinius clan that there is a limit to their loyalty.

Lucretia nods agreement, explaining that she absolves herself of responsibility for the crime committed against her. However, she continues, she cannot absolve herself from punishment. As a noblewoman, her example is important to wives and daughters throughout Rome. The law dictates that if she has had intercourse with a man other than her husband, she should face the penalty, regardless of the circumstances. If an exception is made for her, then other women might choose to be unchaste or unfaithful, safe in the knowledge that if discovered they could claim they were unwilling, dishonestly citing her example to evade penance.

With the men distracted as they seek to give her solace, she reaches into her clothing. Finding the knife she has concealed there, she wraps her hand around the handle, its blade cold against her skin. With an almost imperceptible thrust, she drives it towards her heart, her body slumping forward as she does so. Her husband and her father shout out in horror, but it is too late.

Overcome with grief, they are also comforted by a sense of pride in her unimpeachable Roman virtue. Lucretia's end, they can console themselves, is heroic in a society where death is preferable to dishonour. From her unintentional 'victory' in the 'contest of the wives' that established her as a paragon of domestic virtue, through to her plea that her honour be avenged, and to her painful demise at her own hand so that her name would not be associated with the immoral conduct of others, she has repeatedly prioritized the wellbeing and good name of her family and her husband above her own personal happiness. In this way, Lucretia comes to represent a Roman ideal of femininity defined by moral rectitude and personal sacrifice. An ideal of femininity that well serves Rome's patriarchal society and the male chroniclers who write its history, despite the impossible demands it makes of its women.

## THE SPARK OF REVOLUTION

As Livy tells it, Collatinus's friend Brutus now spearheads the mission to avenge Lucretia. While the others are consumed with sorrow, Brutus removes the knife from her body and holds it aloft, her blood still evident on the blade. He vows to pursue Sextus Tarquinius, his father the king and the rest of the royal family, resorting to whatever violence necessary to ensure the crown is taken from them.

He expresses a hatred for the family, collectively known as the Tarquinii, seeded long before last night's devastating crime. His violent and criminal rise to power aside, the king's extravagant programme of public building has put a strain on the city's coffers, even as the workforce charged with enacting it are treated abominably. His unpopularity is further underscored by simmering discontent that it is a monarch of Etruscan extraction who uses his power to oppress the people of Rome.

Considered until now to be a rather unserious young man, Brutus becomes the lightning rod for the many grievances against the royal family. The assault of Lucretia is the final, appalling nail in the coffin. Under his guidance, the men in the bedroom lift up Lucretia's body and carry it from the house to the local marketplace, where a crowd quickly gathers. In a bold oration, Brutus urges them to action, demanding they take up their weapons as befits good Romans. Leaving Lucretia's father to guard Collatia and appointing others to make sure word of the burgeoning uprising doesn't reach the ears of the king, Brutus and his new followers set off for Rome. There a crowd rushes to the Forum from every quarter of the city to meet him. As he has done at Collatia, he reminds them of the many and varied crimes committed by the king, his wife and sons, and signs up a wave of new names to his fledgling army. Next, he goes to the military encampment at Ardea to recruit more to his cause. The flame of revolution is alive.

## THE *MORES MAIORUM* OF THE ROMAN REPUBLIC

The story of Lucretia demonstrates the importance of feminine virtue in the self-identity of the Roman people, but other key moral codes are evident too. From Collatinus's dignified refusal to brag about his wife to Brutus's determination to uphold the oath he made to Lucretia, the tale is structured along the codes of moral conduct so esteemed by the Romans. The *mores maiorum* (or 'customs of the ancestors') of Rome were numerous, providing a set of clear ethical guidelines for all aspects of life, from domestic to martial. Here are just a few of them.

- *Pietas* – similar to the modern concept of piety, much of *pietas* is about worship, but it also extends to the honouring of tradition and ritual, as well as putting religious considerations above personal desires.

- *Dignitas* – not just carrying oneself with dignity but also demonstrating wisdom and restraint, *dignitas* is the opposite of flippancy and frivolity. It's about the respect you should be shown, and is a measure of your place in the hierarchy: one's *dignitas* depends on the greatness of one's family, but also on one's personal achievements. And the single greatest way to elevate *dignitas* is by winning *gloria* . . .

- *Gloria* – securing glory for oneself can be done by many means, but in ancient Rome the best and fastest path to *gloria* is military conquest. With those at the top of the Senate looking to bring as much *gloria* upon themselves as possible during their brief periods as consul, it's no surprise that the republic finds itself in a state of near-perpetual war.

## BIRTH OF THE REPUBLIC

While Brutus travels to the besieged town, the king is making the opposite journey to Rome, having got wind of the nascent insurrection. But he arrives at the city walls to find the gates closed and a notice of exile against him. By now his reviled wife, Tullia, has already fled, with their sons not far behind, headed for Etruria, the Etruscan homeland. All except Sextus Tarquinius, who makes instead for Gabii, another town 10 miles east of Rome. The prince knows it well, having earlier helped the king capture it by double-crossing Gabii's authorities with claims he was in rebellion against his father. Arriving now as a fugitive, Sextus Tarquinius discovers that Gabii has not forgotten his betrayal. In revenge for his previous duplicity, they slay him.

With the ruling house ousted, the people of Rome have an important decision to make. Do they want to try their luck with a new king, or do they go further still, and cut out the rot of the monarchical system itself? After all, though plebeians have some rights under the current system, the executive power is held exclusively by the man at the top – even the patricians are unable to veto bad decisions. Despite their careful governmental structures, the tyranny of the Tarquinii has shown more clearly than ever that Romans are – and have always been – at the whims of the king, with no recourse to ousting them, regardless of their behaviour or fitness to lead.

So it is that, through a public vote, the citizens of Rome take the momentous decision to end the monarchical system and establish a republic – the *Res publica populi romani* (literally, 'the public thing of the Roman people'). It is the birth of a state not the possession of its rulers but of the people themselves. Executive power now falls to two elected consuls, or praetors as they are called at first. Answerable to the people, or at least to their representatives in the Senate, Collatinus and Brutus are the first to hold the offices.

But the shadow of monarchy is long. Brutus calls on the people to swear an oath that no man will reign here as king again. He redoubles his efforts to remove all vestiges of the Tarquinii clan his revolution has removed from the throne. The fly in the ointment is that among those to carry that family name is his co-consul, Lucius Tarquinius Collatinus, Lucretia's own widower and cousin of the man who wronged her. Wary of upsetting public opinion, and taking the counsel of those around him, Collatinus reluctantly steps down. The path is set for the new republic, which will hone its own legal system and methods of government over the coming five centuries.

## THE IDEAL MAN

While Lucretia represents an ideal of Roman womanhood, the early Roman Republic also throws up several male role models of *virtus* (a generalized concept of 'virtue' but with particular emphasis on martial courage and a willingness to put the needs of the state over personal interests). One such example was the junior military officer Horatius, who was said to have led a heroic defence of a strategically vital bridge against an overwhelming force of Etruscan raiders in the late sixth century BC. Another is Cincinnatus, a patrician statesman and military commander. By 458 BC he was retired, seeing out his years on his farm (farming itself being a noble pursuit in the still largely agrarian Roman society). However, when a large Roman army found itself besieged by the enemy Aequi tribe, Cincinnatus was named dictator and granted special powers as exclusive leader for six months so that he might oversee defeat of the Aequi. According to the histories, he masterminded a victory in a matter of days. Immediately after that, he showed his commitment to the resistance of sole power (the power of kings) by surrendering his dictatorship in a little over two weeks so as to return to his quiet life of farming – a demonstration of *virtus* that accorded him legendary status in the annals of Rome.

That is how the republic is breathed into life, according to the historical narrative crafted by those working in the period of transition from republic to empire some half a millennium later. It is a story that emphasizes the heroic nature of Rome's past – its commitment to justice and fair rule, played out around the story of a woman who comes to represent all that is good in the Roman formulation of womanhood. It also serves as a cautionary tale, warning against arrogance and entitlement, and reminding the powerful that even they will face consequences if they fail to respect the rule of law.

However, the complete absence of contemporary primary written evidence – virtually all the records Rome did keep disappeared when the city was sacked by the Gauls, their old adversaries from the west, in 390 BC – makes it impossible to corroborate the accounts of Livy and his contemporaries. Many modern historians regard the story of Lucretia and the subsequent overthrow of the royal family as a neat narrative that hides a truer story of gradual transition from monarchy to republic. Again, it is also a story written during the heyday of the Roman Republic, and therefore seeks to reinforce its self-identity, its rejection of kings, and its commitment to widening access to power. Some challenge the notion that the monarchy was ever all-powerful, instead regarding early Rome as an oligarchy in which power lay with a wider, albeit exclusive, group of aristocratic patrician families. After all, the republic which emerges still exempts a great swathe of its population from the full rights of citizenship on account of age, sex or social background. It is not therefore a democracy but an evolution of the previous oligarchy, in which power remains with a relatively few well-born families.

In such a light, the overthrow of Tarquinius Superbus can

be viewed not so much as a popular revolution, but rather the replacement of one patrician clan by an alliance of several others. Even celebrated cornerstones of the republic, including the Senate and the division of the population into voting groups, are already there during the era of the kings.

This is not to undermine the impact the transition from monarchy to republic has on the fate of Rome and, by extension, the world it comes to dominate. But it does demand that we treat the accounts of Rome's early history with due caution. The tale of Lucretia does not give us an historically factual account, but it has much to tell us about Rome's values, especially around femininity, and – just as with Romulus – the story it later wants to put out into the world about itself.

# 3

# APPIUS CLAUDIUS CAECUS: ALL ROADS LEAD FROM ROME

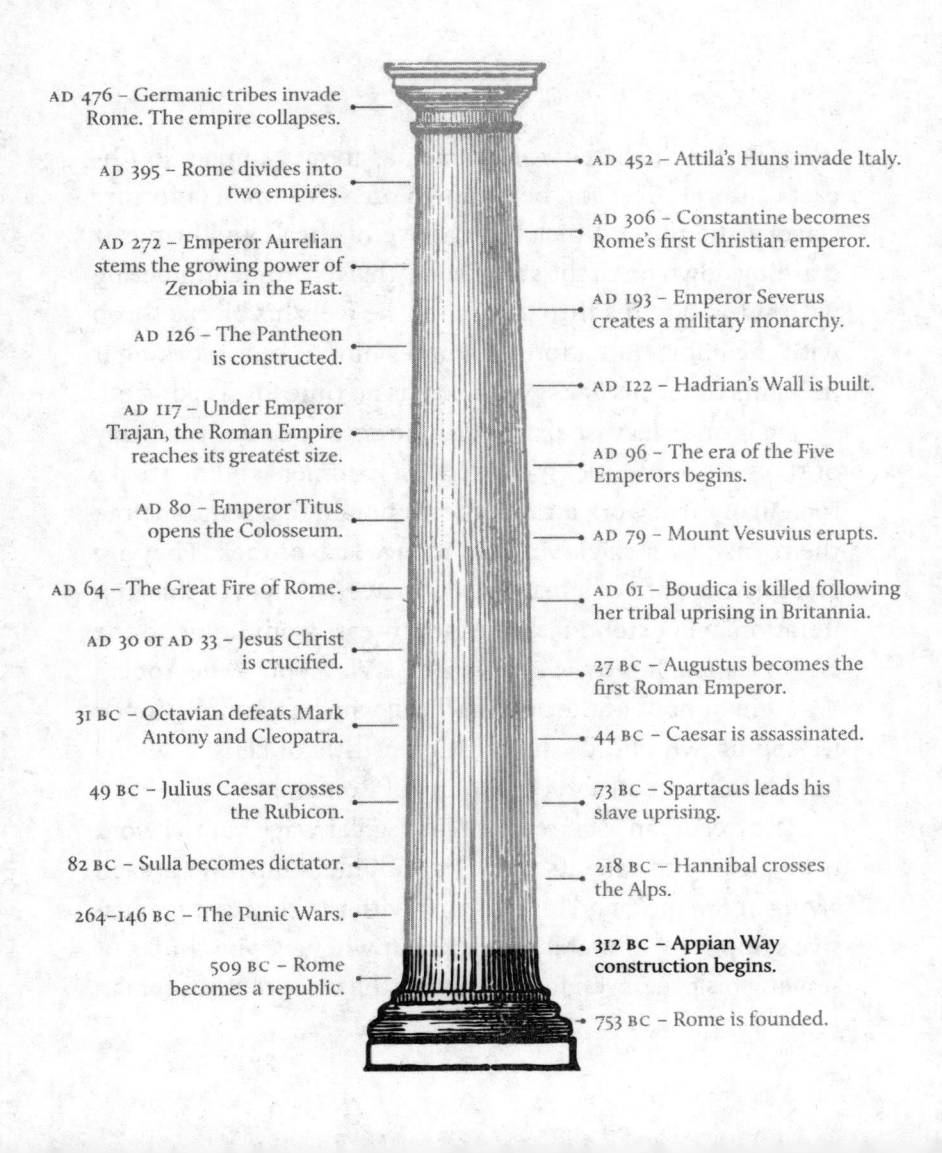

- AD 476 – Germanic tribes invade Rome. The empire collapses.
- AD 452 – Attila's Huns invade Italy.
- AD 395 – Rome divides into two empires.
- AD 306 – Constantine becomes Rome's first Christian emperor.
- AD 272 – Emperor Aurelian stems the growing power of Zenobia in the East.
- AD 193 – Emperor Severus creates a military monarchy.
- AD 126 – The Pantheon is constructed.
- AD 122 – Hadrian's Wall is built.
- AD 117 – Under Emperor Trajan, the Roman Empire reaches its greatest size.
- AD 96 – The era of the Five Emperors begins.
- AD 80 – Emperor Titus opens the Colosseum.
- AD 79 – Mount Vesuvius erupts.
- AD 64 – The Great Fire of Rome.
- AD 61 – Boudica is killed following her tribal uprising in Britannia.
- AD 30 or AD 33 – Jesus Christ is crucified.
- 27 BC – Augustus becomes the first Roman Emperor.
- 31 BC – Octavian defeats Mark Antony and Cleopatra.
- 44 BC – Caesar is assassinated.
- 49 BC – Julius Caesar crosses the Rubicon.
- 73 BC – Spartacus leads his slave uprising.
- 82 BC – Sulla becomes dictator.
- 218 BC – Hannibal crosses the Alps.
- 264–146 BC – The Punic Wars.
- **312 BC – Appian Way construction begins.**
- 509 BC – Rome becomes a republic.
- 753 BC – Rome is founded.

It's 312 BC near the city of Terracina, about 35 miles southeast of Rome. The sun beats down on a freedman (a former slave) as he raises a pick high above his head and brings it crashing down on to the stone beneath. His brow shimmering with sweat and his throat parched, he feels his biceps throb with the effort. But a foreman urges him to keep working if he wants to see his day's pay. There is no time for slacking off.

He is one of a vast army of labourers armed with an array of tools – not just picks, but spades, hammers and mattocks too. All of them work away at the mountain that stands before them, inch by inch carving out a huge slab of rock. They are creating the path of a magnificent new road that, in this first iteration, will extend 132 miles south-east from Rome to the city of Capua. It is to be known as the Via Appia – the Appian Way – in honour of the public official who has commissioned it: Appius, who holds the prestigious title of censor, giving him power over all sorts of aspects of Roman life.

The freedman is grateful for his regular wage but the work is beginning to take its toll. His shoulders burn with each swing of the pick, and his ears ring with the constant percussive symphony of metal on rock. But whenever he thinks of slowing his pace, even for a moment, the voice of the foreman booms out again. The mountain presents a mighty impediment to progress, but he is there to ensure that his workers overcome it. Besides, they have dealt with every other challenge they've faced so far. These labourers have already helped lay the road on the approach to Terracina over the boggy Pontine Marshes, digging trenches, filling them with stones and compacting them with rollers driven by oxen. These last few months the road has grown steadily, an engineering marvel as it builds layer by layer. There are as many as five in all, a mixture of gravel, larger stones, sand, clay and lime, and then a final covering of large basalt polygons fitted intricately together to form an almost perfectly smooth surface.

The freedman redoubles his efforts, as behind him other workers dig ditches either side of the road, wide enough apart for two carts to pass each other. What they rip out of the ground is used in the construction of the road itself, while the ditches provide drainage. The Via Appia is built to crest at its centre, so that water drains off to either side. As he begins to feel weary again, the worker reminds himself of the words of his superiors: this road is for the greater glory of Rome. The censor, Appius, has a grand vision that this route will unite the city's expanding dominions on the Italian peninsula. It will become a thoroughfare not only for travellers and traders, but for the army too. No longer will military adventures be constrained by unpassable marshland or mountain. Instead, a paved road like none before it will allow troops to march out and dominate the region, proving the might of the Roman Republic.

The freedman leans on his pick for a moment, taking a long drink from a flask containing cheap vinegary wine passed to him by his neighbour. It burns his dry throat as he gulps it down. He closes his eyes and feels the mid-afternoon heat on his neck. Hours more until he can rest. Then it is back to work at the foreman's familiar bellow, his pick arcing through the air once more. Rome has plans for itself on the grandest of scales, and Rome will not wait.

## FOUNDATIONS OF A GREAT STATE

The Via Appia stands as one of the great infrastructural achievements of ancient Rome, with long stretches still in use today. The road's construction marked Rome's progression from its status as important regional player towards its eventual position as major world power. The sheer magnitude of the project speaks of the ambition that fuelled it, but also of a sophisticated grasp of what was required to establish the republic above its many rivals. Military might was, naturally, integral to establishing Rome's dominance in the region, but it thrived in no less a part because of the strength of its infrastructure. This extraordinary paved road (and the many more that the Romans subsequently built, until they had a network of some 50,000 miles) served to make administration, trade and military excursions more efficient.

It was emblematic of Rome's ability to think big and its willingness to embrace innovation and invention. Roman society was not the first to conceive of the idea of roads but it created a network unprecedented in history. Similarly, it led the way in many other disparate fields of building and civil development. And as it strove for mastery of the world, Rome became a potent force for modernization and progress wherever they served its interests.

*

*That the Via Appia was named after a single historical figure, Appius Claudius Crassus (also known as Caecus), confirms the importance of the 'Great Man' idea in Roman society, that here was a superpower built primarily on the virtue of powerful individual men. But just who was Appius? What drove him to instigate a flurry of major public building works? And with what results for Rome, at a time when the city was still arm-wrestling with its neighbours for dominance of the Italian mainland?*

## INNOVATION IN THE TIME OF THE REPUBLIC

By the time of the Via Appia's construction, the republic has experienced almost two centuries of both development and tumult. Domestically, there has been the evolution of a complex legal code, beginning with the so-called Twelve Tables. Established around 450 BC, this comprehensive set of written laws, rights and regulations is publicly displayed to allow transparency and, in theory, equal application of secular law regardless of class. It's the beginning of the great Roman legal tradition, and destined to provide the framework for judicial systems around the globe.

There has also been much change in political organization. It is true that power still largely resides with a few patrician families, but no one individual can enjoy, or exploit, it in the way that the kings once had.

Power now resides in a layered system of magistracies (public offices), most of which are elected for only a year. At the top of the pyramid are the two consuls – in essence, Rome's chief executives. Next comes a level of praetors, who are in charge of the running of the judicial system. Below them, the aediles, responsible for various aspects of urban affairs from the repair of infrastructure to the regulation of trade and putting on public events. Finally, at the base of the magistracy pyramid, the quaestors, numbering up to twenty in any given year and each charged with a particular aspect of financial oversight.

The single most important political institution is the Senate, its name derived from the Latin *senex*, meaning 'old man'. The Senate plays a major role in hands-on, day-to-day administration as well as serving an advisory function. In practical terms it is far more important now than in the days of the monarchy, and its members are identifiable by the togas they wear, adorned with a thick purple stripe.

Full citizenship is the privilege of just a small section of the population, extending only to free adult males who have passed the census and its demands concerning wealth, family background and moral virtue. Since very shortly after the creation of the republic there has been tension between the patricians, with their stranglehold on the senior political offices, and the much larger number of commoners, or plebeians, who demand to be better represented in the system. This struggle comes to be known as the Conflict of the Orders, but now, deep into the fourth century BC, the plebeians have made up valuable ground. Intermarriage between the classes is at last permitted, and many more public offices are, at least in theory, open to citizens from outside the patrician class. Most importantly, the plebeians can now call on their own elected officials – or 'tribunes' – to stand up for their interests and represent individuals in matters of the law. Those in slavery, including former citizens forced into servitude through debt, still have no legal rights and can face branding, beating and even summary execution for insubordination. There is still work to be done, but the class divide is narrowing.

Away from Rome, the authorities are in an almost permanent state of warfare with their neighbours in the region – chiefly, but not exclusively, the Latins, Etruscans and Samnites. Each aims to hold the balance of power on the peninsula. Rome is by no means the clearly superior military force, but it has a martial doggedness and political wiliness that have seen it make inroads. What sets it apart is, on the one hand, its mastery of divide-and-conquer tactics, and on the other hand its skill at persuading potential rivals into compacts. While it focuses on defeating a particular enemy, it will pursue alliances with other tribes; then, when victory has been secured, it may decide to turn its attention back to overpowering one of its supposed allies.

But rather than simply enslaving those it conquers and imposing harsh terms of taxation or tribute, as is the norm among warring states, Rome instead frequently pursues integration – and on much better terms than any other military power can offer. It regularly extends Roman citizenship (or partial citizenship) to the defeated and declines to demand tribute, while offering vanquished cities ally status. This gives those it conquers a chance to share in Rome's expansionist project, and access to its lucrative trade routes and markets. By encouraging its own citizens to move into conquered territory as a form of colonization, Rome binds distant outposts to itself. In return for these relatively merciful approaches, the vanquished foe is required to hand over control of its military and send its men to serve in the Roman army. Should an enemy state reject Rome's terms, they risk the severest of reprisals, including the threat of complete annihilation. Rome, then, has an almost inexhaustible supply of troops and a network of pliant client-states that feeds into its policy of further expansion – a system that gives it a unique advantage over its major rivals.

While the young Appius is still working his way up the ranks, hostilities with the so-called Latin League, an alliance of states in the region immediately surrounding Rome, are reaching their peak. The league meets the republic's army in the Latin War of 340–338 BC, with Rome emerging victorious. War with the Etruscans, however, is very much ongoing, and hostilities with the warrior-like Samnites (a federation of several cities) to the south of Rome have ramped up too. A lengthy conflict broke out a few years before the Latin War when Rome leapt to the defence of the state of Capua against the attacking Samnites, with a fragile peace negotiated after two years of fighting. Relations have nonetheless remained tense for the last fifteen years, with the two states jockeying for influence in central and southern Italy. In 326 BC events come to a head again with Rome's decision to intervene in a dispute between the Samnites and another of the cities under its control, Neapolis (modern-day Naples). The powers are once again at war with each other.

## THE BATTLE OF THE CAUDINE FORKS

It's 321 BC, and Rome's army is on the march into the Samnite heartlands. Well marshalled and battle-hardened, its soldiers are confident of winning victory quickly, even as they are confronted by the intimidatingly rugged terrain of the Apennine Mountains.

Before them lies a pass known as the Caudine Forks. It

is narrow, far too slim to accommodate the army comfortably, and on either side steep mountains slope upwards. The Roman commanders make the decision to dispense with their usual marching formation and instead eke a way through in a straggly column. It is far from ideal, but they are not overly concerned. They have received intelligence from some herdsmen they met on their way here who have told them the whereabouts of the enemy. Once through this mountain pass, they are confident of taking the enemy by surprise.

The men quickly fill the pass, struggling to keep moving while being squeezed uncomfortably together, when there is sudden noise up ahead. The unmistakable sound of military boots crunching on the gravelly ground. The Romans stop in their tracks as massed ranks of Samnite warriors come into view. The herdsmen, they realize, have laid a trap for them. With no way forward and entirely out of fighting formation, the command goes up for the Romans to retreat. But as they turn, they realize with horror that the entrance behind them has been blocked by more Samnites. They are trapped, like rats in a cage, and to fight will be tantamount to suicide.

There is nothing for it but to try to negotiate with the enemy. The Roman command engages with the head of the Samnite forces, Gaius Pontius, who exacts a tough settlement. He demands the return of all Samnite territories recently lost to the Romans, along with a promise that there will be no further Roman aggression. To compound his enemies' humiliation, Gaius Pontius also forces them to pass under a yoke constructed of spears – a symbol of their bestial servitude.

Not a single soul has been lost in battle but the encounter goes down as one of Rome's worst military failures. When the army at last makes it back home, they are received in disgrace.

Within the city, the political elite determine that they can never suffer such an undignified reverse again, fearful that their hard-earned martial prestige will be lost for ever. There is a thorough review of how the military operates, from its leadership structure and tactical know-how to its adaptability and intelligence evaluation. The path is set. Rome will do whatever is required to make sure that the shameful defeat at Caudine Forks is never repeated.

## THE AGE OF APPIUS

It's now 312 BC, less than a decade since the humiliation at Caudine Forks, and Appius Claudius Crassus has just been elected to the office of censor. It's a prestigious magistrate's post, making him responsible for everything to do with the census, that vital record of Rome's citizens and their property. The role also extends into the realm of advising on public morality and looking after aspects of the public finances. Given that no other official can overrule the censor in his areas of authority, it makes Appius a very powerful man indeed.

He strokes his thick beard as he contemplates the hard work that lies before him. This posting is the latest step up the *cursus honorum* ('course of honour'), another significant rung up the career ladder for this scion of the Claudii, one of Rome's great patrician families. A veteran of the Second Samnite War, which still rages, he has striven hard to get here, holding several junior government postings and serving as a military tribune. However, he follows more in the tradition of Rome's philosopher-rulers rather than their great military leaders, an astute political strategist and a talented communicator rather than a battlefield commander.

Despite his own high birth, he embraces the growing influence of the plebeians. In the months after his election he begins to formulate reforms that will give them still greater powers. He extends voting rights and sets out amendments that will allow the sons of freedmen – a distinct social class of former slaves who have earned or been granted freedom – to sit in the Senate for the first time. But these are controversial developments that cause friction with some of his patrician brothers, who are unwilling to cede more power down the social scale. Nonetheless, his efforts to further democratize Rome pale into relative insignificance when compared to the magnitude of the huge building projects he wastes no time in getting off the ground.

The city's experience against the Samnites at Caudine Forks has highlighted weaknesses in Rome's ability to get its troops where they need to be quickly. The requirement is clear for a more joined-up approach to winning and maintaining territories. Appius presses for the establishment of more Roman colonies across Latium, in which Rome sits, and in the region known as Felix Campania (literally, 'Happy Countryside'), just south of Rome. These, he hopes, will help strengthen Rome's hand against the Samnites and Etruscans.

Yet still the question remains, how can Rome more easily transport an ever-growing army, and also facilitate the trade that will keep itself and its burgeoning dominions fed and content? The answer, Appius persuades his fellow powerbrokers in the city, is to build a road bigger and better than any previously imagined.

## GAME-CHANGER

Capua is chosen as the natural destination for the road, being the capital of the contested Felix Campania region. Not much over 100 miles from Rome along a mostly coastal plain means the route to the settlement is a defensible one, less vulnerable to Samnite ambush than the existing, limited inland paths. By the time it is finished, the new paved superhighway will allow troops to cover perhaps 25 miles a day, and will be strong enough to withstand them. A fearsome prospect, for the Samnites. It will come at a price, of course – over 250 million sesterces, enough to buy 625,000 tons of wheat – but it will be money well spent. Brilliantly engineered, its architects are using the latest surveying expertise and equipment to ensure it is as straight and direct as the natural landscape allows. Even better, the material excavated to open its pathway can be recycled in the innovative construction of the multi-layered road itself. Not only will it give Rome an advantage in its current conflict, it provides a blueprint for future road-building schemes too. This is investment in a bright new future.

But though this is a project of unprecedented scale, Appius is a man with his eye on his legacy. He's determined to make the most of his brief moment of power, and he wants to secure immortal glory by developing not only Rome's political systems and military capability, but also its municipal infrastructure.

The Romans already lead the ancient world in the development of urban sanitation, epitomized by the city's revolutionary sewer system, the Cloaca Maxima. But now, almost at the same time that work begins on the road, Appius and his co-censor, Gaius Plautius Venox, commission a mighty aqueduct. For some time, Rome's water supplies have been under strain from a combination of the rapidly rising population, drought and contamination. The plan is to bolster supplies by transporting fresh spring water from high ground in the Sabine Hills some 10 miles to the east of the city.

In order to route the water into Rome on a downward course, as gravity demands, most of the channel's stone-lined length is underground, which is no bad thing considering the Samnites might wish to attack it. But on the immediate approach through the hills of Rome there are sections that have to be elevated on spectacular arches – an historical architectural feature that the Romans have refined to perfection. Using tufa rock quarried from the local hills, Appius's builders are innovators in cement production too. From a mixture of lime and volcanic rock they are able to produce a formidably durable material that makes possible the construction of such grand structural wonders.

The aqueduct project demands an engineering expertise rivalling that on display in the road-building works. The feat of engineering is such that its designers manage to plot a course that drops only 10 metres along its entire route before arriving into a series of reservoirs within Rome's walls beneath the Palatine Hill. From there it is distributed to a mixture of private and public establishments. In finding a way to build Rome's first aqueduct, its creators pave the way for a further ten aqueducts of increasing sophistication. In terms of state planning and building, 312 BC has been nothing short of an *annus mirabilis* (remarkable year).

Strictly speaking, though the censorship enjoys a lengthier tenure than most public offices at eighteen months long,

Appius's term is up before either the road or aqueduct are entirely completed. However, he is keen to see the job through and takes advantage of a series of procedural issues to delay his resignation from the post. By 308 BC he is still in place, a longevity reflected in the accolade of having both projects named in his honour: the Via Appia and the Aqua Appia.

### NEW NEWS

Post-dating Appius by some 200 years, another striking Roman innovation is the *Acta Diurna* ('Daily Acts'), a forerunner of the modern newspaper. A daily gazette of public notices and announcements (from births, marriages and deaths to the latest gladiatorial results), along with some gossip too, it is inscribed on stone and metal tablets and displayed for a day or two in prominent public places, such as the Forum in Rome. From 59 BC Julius Caesar makes a goodwill gesture to his public by also allowing publication of the previously secret *Acta Senatus* ('Acts of the Senate' – minutes from its meetings), commencing an era of, if not exactly a free press, at least a nod to greater transparency. Sadly, despite *Acta Diurna* being extensively archived, no editions have survived to the present day.

## LEGACY

The effectiveness of the Via Appia in conveying troops contributes towards the defeat of the Samnites and the conclusion of twenty-two years of fighting in 304 BC. By now Appius has served the first of his two terms as consul, arguably the most prestigious position in Roman society, and he continues to hold high offices for several decades to come, during which time the Samnites are conclusively defeated in a third and final war.

Around 280 BC he enjoys a final glorious moment in the spotlight. Rome has been at war with the Greek king Pyrrhus of Epirus, who has invaded southern Italy in a bid to counter Roman expansion. The two sides have recently clashed at the battle of Heraclea, with Pyrrhus claiming a famous victory. It has, though, come at great cost to him, with thousands of his men slain – a hollow win that gives us a new phrase: Pyrrhic victory. The Greeks send an envoy to Rome to sue for peace, and Appius gets word that there are many in the Senate willing to accept terms. Now in old age, and with his sight said to be failing (his cognomen, which functions something like a nickname, is Caecus, meaning 'blind'), he is carried to the Senate in a litter. Surrounded by his contemporaries, he gives an impassioned speech in which he urges Rome not to give in to the enemy, famously proclaiming: 'Every man is the architect of his own fortune.' His oration hits a nerve. Rome rejects the peace deal, holds firm, and within five years casts Pyrrhus out of Italy, all his gains lost.

However, when Appius dies in 273 BC at the age of sixty-seven, it is for his two grand infrastructure projects that he is most celebrated. His aqueduct by now brings some 20 million gallons of water into the city per day, while the road that bears his name grows longer and longer until, around a decade after his death, it reaches its furthest point, 350 miles away from Rome in the port city of Brundisium on the Adriatic coast (modern-day Brindisi, on the heel of Italy). Outstanding achievements in their own right but also totems of a civilization on the up, visionary and ambitious. In the long arc of Rome's progress, Appius's extraordinary public works stand out as monuments of a state on the cusp of dominating the Mediterranean.

# 4

# FABIUS MAXIMUS:
# FIRST ITALY, THEN THE WORLD

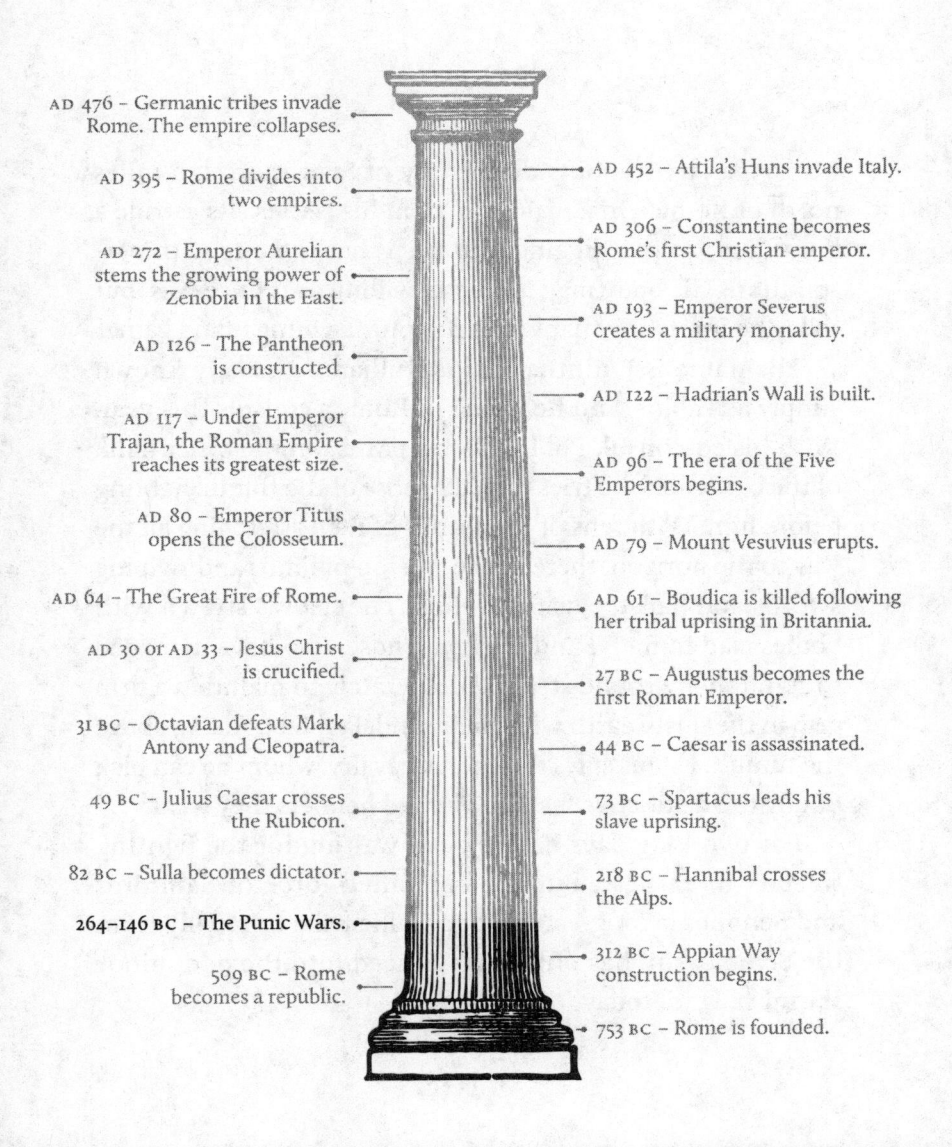

AD 476 – Germanic tribes invade Rome. The empire collapses.

AD 452 – Attila's Huns invade Italy.

AD 395 – Rome divides into two empires.

AD 306 – Constantine becomes Rome's first Christian emperor.

AD 272 – Emperor Aurelian stems the growing power of Zenobia in the East.

AD 193 – Emperor Severus creates a military monarchy.

AD 126 – The Pantheon is constructed.

AD 122 – Hadrian's Wall is built.

AD 117 – Under Emperor Trajan, the Roman Empire reaches its greatest size.

AD 96 – The era of the Five Emperors begins.

AD 80 – Emperor Titus opens the Colosseum.

AD 79 – Mount Vesuvius erupts.

AD 64 – The Great Fire of Rome.

AD 61 – Boudica is killed following her tribal uprising in Britannia.

AD 30 or AD 33 – Jesus Christ is crucified.

27 BC – Augustus becomes the first Roman Emperor.

31 BC – Octavian defeats Mark Antony and Cleopatra.

44 BC – Caesar is assassinated.

49 BC – Julius Caesar crosses the Rubicon.

73 BC – Spartacus leads his slave uprising.

82 BC – Sulla becomes dictator.

218 BC – Hannibal crosses the Alps.

**264–146 BC – The Punic Wars.**

312 BC – Appian Way construction begins.

509 BC – Rome becomes a republic.

753 BC – Rome is founded.

It's 295 BC, a little outside the city of Sentinum, 120 miles north of Rome. On a plain, a man in his sixties sits astride a horse, his armour digging into flesh that is damp with perspiration. His body may not be as willing as it once was, but today he is proving that war is not only a young man's game.

His name is Quintus Fabius Rullianus, usually known simply as Fabius, and he is one of Rome's consuls this year. With his co-consul, Publius Decius Mus, on the other flank of the battlefield, he tries to make sense of the frantic fighting before him. With tens of thousands of men stretching all the way to the horizon, there is a confusion of limbs and swiping swords and hailstorms of javelins. The field is strewn with bodies clad in metal and leather. Those who have managed to stand their ground struggle desperately to maintain a firm grip in the dusty earth with their sandalled feet. Rising above the tumult, Fabius spies the enemy cavalry, whom he can pick out by the distinctive feather-plumed helmets they wear.

For two long days he has been waiting for the fighting to start in earnest. But the combined force of Samnites and Senones (a long-established Gallic tribe originally from the Seine basin) has only been enticed into the odd minor skirmish. Until today.

With much greater experience than Decius Mus, Fabius is able to pick out patterns in the chaos that has erupted. The divisions under his command face the Samnites, an adversary he has encountered often over the decades. There is something almost comfortingly familiar about them. For now, his men are doing well in the struggle. He knows the Samnites like a quick attack, so he has held his own lines back in a strong defensive formation, urging the enemy forward in wave after ineffective wave until they have started to tire.

Across the battlefield, things are going less well for Decius Mus, a more impetuous man than his older colleague. His divisions face the Senones. The Roman cavalry have made some thrusting charges, but now they have pushed too far, losing their shape as they face the Gauls' chariots. A messenger races to Fabius to tell him that the Roman horses have been spooked and are scattering, forcing Decius Mus's cavalry into retreat.

As he squints across the plain, Fabius is horrified to make out the figure of Decius Mus racing into the heart of the battle on his steed. Though it is utterly reckless, he understands the move at once: the young consul has chosen to risk his own life in a grand gesture to rally his men. He is literally making a sacrifice of himself to the gods of war. Sure enough, he is struck down, ripped from his horse's back, destined to die in the dirt. Reckless it may be, but death in combat is the mark of a true Roman warrior. The act renews the spirits of his men, who throw themselves back into the fray.

Fabius sees an opportunity. His own divisions now definitively have the better of the wearying Samnites. He signals to his cavalry to follow him and then, digging his heels into the lean belly of his horse, he gallops over to the other side of the battlefield, the breeze streaking through his hair as his heart races. Circling around, he leads his men behind the lines of the Senones and launches a bold surprise attack. As one, the Senones raise their shields above their heads to form a protective screen, but it crumbles against the onslaught of Roman sword and lance.

With both flanks of the opposing force now in disarray, it is only a matter of time before Rome can claim the victory. Flooded with adrenalin, Fabius throws his fist into the air and roars – for the conquest, for the glory of Rome, and for one more glorious triumph on his unrivalled record of military success. Because whatever the political goings-on in Rome – a different sort of battlefield he has navigated with aplomb for many years now – there is nothing quite like the exhilaration of smiting the city's enemies in the field. And though this victory does not signal the end of Rome's long war with the Samnites, it is a pivotal moment towards its conclusion.

*Were it not for Fabius and his military acumen, it is quite possible that Rome's forces would have been beaten by the larger enemy here. Not for the first time, the fate of Rome had seemed balanced on a knife edge. Had Fabius lost control at Sentinum, the consequences might have been catastrophic: devastating losses, a humiliating peace treaty, rebellions or alliances of other Italian tribes. Worse still, if forced into a defensive position and with its troops shattered, Rome itself could have been vulnerable to invasion.*

*However, as Fabius surveys the bloody scene before him at Sentinum, he reassures himself that such speculation is unnecessary. It is the Romans who will notch up the victory, taking another step closer to achieving hegemony over the entire Italian peninsula. And, once that is achieved, whole new vistas will open up, giving Rome the chance to establish itself as a global superpower.*

*Watching on as what is left of the Samnites and Senones retreat, many of them cut down by his own men as they flee, he may be justified in pondering just who can stop Rome now. But what military challenges did Rome have to overcome to reach this point? And how did celebrated military figures like Fabius drive Rome's progress?*

## FABIUS, MILITARY SUPERSTAR

Fabius has the good fortune to be born into one of the city's powerful patrician families, the Fabii. By the 320s BC, as he is coming into his thirties, he is beginning to make waves in public life. At the start of the decade, a number of prominent men in government are struck down by a mystery ailment. Based on intelligence supplied to him, Fabius uses his position as a junior magistrate to accuse 170 high-born women of complicity in a plot to poison Rome's male elite, resulting in mass convictions. Whatever the truth of these wild claims, Fabius is suddenly propelled to the frontline of Roman politics. Within the city's patriarchal hierarchy, his attack on such a large contingent of women proves no brake on his advancement.

By the time the Second Samnite War breaks out a few years later, he has risen to the position of *magister equitum*, or 'master of horse'. The role puts him second-in-command to Papirius Cursor, an accomplished general now serving as dictator – a short-term posting introduced only in times of emergency that allows him to wield power greater even than that of the consuls. Papirius is specifically charged with overseeing the conflict with the Samnites, in which Rome hopes to weaken the rebel tribe, ultimately bringing it under Roman control. And with his immediate boss in such a crucial role, Fabius himself is also now positioned right at the heart of power.

Yet even this is not enough to sate Fabius's desire to influence events. In 325 BC Papirius decides to leave his Roman camp in Samnium, land of the Samnites, to return to Rome for a consultation. Except it's not other statesmen or even more experienced elders from whom he seeks advice: instead, he turns to the sacred chickens. It is customary for these particular poultry, specially reared by priests, to be used as a kind of oracle; ceremonially slaughtered after a question has been put to the gods, their blood and entrails are studied for omens before any major political or military decision is made. Fabius, meanwhile, has been holding his position back in Samnium. But he is restless in camp, especially when he is told by his scouts that the enemy are unprepared for combat. He decides to take matters into his own hands and draws the Samnite army out into a battle not far from the town of Imbrinium.

For a while it seems like he has made a terrible mistake. A succession of Roman advances are repelled, until at last a desperate cavalry charge throws the Samnites into disarray. Fabius notches up a famous victory by the skin of his teeth. Papirius, however, is incensed by his insubordination. The threat of execution hangs over Fabius, and it is only the intervention of the Senate, acting on popular sentiment, that saves him.

Three years later, in 322 BC, Fabius's rehabilitation is complete when he is elected consul for the first time. With no immediate crisis at hand, there is no current need for a dictator, so he finds himself with no one above him in a superior position. So now he takes the fight to the Samnites with renewed gusto, winning one encounter after another. Along the way he ravages both the Lucerians and Apulians, long-standing allies of the Samnites. Back in Rome, the Senate awards him that greatest of honours, a triumph, in which he and his army are granted the right to process into the city to receive the adulation of the people. His victories help balance out the ignominious defeat at Caudine Forks in 321 BC – in which Fabius is not involved – and help pave the way for a peace, or at least a ceasefire, between the two sides in 319 BC.

## A RARE DEFEAT

By now Fabius has no command of his own. However, when hostilities reignite around 315 BC, he is not merely returned to the fray but is made dictator. Things go well for him when he masterminds the capture of the Samnite city of Saticula, which has held out against a siege for the past year. Hammering home his advantage, he takes a series of nearby towns and strongholds for good measure. It feels like any force under Fabius is indestructible, his record of unbroken success now stretching back over many years. So when he hears that one of the towns in Latium has defected to the Samnites, he marches into the region with customary confidence. However, at a location named Lautulae, he is bested by a Samnite army. When news spreads of the defeat, it spurs others to rise up against their Roman occupiers. Rome, after all, has essentially imposed a glorified protection racket upon large swathes of the peninsula, forcing smaller tribes or settlements to accept Rome's control if they want it to guarantee their safety against invasion. In reality, though, the main risk of invasion comes from Rome itself. As such, the offer is one that ever-increasing numbers of towns and cities have been unable to refuse. But if Rome's greatest general can be beaten like this, perhaps Rome's offer of protection – and the implicit threat in refusing it – is becoming more negotiable.

Fabius licks his wounds after the defeat but, though he relinquishes the dictatorship as is customary (the post is time-limited to a few months), he has no intention of exiting the scene. Crucially, the faith his citizens have in him does not waver either. He is back on the battlefield within a year, wiser for the experience of his defeat and determined it will be the only loss he ever gets on his scorecard. It is as if he is the personification of Rome's hunger to conquer and expand. He marches to Sutrium to take on an Etruscan force working in alliance with the Samnites. Seizing the high ground, he masterminds an assault that sees the enemy crumble beneath an aerial bombardment of javelins and stones, followed by a terrifying downhill charge by the massed Roman ranks. From there, he moves northwards, raiding along the way and putting to the sword local rag-tag forces. The stain of Lautulae is soon erased.

In 310 BC he is elected consul again, glorying in inflicting yet more damage not only on the Etruscans but the Umbrians, who also stand against Rome. In one memorable day at Lake Vadimo a little north of Rome, he destroys what the historian Livy will much later say is the largest force the Etruscans ever muster, killing as many as 20,000 men in a day. A devastating blow from which the Etruscans never fully recover.

However, Rome is faring less well in Samnium, where his co-consul Marcius Rutilus has command. Prioritizing the needs of the state over personal feelings like a good Roman should, Fabius agrees to his old nemesis Papirius being appointed dictator for another term, with a remit to make up lost ground against the Samnites. It is a masterstroke, with Papirius immediately making gains. Before the year is out, both men are awarded a triumph and Fabius, unusually, retains the consulship for yet another term.

He carries on his military exploits, leading his troops in Campania and then into Umbria and Etruria. His mastery of the northern theatre of war is such that the Etruscans and Umbrians now seek peace. Rome rewards Fabius in 306 BC by making him proconsul, a title that affords him the powers of a consul without holding the office itself. It effectively extends Fabius's right to lead his army even as his term as consul expires. Within two years the exhausted Samnites are also seeking to agree terms to end the fighting. As the Second Samnite War draws to a close, Fabius is made censor, and begins to unpick some of the pro-plebeian reforms that have been instigated by Appius Claudius Caecus. Fabius may be a hero of the people but he is also a son of the patricians.

## SAMNITES, PART III

While his contemporaries might justifiably be considering retirement, Fabius has no intention of stopping – especially when the Third Samnite War erupts as Rome and the Samnites jockey for power in Lucania in southern Italy. In 297 BC, a year into the conflict, Fabius is made consul yet again.

The town of Tifernum lies in the upper valley of the Tiber, 100 or so miles north of Rome. Fabius leads an army of 20,000 men into the area, while his latest co-consul, Decius Mus, heads a force of similar size further south. The Samnite army, meanwhile, numbers perhaps 25,000. Fabius is readying his troops for a day's march when he is approached by a party of scouts, who inform him that the Samnites want to take out each consul's army one at a time. Their plan is to lure Fabius and his divisions into a confrontation by ambushing them with a small advance party. Then, once the Romans are engaged, they will flood the battlefield with the rest of their men, who will be hiding in the hills beyond.

Considering his options, Fabius reorganizes his men into a highly defensive quadrangular formation, and leads them towards where he now knows the enemy to have secreted themselves. However, he halts his advance short of the valley where his army would be most exposed. The Samnites are left in a quandary. Their opponents are not in the vulnerable position they had hoped for, but if they delay their planned attack, they fear that Decius Mus will join his troops with those of Fabius, giving the Romans a huge numerical advantage. The Samnite commanders decide they have little choice but to come out of their hiding place and take their chances against Fabius in traditional battle lines.

Fabius accepts the battle, but is soon nervously watching the enemy gain the upper hand. The prospect of adding another defeat to his record is real. But he has a plan to shift momentum. He instructs a trusted officer to lead a division of *hastati* (spear-wielding infantry) into the hills behind one of the Samnite flanks. In their light chainmail and armed with their spears and small shields, they move stealthily across the terrain, exiting the main arena of the fighting without being spotted. Back on the battlefield, a Roman cavalry charge is disastrously repelled, and a Samnite counter-attack seems poised to break the Roman lines. But when the *hastati* suddenly appear on the hills behind, the Samnites assume these are in fact the newly arrived reinforcements of Decius Mus. The Roman ground troops assume the same, and the misunderstanding provides them with a surge of renewed hope even as the Samnites are drained of theirs. Fabius watches contentedly as the Samnites rush into retreat, terrified of annihilation by a combined Roman force that is, in truth, merely an illusion: Decius Mus and his men remain somewhere distantly south. Regardless of how it comes about, Rome carries the day when defeat has seemed the more likely result.

Too weary to pursue the fleeing enemy, the Romans withdraw from the field, happy to have slain over 3,000 of the foe. The Samnite army, though, lives to fight another day.

## ENDGAME

Rome has effectively been facing long, drawn-out wars on two fronts, countering the Samnites and the Etruscans (along with other more minor opponents), but over the coming months Fabius builds on his hard-won advantage, taking still more towns and cities. However, Rome's rivals now redouble their efforts, the alliance between the Samnites, Etruscans and Umbrians reinforced by the addition of the Senones from Gaul. On the chessboard of peninsula hostilities such alliances are fluid, but for now there is unity among Rome's enemies, convinced that the time has come to stymie Rome's prolific expansion.

With a mandate to take on this coalition, Fabius is elected consul for a remarkable fifth time in 295 BC, alongside his old comrade Decius Mus. They lead their troops into Umbria for a showdown, where the stage is set for another Fabius tactical masterclass. He instructs several generals currently defending Rome to launch incursions into Etruria instead. The Etruscans withdraw back to their home territory to the north to fend off these raids, taking their Umbrian partners with them. Fabius is therefore left to confront a much weakened, though still powerful, force of Samnites and Senones. It will be a tough fight, but had the Etruscans and Umbrians been lining up alongside them, it would likely be unwinnable. At least Rome now has a chance – one Fabius hopes to exploit at Sentinum.

When the bodies are eventually counted after that famous battle, the estimated 25,000 enemy lying dead is almost triple that of the Roman losses. In light of this touchstone victory, Fabius and his troops return to Rome for the third triumph of his career. Yet still he does not rest, notching up further victories elsewhere on the peninsula. The Samnites, meanwhile, refuse to disappear altogether.

Command of the Samnite army passes to Gaius Pontius, the man behind the humbling of Rome at the Caudine Forks almost three decades previously. As Livy tells it, in 292 BC Pontius faces a Roman army led by Fabius's son, Fabius Gurges, who is one of this year's consuls. Hungry to claim victories of his own and shrug off the long shadow cast by his father's many successes, Gurges is reckless and walks into a surprise attack, his forces sucker-punched by the Samnites. Fabius senior now takes de facto command of the Roman troops, drawing on all his experience to overturn the defeat. The two old dogs of war, Fabius and Pontius, square up for the last major battle of the Third Samnite War. Exactly how the fighting plays out is uncertain, but it is Fabius who emerges victorious, while Pontius's side suffers heavy casualties. Fabius and his son make the long journey back to Rome, capturing still more towns along the way.

Back in their home city, the grateful citizens turn out yet again to shower them and their army with plaudits. However, Fabius notably rides into Rome behind his son. This is to be Gurges's triumph, no matter how much it has been dependent upon his father. It is said that Pontius is paraded through the streets too, the celebrations climaxing with his beheading.

This is to be the last great battlefield triumph of Fabius that history records, yet it is not the end of his public service. Perhaps as late as the 270s BC, by which point he is truly a venerable old man, he holds the highly honoured position of *princeps senatus* ('leader of the Senate'). He is accorded a cognomen too – the first in his line to be called Maximus, 'the Great'. His record of battlefield victories – perhaps as many as three dozen – is one that goes unrivalled for centuries.

## ITALY AND BEYOND

The Samnites are effectively ended as a major fighting force. Rome's other foes continue to show resilience, however. Hostilities with the Etruscans, already having rumbled on for more than two centuries, do not conclude in Rome's favour until the mid-260s BC, with the Umbrians subjugated not long after. At last, central Italy is under the Roman yoke, and the rest of the peninsula, save for a few outposts, soon follows suit. Rome can now look to outward expansion. To the north, beyond the Alps, are the Gauls and the Germanic tribes. To the south and west, mighty Carthage, a truly formidable opponent, straddling North Africa and Europe, where it dominates the southwestern Mediterranean. To the east are the Greek cities and the kingdoms which emerged following the death of Alexander the Great, who only a few decades ago looked to establish Macedon as the greatest empire of the age. Though the Greek world is always divided, the successor kingdoms individually and collectively pose a potent threat; Rome has already had to defend against their incursions into Italian territory.

## THE GAULS

The Gauls proved a fearsome adversary of Rome, making forays into the Italian peninsula from their homeland further north, a vast area roughly comprising the territory of modern-day France and parts of Belgium, Switzerland, Germany and Austria. Culturally and linguistically, the Gauls were part of the Celtic civilization. From the fourth into the third centuries BC, spearheaded by the Senones tribal group, the Gauls established a strong presence south of the Alps in northern Italy. Around the summer of 390 BC Rome came face to face with the invaders at the battle of the Allia, about 10 miles north of Rome itself. The Senones overwhelmed the defenders and proceeded to loot and burn much of Rome, and when they failed to take the citadel on the Capitoline, they laid a siege. After several months, and with both sides beset by hunger and disease, Rome paid the Gauls to leave, although the historical sources disagree on whether the Gauls were eventually chased away or not. As for the Roman authorities, they set about reinforcing the city's fortifications to avert any repeat of their humiliation.

But Rome is not cowed. Its ambitions to expand its influence around the Mediterranean are driven by the prospect of extravagant power and wealth, unattainable by remaining within the borders of the Italian boot. In 264 BC Rome takes on the Carthaginians and defeats them in a landmark contest on Sicily – a fledgling venture away from the mainland that marks the start of the First Punic War, the initial phase of an epoch-defining conflict that cements Rome's rise among the world's major powers.

A superstar of his day, Fabius's fame has not lasted in the way of other notables of ancient Rome. As with so much of early Roman history, there is dispute among chroniclers about the exact details of his exploits. His campaigns against Pontius are particularly contested. Nonetheless, it is upon such figures that Rome's glories are built, individuals who possess undoubted political and military skills but who, perhaps more importantly, drag Rome to triumphs in battles of endurance. Fabius wins fabulous victories, but his armies are frequently put to the test. They cannot rely on simply overwhelming the enemy with shock and awe. Instead, they grind out results even when the odds seem stacked against them, holding fast in wars of attrition that last years, decades or even centuries.

By now the Roman state has sound foundations and sophisticated political structures. Increasingly, it boasts impressive infrastructure too. Its wily policy of conquering and assimilating has gained it the physical territory and personnel necessary to become a significant military force. Yet its domination of the Italian peninsula has been no foregone conclusion. Instead, it is an achievement centuries in the making and rooted in the kind of ambition and doggedness that will come to define many of its leaders, epitomized by figures like Fabius Maximus.

# 5
# HANNIBAL: THE ADVERSARY

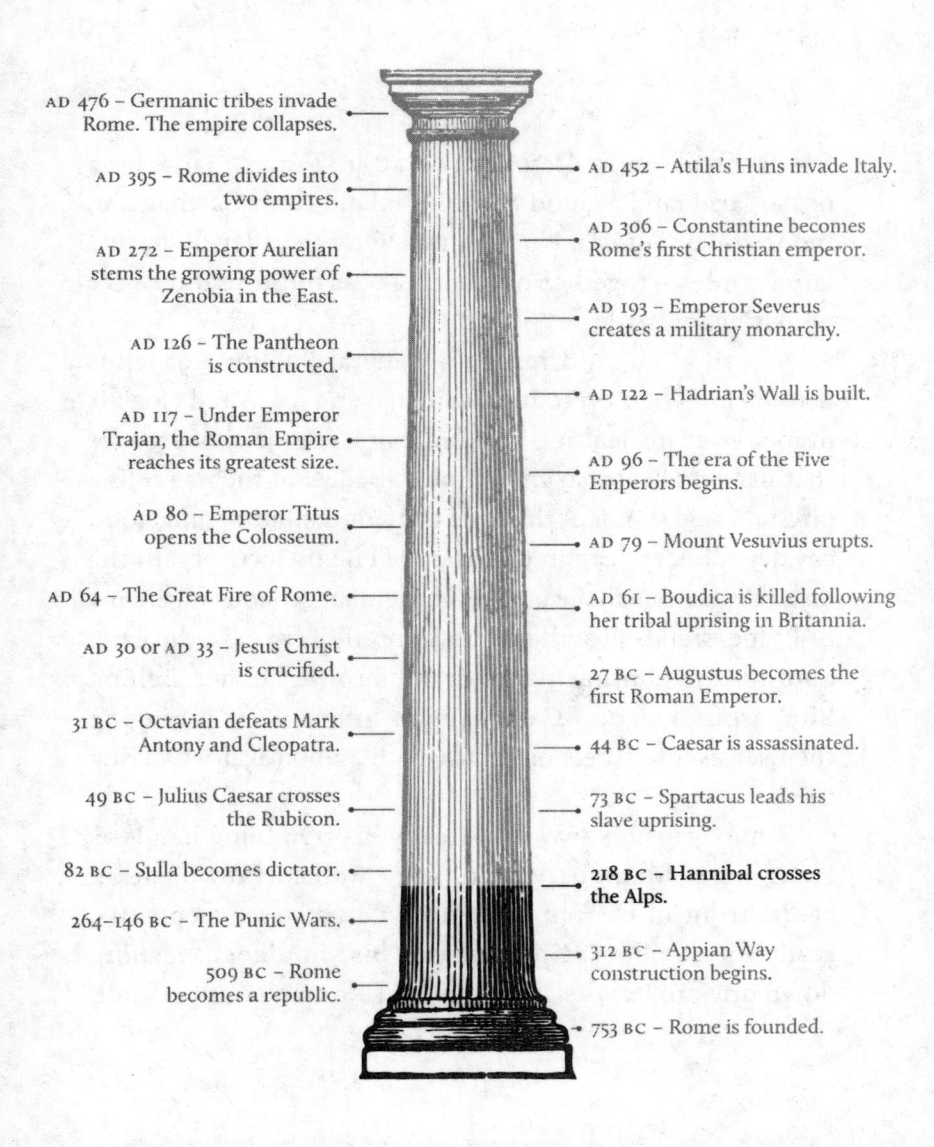

- AD 476 – Germanic tribes invade Rome. The empire collapses.
- AD 452 – Attila's Huns invade Italy.
- AD 395 – Rome divides into two empires.
- AD 306 – Constantine becomes Rome's first Christian emperor.
- AD 272 – Emperor Aurelian stems the growing power of Zenobia in the East.
- AD 193 – Emperor Severus creates a military monarchy.
- AD 126 – The Pantheon is constructed.
- AD 122 – Hadrian's Wall is built.
- AD 117 – Under Emperor Trajan, the Roman Empire reaches its greatest size.
- AD 96 – The era of the Five Emperors begins.
- AD 80 – Emperor Titus opens the Colosseum.
- AD 79 – Mount Vesuvius erupts.
- AD 64 – The Great Fire of Rome.
- AD 61 – Boudica is killed following her tribal uprising in Britannia.
- AD 30 or AD 33 – Jesus Christ is crucified.
- 27 BC – Augustus becomes the first Roman Emperor.
- 31 BC – Octavian defeats Mark Antony and Cleopatra.
- 44 BC – Caesar is assassinated.
- 49 BC – Julius Caesar crosses the Rubicon.
- 73 BC – Spartacus leads his slave uprising.
- 82 BC – Sulla becomes dictator.
- **218 BC – Hannibal crosses the Alps.**
- 264–146 BC – The Punic Wars.
- 312 BC – Appian Way construction begins.
- 509 BC – Rome becomes a republic.
- 753 BC – Rome is founded.

It's daybreak on 19 October 202 BC in Zama, a large area of flat, arid land around 80 miles inland from Carthage, in modern-day Tunisia, North Africa. On the valley floor, two large armies – together numbering tens of thousands – are preparing for battle.

A bead of sweat drips from General Publius Cornelius Scipio's long hair on to his clean-shaven face. A red cloak is draped over his leather-muscled cuirass, a piece of armour that fits over his torso and mimics an ideal of the masculine physique. He stands at the head of 29,000 infantry and 6,000 cavalry soldiers deep in the heart of enemy territory. In the distance, Hannibal, the great Carthaginian general and enemy of Rome, stands proudly at the front of his troops, the early autumn sun glinting off his ornate bronze helmet. Behind him, around 36,000 Carthaginian infantry are arranging themselves into three long lines, with 4,000 cavalry flanking them.

Scipio grips his sword to steady his trembling hands as Hannibal's infamous weapons are walked into position at the front of the opposing army: eighty war elephants, ready for combat. Scipio squares his shoulders, pushing down any anxiety, as the sounds of Roman trumpets and the cries of men and animals reverberate across the valley floor. Then, Hannibal raises his sword and his war elephants are unleashed. Shaking the ground, they charge towards the Roman lines.

*One of the greatest battles of the ancient world has begun. In the words of Livy: 'Before night fell, they would know whether Rome or Carthage would make laws for all the nations; the reward for victory was not just Italy or Africa, but all the world.' But how did we get here? How has Rome found itself in a winner-takes-all battle with the Carthaginian Empire? For Hannibal, it's a story that takes seed nearly four decades earlier.*

## HANNIBAL'S OATH

It's 239 BC, thirty-seven years before the battle of Zama, and nine-year-old Hannibal has been summoned to meet his father in Carthage, the epicentre of the Carthaginian Empire. The meeting spot is a temple surrounded by a tranquil courtyard, its walls featuring vividly coloured paintings, some detailing elegantly dressed people captured in conversation. A statue of Baal, the city's chief god, looks down on the scene. In this peaceful place, the sounds of the bustling city outside feel distant.

Young Hannibal's gaze is drawn to a small altar in the courtyard's centre where stands a man with a thick, dark, wavy beard, wearing decorative military clothing. It's the first time Hannibal has met his father, Hamilcar Barca, the great Carthaginian general, as the older man has been away fighting in Sicily. Now, Hamilcar stoops down and fixes his determined eyes on his child. He is about to embark on an expedition to

Iberia, in modern-day Spain, to expand Carthage's territory, and he wants his son to join him.

It is only two years since Carthage suffered defeat in the twenty-three-year-long First Punic War between the rival empires of Rome and Carthage. Hannibal has heard the stories of his father's heroic defence of the island of Sicily, and his dismay at losing the territory to the Romans, who now have access to its plentiful resources as well as controlling the sea straits that pass north and south of the island. Carthage had begun the war with the superior navy, while Rome boasted the better army. However, the shrewd Romans turned their weaker sailing skills into a strength, avoiding technical sea battles in favour of simply ramming the Carthaginian ships and using gangplanks to overrun them with foot soldiers. Rome won the war and seized control of Sicily despite the best efforts of Hannibal's father, who has been left resentful that he was given insufficient military support to overcome the enemy.

Now, as Hannibal excitedly agrees to join him on his new campaign, Hamilcar takes the boy's hand and lays it on the sacrificial altar. The child's small fingers splay out among the remnants of an animal sacrifice as he swears an oath: 'I will never be a friend of Rome.'

## YOUNG HANNIBAL

Sicily's natural resources are now flowing around Rome's expanding territories. To make up for the corresponding loss to Carthage, Hamilcar and his sons, including Hannibal, travel to Iberia – what is now Spain and Portugal – intent on seizing land from the indigenous populations and exploiting the area's rich mineral wealth. He's successful in conquering much of southern and eastern Iberia and uses the plunder to strengthen Carthage's military. In 228 BC, however, Hamilcar dies (probably by drowning in a river), and seven years later Hannibal's brother-in-law is assassinated by a Gaul. Aged just twenty-six, Hannibal now takes charge of the Carthaginian army and begins planning revenge on the Romans.

Early in 219 BC he attacks Saguntum, an Iberian city with ties to Rome, then orders his army over the Ebro river. Lying 100 or so miles south-west of what is now Spain's border with France, the waterway is a natural boundary line that Carthage had agreed not to cross at the end of the First Punic War. Recognizing that any further incursions north could bring the Carthaginians a little too close for comfort to their own northern territories, Rome is furious at the antagonistic move. So it is that by the following spring – twenty-three years on from the concluding horrors of that first war – the Second Punic War erupts, engulfing the Mediterranean once again in violence.

As Hannibal begins his advance on the old enemy, Rome's key advantage over Carthage is its ability to rapidly raise armies from among its Italian half-citizens and allies. It is this allied network that provided Rome with the manpower it needed to see out almost a quarter of a century of attrition in the First Punic War. To defeat Rome, Hannibal believes he must get inside Italy and secure some battlefield victories. If that pays off, he thinks, it will then inspire Italian townships to switch allegiance to him in a bid to regain their traditional ancestral freedoms. The plan is far-fetched to say the least.

Getting into the Italian peninsula in the first place is no small matter. A seaborne invasion will likely be quelled immediately by the now dominant Roman navy, and there is no navigable overland route from Iberia to Italy that doesn't pit his army against the mountainous Alps that sit north of the Italian peninsula. The Romans themselves are convinced this route is impassable because of the freezing temperatures and fierce tribes found within the mountains. Hannibal is unconvinced by such scepticism; after all, the deity Hercules is said to have crossed the Alps in days gone by. If Hercules can do it, why can't he?

## VOYAGE THROUGH THE ALPS

In late autumn 218 BC Hannibal and his troops (along with some miserable, bound Celt prisoners he has picked up along the way) set off from Iberia for the Alps, but getting to the foothills is perilous. First, his army must navigate the high passes of the Pyrenees, where they endure attacks by wild tribesmen. Then they are forced to battle a large army of Gauls when crossing the mighty Rhône river. Several days after discreetly entering the Alps, some of his soldiers, wearing full armour, plummet down a precipice to their deaths after attempting to traverse a narrow icy pass. A little later, several panicked pack animals carrying supplies meet a similar fate. And while the sight of war elephants thousands of feet up in the mountains is a terrifying spectacle for tribes who have never seen such a creature before, the elephants themselves are struggling too. Spooked by the unfamiliar sights and sounds around them, not to mention the freezing temperatures, the massive beasts are proving almost impossible to handle.

Soon, they are approached by a mountain chieftain who

has travelled to meet Hannibal. Explaining that this is dangerous territory, he offers guides and supplies to assist him on his journey. Without even a navigable map of the Alps, Hannibal welcomes the offer, albeit cautiously. For a while the guides seem to aid progress.

After several days of trekking, the army enters yet another narrow pass. Icy rain hits the young general's face as he looks up at the rugged, sheer, overhanging cliffs. What he sees makes him immediately regret his decision to come this way. He steps back in horror, scrabbling for his sword, as war cries resonate through the landscape and the silhouettes of hundreds of tribal warriors appear on the ridgeline. A volley of boulders and rocks strikes the Carthaginian soldiers strung out along the narrow valley pass in front of and behind their leader. Regaining his composure, Hannibal screams orders at the elephant handlers and cavalry soldiers in advance of him, then turns to see the elite infantry already slashing away at the attackers to his rear. They must hold the line or face being overrun. Throughout the night Hannibal's men remain trapped in the pass, defending themselves against wave upon wave of attack, but as the hours pass the skirmishes lessen in their intensity.

By sunrise the Carthaginians have turned the tide and overwhelmed the enemy. As they set about stripping the warm winter furs off the tribesmen's bodies, Hannibal himself searches among the dead and confirms what he already suspected – that it was none other than the treacherous mountain guides who led his army into this ambush. The Carthaginian death toll could have been far worse if Hannibal hadn't entered the pass with some of his best men deployed at both the front and back of his stretched-out army.

Nonetheless, they have paid a heavy price, losing men, horses and elephants.

After nine days of hiking through the mountains – occasionally going in the wrong direction – the demoralized Carthaginian army finally catches a glimpse of the green pastures of Italy's Po Valley on the horizon. Winter snows will make their descent perilous, but the horrors of the Alps are almost over. Soon they will be in the Italian foothills, preparing their march south, to Rome.

## AN ENEMY IN ITALY

When Hannibal finally arrives in Italy, he dismounts from the only surviving elephant and plunges his arm into a river, its icy cold waters swollen by the winter snow and rains. His feet are damp from squelching across the flat, muddy marshland, but they are of less concern to him than his right eye. It's red and sore and has been irritating him for days, aggravated by the swampy conditions. In fact, he is suffering a severe bout of ophthalmia that will leave him permanently blind in that eye.

But at least he's survived, which is more than can be said of half of his men. Though he set out with a combined infantry and cavalry force of over 60,000, after losing so many to skirmishes, accidents, the conditions of the trek and desertion, he is now down to a mere 25,000 men and 6,000 cavalry. But his expedition must continue, whatever his suffering and that of his men. Rome must be brought to its knees.

Hannibal's unexpected arrival sends shockwaves across the Italian peninsula, with two hastily assembled armies sent out to confront the Carthaginians. The odds stacked against him,

Hannibal stages gladiatorial death matches between some of his captured Celt prisoners. There is freedom on offer to the victorious, and he hopes the spectacle will inspire local tribal groups to join with him against the tyranny of ever-expanding Rome. He barks at his own men that the prisoners forced to fight are no different from them, trapped in a situation where only absolute victory will secure their liberty. When one of the local tribes, the Taurini, refuses to join his force, he makes an example of them, slaughtering them all, including women and children. The message is clear: join Hannibal or die.

## THE BATTLES OF TICINUS AND TREBIA

Behind enemy lines, heavily outnumbered and without a proper supply chain, Hannibal must do whatever he can to keep his soldiers going if they are to have any chance of surviving the coming Roman onslaught. By late November 218 BC he is close to the Ticinus river in northern Italy. This year's Roman consul, Cornelius Scipio, leads out an army to engage the Carthaginians. To his surprise, as the two forces line up readying themselves for combat, the Carthaginians almost instantaneously charge the Roman line. The unexpected strategy creates confusion among the Roman soldiers. Seizing upon this moment of weakness, Hannibal's cavalry encircles the enemy and attacks them from behind as part of a manoeuvre called a double envelopment. Writing around 200 years after the fact, Livy describes how, amid the chaos, Scipio's sixteen-year-old son, who shares his father's name, charges forward when he sees his father fall, risking his life to ensure that his father is able to escape. The consul and his son live to fight another day but the engagement goes down as a

Carthaginian triumph. Emboldened by Hannibal's victory, the local Celt tribes flock to join him.

It is not long before Hannibal faces a second Roman army, this time at the Trebia river. In another moment of tactical brilliance he decides to turn one of the Romans' main strengths – their bravery – into their central weakness. At dawn on 23 December, guards protecting a Roman camp near the river sound the alarm. A dispatch of Hannibal's Numidian cavalry are firing projectiles into the camp. The angered Romans hastily make chase, despite their empty stomachs and lack of preparation. Courageously, they wade through the cold river in pursuit of their prey but, unbeknown to them, the Numidians are only pretending to retreat. In reality they are luring the Romans into a trap. Having crossed the river, the Romans stand in sodden clothes in almost freezing temperatures. To their horror, Hannibal's army are lining up over the brow of the riverbank in the near distance, arranging themselves in battle formation. The cold, wet, hungry Romans now face a prepared, rested, fed and dry Carthaginian opponent. As battle commences, a further 2,000 elite Carthaginian troops emerge from hiding spots further down the riverbank, capitalizing on their advantage to win the battle. Once again, Hannibal demonstrates near perfect military planning and execution.

## LAKE TRASIMENE AND CANNAE

The following summer Hannibal raids a series of villages on the shores of Lake Trasimene, a little over 100 miles north of Rome, in another bid to lure a Roman army from its encampment nearby. The Roman leader, Consul Gaius Flaminius, is advised to await reinforcements. But he has a reputation as a hothead, and when he sees the destruction he orders his soldiers to confront Hannibal at first light. However, Hannibal has the measure of his rival. Predicting Flaminius's actions, he commands his troops to leave camp in the dead of night and hide in the hillsides north of the lake. As Flaminius's army marches along the northern shore later that morning, Hannibal's men descend from the hills, pinning the Roman soldiers against the water's edge. The stunned Roman army is massacred; the few that initially escape into the lake either drown in their heavy armour or are forced into the shallows where they are butchered by the Carthaginian cavalry. Some sympathetic Roman historical accounts suggest that Flaminius's men have been fatally disadvantaged by the descent of a thick fog, but it is difficult to avoid the conclusion that Hannibal bested his enemy by making better decisions.

A little over a year later, in August 216 BC, Hannibal has made his way down the eastern side of the peninsula towards the ankle of Italy. Knowing that his army is still too small to take on the heavily defended fortifications of Rome itself, he is concentrating on breaking its alliances and bringing smaller tribes under his own command.

To stop him, a vast 80,000-strong Roman army amasses in Cannae, in south-east Italy. Hannibal may be a military genius, but his men are now outnumbered two to one. Rome's network of allies pulls together again, yet to their horror Hannibal uses his signature move, a double envelopment, to claim another extraordinary victory. As the Carthaginian general's reputation is cemented for ever more, half of Rome's fighting force is massacred, and Rome itself seems on the brink of collapse.

## QUINTUS FABIUS BECOMES DICTATOR

On hearing about the devastation at Cannae, hundreds of mothers and children gather at the gates of Rome, eyes fixed on the horizon, desperately hoping to see their sons, husbands and fathers as the returning army appears in the distance. The sounds of mourning and wailing fill the streets. It's reported that at least one mother drops dead of heartbreak as the awful truth becomes clear: tens of thousands of Roman lives have been lost.

In the days following the battle, the panicked Roman Senate convenes an emergency meeting. In a bid to restore calm, the senators decide to elect a member of one of the great patrician families as dictator, to see them through the crisis. They choose **Quintus Fabius Maximus**, the grandson of Fabius Maximus, hero of the wars against the Samnites and Etruscans. Quintus Fabius's term as dictator is limited to six months, but he is expected to lay aside his new powers as soon as the emergency has passed.

With the atmosphere in the city on a knife edge, Quintus recognizes that in order for faith in their leaders to be restored the people are in need of someone, or something, to blame. He declares that Rome's four recent battlefield failures against Hannibal are the result of the city's lack of religious observance, and embarks on a harrowing series of measures to cleanse Rome and restore the city's divine favour – to re-establish their collective *pietas*. So the story goes, he bans public mourning and has a Vestal Virgin buried alive for breaking her oath of celibacy and offending the gods. He continues his mission by punishing other allegedly sinful men and women in the same way. Yet despite his brutality, Quintus's actions do not cause much of a stir in the city. Rather, having identified scapegoats, he appears to be unifying its citizens.

> ## VESTAL VIRGINS
>
> The Vestal Virgins were an important all-female priesthood in Rome, dedicated to Vesta, goddess of the home and hearth. The order was said to have been established in Rome by Romulus's successor, Numa Pompilius, and initially numbered just two priestesses, although this would eventually grow to six. The priestesses were selected when pre-pubescent, freed from ties to their families and expected to serve for at least thirty years, when they could retire with a pension and marry if they so wanted. In the interim, they pledged to remain celibate under threat of punishment of death. Their duties included maintaining the fire in the sacred hearth of Vesta's temple at all times. Should it go out, it was feared Vesta would withdraw her protection from the city. If Livy is to be believed, the Vestal Virgins actually pre-dated Rome's foundation, with Romulus and Remus's mother, Rhea Silvia, said to have been assigned the office in Alba Longa before she conceived the famous twins.

Quintus is, however, cautious about engaging Hannibal in another direct confrontation. Instead, he plans to quell the Carthaginian incursion through more attritional tactics. Rather than chase open battle, he targets Hannibal's supply lines, reasoning that the Carthaginians will weaken in time.

Soon enough, with no field battles to fight or negotiations to make, Hannibal finds himself somewhat isolated.

Rome now launches an attack on the city of Capua, which has sided with Hannibal. After crushing its defenders and murdering its senators, the Roman authorities then set about selling Capua's inhabitants into slavery. There is a growing sense that, following the disastrous battle losses against Hannibal, Rome is at last turning the tide of the war. But the republic needs a hero to vanquish Hannibal once and for all, someone who can display *virtus*, that fabled Roman concept encompassing valour, masculinity, excellence, courage, character and worth.

## PUBLIUS CORNELIUS SCIPIO

Publius Cornelius Scipio is born into one of the great patrician families in Rome. His father, grandfather and great-grandfather were all consuls. Having saved his father's life at the battle of Ticinus, Scipio has spent the last few years developing a reputation in Rome for bravery and loyalty. In 210 BC he is given control of his father's demoralized army in Hispania, a role Rome's military generals deem something of a suicide mission. But against the odds, the young general changes the course of the war there with several decisive victories. Most spectacularly, he oversees the successful siege of New Carthage, the power base for Carthage in the region. Using a combination of terror tactics and wily diplomacy, Scipio then defeats Hannibal's brother, Mago Barca, in battle in 206 BC, securing control of vast territory and resources, including a silver mine. Scipio returns to Rome a year later, where he hatches a bold plan to lure

Hannibal out of Italy by mounting an invasion of Hannibal's homeland, hoping he will return to defend it. After two years of fierce debate, the Senate finally agrees to support his daring scheme.

It begins in 204 BC. At the prow of a Roman transport ship travelling at speed across the moonlit Mediterranean Sea, Scipio scans the dull silhouettes of hundreds more vessels surrounding him. Between them, the ships carry 35,000 tightly packed Roman soldiers. His invasion force is on a one-night journey from Sicily to a North African town near Carthage. On arrival, havoc breaks out as the Romans set about terrorizing the local population.

Scipio's first military objective is to seize the town of Utica (a little way north-west of modern-day Tunis) to use it as the Roman base of operations for their wider invasion. But, in contrast to Hannibal's devastating early victories in Italy, the Romans fail to take their target and are forced to encamp on a nearby peninsula. It's not the start the mighty hero of Rome has hoped for, and it seems as if he may have no choice but to capitulate in light of this defeat.

In the spring of 203 BC, lookouts at the main Carthaginian military camp located out in the desert raise the alarm when they spy a small detachment of Roman soldiers and slaves approaching, led by Scipio himself. The Roman general enters through the wooden palisades and is ushered in to meet the Carthaginian leaders. Scipio declares that he has made the 7-mile journey from his own camp to enter peace negotiations. It seems he believes the war can never be fully won and, having seen the might of Carthage, he doubts the Romans can defeat them. It's an unexpected and astonishing confession, but the Carthaginians welcome him and talks begin on an agreement that would see Hannibal exit Italy in return for Scipio leaving North Africa.

As the negotiations continue, the men who have accompanied Scipio but are not allowed into the talks roam freely around the camp, their eyes darting left and right as they walk past row upon row of simple huts. They appear to be slaves, but on returning to the Roman camp they take off the coarse tunics they've been using as disguises, put on their usual officers' clothing and immediately get to work drawing detailed plans of the enemy camp. They map out the complex network of passageways that connect the rows of thin-walled, thatched-roof huts housing some 93,000 troops.

The deception is finally revealed late one night, after several weeks of seemingly upbeat negotiations between Scipio and the Carthaginians. Without warning, a volley of flaming arrows fizzes through the sky and sets alight those same thatched roofs. Out of the darkness, panicked shouts ring out across the desert. Roman soldiers soon flood through the camp's passageways and into the huts, where they indiscriminately slaughter the inhabitants. Many of the Carthaginians, still believing the inferno has started accidentally, are slain as they attempt to dampen the flames. By sunrise perhaps tens of thousands of Carthaginians lie dead in the dust.

In the wake of this attack, a ship leaves Carthage for Italy, summoning Hannibal to come home. After fifteen years of roaming the Italian peninsula, Hannibal agrees, arriving with 12,000 soldiers poised to defend their homeland. He nonetheless receives a muted welcome from a terrified population. In a strategic game of cat-and-mouse, Scipio has blockaded a river valley that provides Carthage with most of its food supply.

Hannibal acts quickly, assembling extra soldiers, cavalry and war elephants from local towns. In the autumn of 202 BC he meets with Scipio, offering the Romans an opportunity to return to Italy without further bloodshed. But Scipio is said to reply: 'It is that you must submit yourselves and your country to us unconditionally or conquer us in the field.'

The stage is set for the ultimate showdown between the two great empires.

## ZAMA

The rival armies face off in the locale of Zama, not far from the border of modern-day Tunisia and Algeria. Hannibal is in the midst of giving his men a rousing speech when he is interrupted by a blast of Roman trumpets and thunderous war cries. Unable to be heard, Hannibal lifts his arm to signal the release of his war elephants. Scipio's battle formation has been designed for this moment. Unlike earlier confrontations where the tightly packed Romans were crushed as they tried to escape the elephants, this time his men are arranged into blocks, broken up with intermittent unmanned channels. The terrified elephants rush straight for these exit routes, stampeding harmlessly through the Roman lines before fleeing into the desert. Just moments into the battle, Scipio has rendered Hannibal's chief instruments of terror useless.

Now Scipio turns to his own secret weapon. For years the Numidian cavalry, renowned for their mastery at fighting with javelins, have stood alongside Hannibal. But the wily Scipio has played his own long game, wooing the Numidian leaders so that many have now changed their allegiances to him. Scipio's own Numidian cavalry charge at Hannibal's lesser cavalry force, pursuing them deep into the desert. With both cavalries thus occupied, the infantry clash.

Without the support of their mounted troops, Scipio's smaller army struggles to hold its ground. Emboldened to an extent by their home advantage, the Carthaginians fight with a passion driven by the knowledge that not only are their own lives at risk, but those of their loved ones living here in North Africa too. Slowly, the Romans find themselves being flanked by Hannibal's chillingly familiar double envelopment strategy. Scipio rushes reinforcements to the centre of the battlefield, where Hannibal's elite soldiers are making ground.

By now Hannibal's battlefield mastery is in full display. The ground is so blood-soaked that the Roman ranks find themselves slipping on the gore beneath their feet. But suddenly there is renewed hope. In the early afternoon a great dust cloud rises in the distance, followed by the noise of clattering hooves. Scipio's cavalry, having defeated Hannibal's, is on the charge into the Carthaginian back line. They begin to encircle the battlefield until, by nightfall, Rome is victorious.

Protected by his best fighters, Hannibal escapes and returns to Carthage, a city he has not seen for thirty-six years. In the aftermath of Zama, the Carthaginians surrender and the Second Punic War comes to a close. Carthage has to pay a war indemnity of 10,000 talents (equivalent to almost 300,000 tons of silver), their once mighty navy is restricted to a mere ten warships, and their stray elephants are put to death. Reduced to the status of a dependency of Rome – albeit one allowed to make many of its own laws – the ailing superpower will never reclaim its former glories.

Back in Rome, Scipio is granted the great honour of a triumph. Vanquishing the legendary Hannibal is the high point of his career, an achievement that has not just surpassed his father's, but also brought more *gloria* upon his name than anyone else in Roman history. And though the days of a small parade lasting an hour or two are long gone, even by the standards of the day his is no ordinary triumph. Days long, the celebrations in his honour include games, feasts and revelry. The biggest moment, however, is the procession itself, involving countless musicians and the display of vast quantities of plunder. Innumerable prisoners of war follow, terrified in the final hours before their ceremonial executions. Finally, with tens of thousands lining the streets, the man of the hour himself appears: Scipio Africanus, the conqueror of Africa, standing atop a chariot emblazoned with ivory and gold and pulled by four decorated horses. An effigy of a phallus hangs beneath the chariot, placed by the religious order of the Vestal Virgins to ward off the evil eye. Behind Africanus, a slave stands holding a golden crown above his head. A later account by the early Christian historian Tertullian claims that the slave would also whisper to the general as he proceeded around the city – *Respice post te. Hominem te memento.* (Look behind you. Remember that you are a man.) There's good reason to offer this reminder. The dazzling purple and gold of Scipio's toga tells the people of his standing in the mortal world. But with his face painted with red pigment in reference to the great Jupiter, he himself appears less of a man and more like a god.

According to Livy, around 183 BC, after several years living in exile, Hannibal – now in his mid-sixties – removes his ring from his finger, detaches its gemstone and reveals a small poison-filled compartment. Rome's great nemesis seemingly dies by his own hand, although there are differing accounts around the exact circumstances of his demise. To the surprise of many, Hannibal dies a changed man. Weary of the horrors of conflict, in his final years the famous warmonger has become an outspoken advocate for peace.

With its leaders driven as they are by the relentless desire for glory, the Roman Republic doesn't share his new ideals. And though Scipio has raised the bar of what can be achieved by one general, he has also ensured that his descendants must go even further if they are to match his legacy and bring honour upon their own names. In 146 BC Scipio's grandson, Scipio Aemilianus, razes Carthage to the ground, killing or enslaving every inhabitant of the city. That same year Rome sacks the Greek city of Corinth, signalling a major staging post in its conquest of Greece. With Carthage and the Greek world thus subdued, the march of Rome appears unstoppable.

# 6

# SULLA:
# A CRUMBLING REPUBLIC

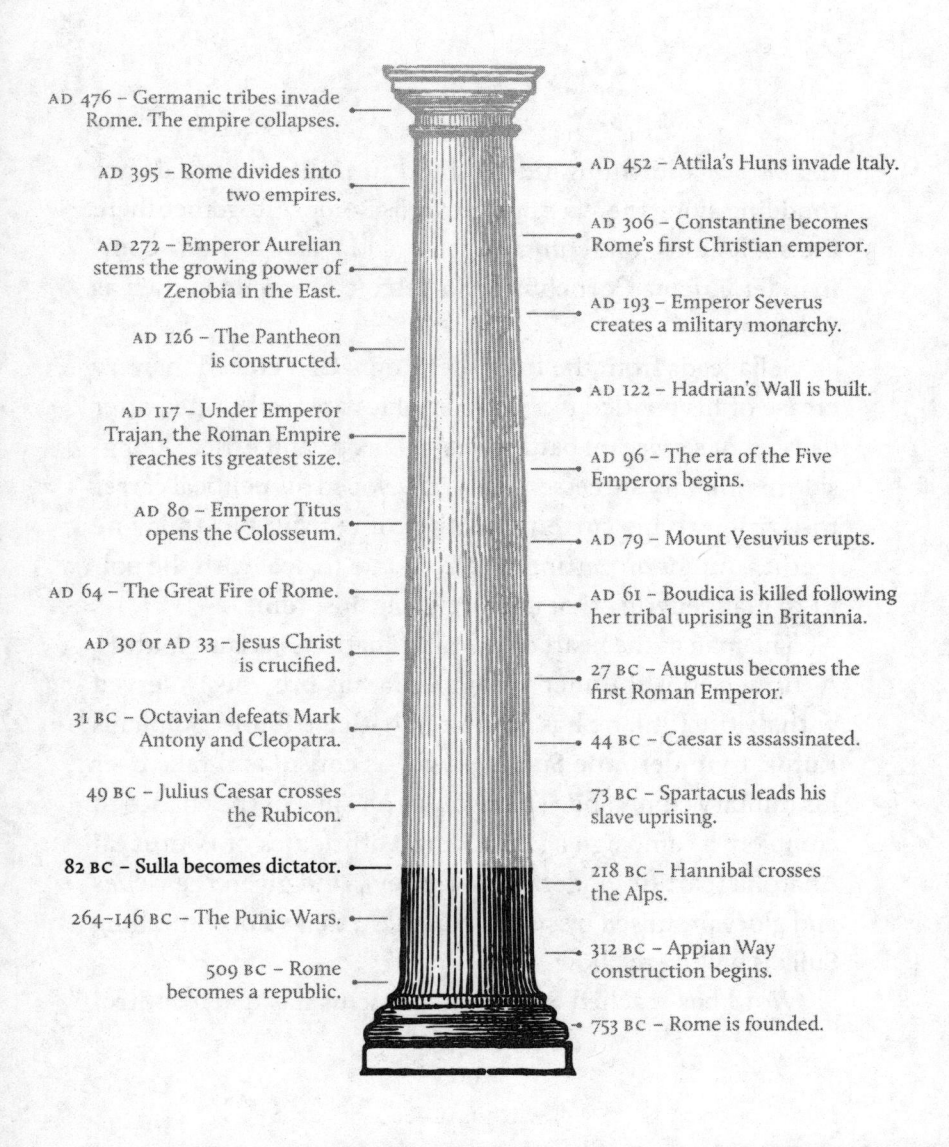

AD 476 – Germanic tribes invade Rome. The empire collapses.

AD 452 – Attila's Huns invade Italy.

AD 395 – Rome divides into two empires.

AD 306 – Constantine becomes Rome's first Christian emperor.

AD 272 – Emperor Aurelian stems the growing power of Zenobia in the East.

AD 193 – Emperor Severus creates a military monarchy.

AD 126 – The Pantheon is constructed.

AD 122 – Hadrian's Wall is built.

AD 117 – Under Emperor Trajan, the Roman Empire reaches its greatest size.

AD 96 – The era of the Five Emperors begins.

AD 80 – Emperor Titus opens the Colosseum.

AD 79 – Mount Vesuvius erupts.

AD 64 – The Great Fire of Rome.

AD 61 – Boudica is killed following her tribal uprising in Britannia.

AD 30 or AD 33 – Jesus Christ is crucified.

27 BC – Augustus becomes the first Roman Emperor.

31 BC – Octavian defeats Mark Antony and Cleopatra.

44 BC – Caesar is assassinated.

49 BC – Julius Caesar crosses the Rubicon.

73 BC – Spartacus leads his slave uprising.

**82 BC – Sulla becomes dictator.**

218 BC – Hannibal crosses the Alps.

264–146 BC – The Punic Wars.

312 BC – Appian Way construction begins.

509 BC – Rome becomes a republic.

753 BC – Rome is founded.

It's 88 BC, and thousands of men in military sandals are thudding along the Via Appia towards Rome. Altogether there are six legions, marching in personal loyalty to their commander, Lucius Cornelius Sulla Felix (commonly known as Sulla).

Sulla leads from the front, determination etched in every crease of his gnarled face. His wrinkles are well earned after decades of service on battlefields in Europe and Africa. Alongside his military successes he has developed his political career too, rising to his current position of consul. But today he seethes, intent on getting back to Rome to deal with the political manoeuvring that is going on against him.

The man at the heart of the machinations is Gaius Marius. A former consul under whom Sulla has previously served with distinction, he has conspired with a tribune, Sulpicius Rufus, to undermine Sulla's power as consul and take over his military command. That would rob Sulla of the chance to complete a campaign against King Mithridates of Pontus, in Anatolia (part of modern-day Turkey). And given the riches and glory promised by such a conquest, that's not something Sulla is willing to allow.

Word has reached Sulla that Sulpicius has taken control

of the city and is picking off Sulla's allies, killing them and seizing their property. Determined to reassert his authority and avenge this betrayal, Sulla pulls hard on the reins of his horse, urging the beast to pick up the pace. His army behind speeds up to match him.

Up ahead, Sulla spots a pair of officials from the Senate come to intercept him. They demand to know the meaning of this march on Rome. Looking them in the eye, he tells them he has come to rescue the city from tyrants. As they survey his vast force, the envoys plead for peace talks. But Sulla is having none of it. Kicking his heels into his horse's side, he races off, and the officials have no choice but to step aside and allow the thousands-strong army to pass.

Soon, Sulla arrives at a stone post denoting the *pomerium*, the outer boundary of Rome that Romulus himself is supposed to have ploughed. It is weighted with symbolic meaning, and sacred tradition says that no Roman shall cross it bearing arms. But Sulla has no time for the convention today. He leads his army resolutely onwards, even as some of his men step out of their lines, unprepared to break this covenant.

When he arrives at the formidable Esquiline Gate, set into the city's eastern defensive wall, he comes under a deluge of bricks and stones thrown down upon him by citizens loyal to Marius. But this rag-tag bunch are no match for Sulla's well-drilled men, who secure the gate and then pour through it. He barks an order for them to parade through the streets, a reminder to the citizenry that the old order is reasserting itself. Rome echoes to the sound of their regimented procession, during which his troops fire off blazing arrows into the sky. Sulla smiles at the intimidatingly impressive scene.

A messenger reports to him that Marius has sought refuge

in a temple on the Esquiline Hill, and before long Sulla's old ally-turned-foe flees the city altogether, as does Sulpicius. Sulla now summons the sheepish Senate and declares twelve of the chief conspirators against him, including Marius and Sulpicius, as outlaws. Everyone knows Sulla is back in charge. But he has had to break a taboo to make it happen. For the first time in the republic's history, a Roman has led an army into Rome to challenge his fellow citizens.

Sulla has won the day, but the battle for the soul of Rome has many more twists and turns to come. The republic itself, and all that it stands for – including the notion that the state comes before any individual – is in peril.

*For over four centuries the Roman Republic has thrived and prospered. There are many reasons for this, but one vital aspect is its unique political structure. After deposing its kings, Rome has operated a complex system of political checks and balances. In broad terms, the consuls, Senate and the assemblies of the people are sufficiently interdependent that no branch of government is able to overreach, or at least not for any significant amount of time before the system corrects itself. As the historian Polybius notes, the republic boasts a constitution that blends a mixture of monarchy, aristocracy and democracy.*

*Yet, Rome has perhaps become a victim of its own success. It is one thing to maintain the necessary checks and balances in a city of a few tens of thousands. But today Rome is a metropolis of 100,000 and more. Moreover, the territory it controls encompasses most of Hispania, Greece and parts of the North African Mediterranean coast, and is forever expanding further northwards and eastwards. There is a nuanced patchwork of competing interests and agendas among people of vastly differing statuses, ranging from the members of Rome's old ruling families to slaves grabbed during the republic's conquests of distant regions. The faultlines in Rome's long-established, and largely unwritten, constitutional set-up have been showing the strain for a while. But just how have the ideals and institutions of the early republic that spurred Rome's spectacular growth so failed that Sulla has been able to make his power-grab? And with what devastating consequences for the republic itself? A good place to start seeking the answer is in the republic's complicated social make-up.*

## CITIZENSHIP AND DEMOGRAPHY

The question of citizenship in Rome has never been entirely straightforward, with rights differing depending upon several variables, including how one has acquired citizenship, sex, social class and so on. Then there are the distinct rights accorded to citizens of states that have formally allied themselves with Rome, including several on the Italian peninsula who have long loaned their manpower to help Rome's expansion. Their rights, lesser than those of full citizens, are nonetheless considerably superior to those granted to peoples that have otherwise fallen under Roman control. Trying to keep everyone happy, citizens of all types and non-citizens alike, is proving tricky.

Even within Rome, the old social divisions are evolving and changing. There has always been a tension between the patricians and plebeians, but there are nuanced rifts between the old, traditionally powerful families (the *nobiles*) and members of newer families on the up (known as *novus homo* or 'the new man'). A wealthy class of *equites* (or 'knights') has grown rich exploiting opportunities in far-off new territories, posing a threat to the authority of the traditional patrician, senatorial class. Politically, there are now two distinct though not formally recognized camps: on the one hand the *optimates*, intent on defending the old ways centred around senatorial authority, and the *populares*, who see a more expedient route to power by presenting themselves as champions of the people and using popular political institutions (like the tribuneship) to undermine senatorial power.

### ROMAN CITIZENSHIP

Citizenship in the Roman Republic was a complicated matter, impacting your rights to vote and hold public office, your responsibilities (not least to the military), and your property and marriage prospects. The exact nature of these rights and responsibilities evolved over time, but the citizenship classes included:

- *Cives Romani* – full citizens who enjoyed the complete protection of Roman law. Subdivided into the *non optimo iure*, who enjoyed property and marriage rights, and the *optimo iure*, who were also able to vote and hold office.

- *Latini* – originally, granted to Latin peoples (and members of other Roman colonies), giving them rights to trade with and marry Romans and to migrate across Roman territory.

- *Socii* – given to citizens of states who allied themselves with Rome or, in some circumstances, had been conquered. They were bound to pay taxes and provide men for military service, but were given few rights in return beyond protection and the right to share in the spoils of war. Their demand for improved rights lay behind the Social War of 91–88 BC.

- *Provinciales* – for the populations of conquered areas considered by Rome to be worthy of only lesser rights.

On top of all this political jousting, there are important demographic changes too. The republic started out as an agrarian society built upon small farm settlements. Now many of these smallholdings have been swallowed into much larger enterprises, the labour carried out by swelling numbers of slaves. For many Roman citizens born into the expectation of a life working the family farm, that option no longer exists. Instead, they do their military service until it is time for them to retire from active duty, only to find that their family lands have been depleted and the rewards they had hoped for in return for their sacrifice to the republic are no longer there. This mass of disgruntled, landless ex-veterans is another important factor to consider in the political landscape. Then there are the slaves and the conquered peoples, whose lot is worst of all. The republic governs a tinderbox of competing desires and complaints. And it's only a matter of time until something gives.

## TIBERIUS GRACCHUS

In 133 BC Sulla is just an infant, the son of a respected patrician family fallen on hard times. A man named Tiberius Gracchus has just been elected tribune of the plebeians. He hails from one of the city's most esteemed families, his grandfather none other than Scipio Africanus. Gracchus, though, is alert to the sense of disgruntlement spreading through Roman society, and has plans to address it. Whether his solidarity is genuine or he sees it as a strategy to firm up popular support is a matter of debate, but whatever his motivation, his position as tribune gives him the perfect platform.

As tribune, he has the right to propose legislation for consideration by the council of the plebeians. He comes up with a series of land reforms sure to upset many within his own class. He suggests a limit on the amount of state-owned public land any individual can possess, and also a law that would see territory seized by the state during conquests parcelled up and redistributed to Rome's poor and landless. While his proposals are not without supporters in the Senate, they are not going down well with everybody, especially plantation-holders growing rich by exploiting slave labour.

But what really upsets Rome's traditional power-brokers is the way that Gracchus has gone about pushing his changes through. Failing to secure sufficient support from the Senate, he bypasses it and goes straight to the plebeian assemblies. In doing so, he is challenging the status quo in an unprecedented way.

It has long been the case that tribunes possess a veto to overrule any action of an over-mighty magistrate, but now Gracchus's opponents in the Senate use this rule against him. They persuade one of his nine fellow tribunes to veto his reforms, despite a tribune-on-tribune veto being without precedent. The infuriated Gracchus responds by adopting another unheard-of tactic, calling on the citizen assemblies to vote his rival tribune out of office. And what the traditionalists see as a gross overreach doesn't stop there. Gracchus also succeeds in diverting taxes raised abroad, and then announces that he'll be running for another term as tribune, subverting the custom of stepping down after a year. Everywhere, the old rules are being rewritten.

## A VIOLENT RESOLUTION

Gracchus's re-election is on a knife edge, with the Senate accusing him of crimes ranging from misappropriating public monies and acting unconstitutionally to wishing to overthrow the republic. With the stakes high, he makes his way to the Capitoline Hill to hear the results. When he arrives, there is already a large crowd, a tense mixture of his supporters and opponents.

Over the hubbub, he spots a senator friendly to his cause who tells him that the Senate has met this very morning and plans to have him killed. As Gracchus aims to get word of the danger to his inner circle, he raises his hands towards his head. It's an innocent enough gesture, yet one of his enemies in the crowd starts a rumour that Gracchus is signalling his desire to wear a crown – in other words, to make himself king. A messenger carries the 'news' back to the Senate, where one of its members, Gracchus's own cousin Scipio Nasica, sets out for the Capitoline with a quickly assembled mob armed with canes and stones.

When Gracchus spots them, he and his followers attempt to flee but several are knocked over in the panic. Gracchus stumbles too, and as he flails on the ground he feels a crack across his skull. He puts his hand to the wound, blood smearing his fingertips. Out of the corner of his eye he sees its cause – the leg of a stool wielded by a merciless attacker. Before he can recover his senses, another blow lands, then another. Soon enough, pain and fear give way to unconsciousness, from which he will never wake up.

The republic is not used to this sort of political violence, but it feels as if the old system of checks and balances is collapsing.

## GAIUS GRACCHUS

It is not the end for the Gracchus family. A decade later, in 123 BC, Tiberius's younger brother Gaius becomes a tribune. And if anything, he is more confrontational than his sibling. As well as resurrecting land reforms, he wants the state to pay for soldiers' uniforms (until now funded from their wages), and calls for more roads to be built to provide employment and spur agricultural trading. He also wants to give land in foreign colonies to the landless, make juries more representative, and distribute grain to the poor.

But possibly his most controversial idea centres on the knotty issue of greater citizenship rights for Rome's Latin allies, who – trapped in Rome's 'protection racket' syndicate – are growing weary of not seeing the benefits of their cooperation. In Rome, though, there is reluctance to elevate the status of these peoples who will never be, in the eyes of traditionalists, the equals of Romans.

Just as Tiberius Gracchus had sought a second term to see his work through, so too does Gaius. And he gets it. The Senate, still reeling from the opprobrium that came its way after Tiberius's death, is reluctant to take on the younger brother so openly. Instead, some of his enemies put their weight behind another tribune who works to block Gaius Gracchus's reforms while courting many of the same disgruntled groups. Gaius haemorrhages popular support as his second tribuneship draws to a close. Fearful of what his enemies might do to him, he builds a personal bodyguard. But when a particularly fiery political meeting breaks out into fighting, Rome is engulfed by rioting – just the excuse the Senate needs to declare martial law. It is a disaster for Gaius who, along with 3,000 of his supporters, dies in pitched street battles. It's far from a graceful end, made worse by the current consul promising that whoever brings Gaius's head to him will earn its weight in gold. When the head is presented, its bearer is delighted to see the scales tip at 17½lb. But as the suspicious senators inspect it, they discover that the enterprising butcher has removed the brain and filled the cavity with molten lead – a deception they punish with execution.

Ultimately, the Gracchi have failed to push through their radical agendas. Nonetheless, they have highlighted dangerous fissures in the political system. The alarm bells ringing among the traditional elite will not easily be silenced, nor the culture of political violence tamed.

## THE COMING MEN

The schism between the populist *populares* and the traditionalist *optimates* has never been starker. In this inhospitable environment a new name is on the rise: Gaius Marius. He comes not from one of the great patrician families but a relatively humble equestrian background. He has, however, cultivated the patronage of some of Rome's most established names and, crucially, his wife Julia comes from the great patrician Julian clan. Marius is the epitome of the *novus homo*, and in 119 BC he is elected a tribune, then, a few years later, praetor – the rank just below that of a consul, without powers of a commander and judge.

As governor of Hispania Ulterior (the far south of Spain), Marius gains valuable experience of guerrilla warfare as he fights off sporadic rebel incursions. It stands him in good stead when he goes off on campaign against the Numidian king, Jugurtha, in 109 BC. He grows his profile sufficiently that he is elected two years later as consul. A meteoric rise for a *novus homo*. Next, Marius supplants one of his old-school patrons to take command of the military forces in North Africa by vote of popular assembly. This sets him up in opposition to branches of the Senate, who ensure that though he may have the command, he will be denied troops.

This in itself once again brings to the fore a problem that has been growing in Rome for many years – the unglamorous issue of land reform. Thanks to the ever-intensifying competition among the powerful for more and more *gloria*, the republic has been in a near-constant state of war. When it is victorious – which it very often is – wealth and slaves flood in. Consequently, the richest among the patrician class use huge volumes of slave labour and take on ever-increasing areas of land to bolster their wealth, while Rome's many traditional family farms are edged out in the face of such competition. Crucially, according to custom, only landowners can serve in the army, because they are considered to have a stake in the outcome of the republic's conflicts. But with fewer and fewer people now owning land, it's feared that recruitment into the military will dwindle.

Marius now changes that. Promising them land in Rome's expanding territories when they return, he populates his army with willing volunteers and drills them into an impressive fighting force – not the citizen militia of Roman tradition, but more akin to a professional standing army. The impact of this change will one day be recognized as a definitive shift in the power structure of the whole republic. Because unlike the armies of Scipio Africanus's day, these armies of the poor are loyal to the person promising them a share of the spoils. And that's not anyone in the Senate – it's their general.

Ahead of becoming consul for a second time in 104 BC, Marius leads a celebrated victory against Jugurtha, one achieved in no small part thanks to the brilliance of one of his generals, Lucius Cornelius Sulla. Marius's accomplishments are rewarded with four further consulships in the next five years. During this time he and Sulla enjoy success against two potently dangerous Germanic tribes, the Cimbri and Teutones. Their combined force trounced the Roman army a year ago at the battle of Arausio (modern-day Orange in south-east France), in which Rome lost up to 120,000 men – the most damaging defeat in terms of lost personnel that ancient Rome will ever see. Marius's subsequent subduing of them drives his domination of the consulship.

Sulla, though, as a man of patrician background, is sceptical of this *novus homo*, not to mention resentful of Marius getting all the glory for their military successes. Soon, the pair are on a dangerous collision course: Marius the *populare* and *optimate*.

## THE SOCIAL WAR

By 91 BC Marius's political star has been waning for some years, but Sulla's is about to be launched into the stratosphere. A tribune is championing various reforms, including extending citizenship rights to all the Roman *socii* (allies) in Italy south of the Po river. But before there can be a vote on his proposals, he dies in mysterious circumstances – likely murdered. Nonetheless, he has brought the issue of citizenship to the fore again. Fed up with their lot, and still uncertain of the security Rome can offer in light of the reversal at Arausio, several of the *socii*, including the Samnites, split from Rome and begin what will be called the Social War.

Pitching former allies against one another, each side schooled in the same methods of fighting, it is akin to a civil war. Two major theatres emerge, a northern and southern one, and Sulla is sent south to serve under Consul Lucius Julius Caesar. For now he is engaged in a strategy of containment, but in 89 BC, after the death of one of that year's consuls, Sulla is named proconsul and given supreme command in the south. Now he gets on the front foot, laying siege to the defiant city of Pompeii.

It's summer, and from a position high in the surrounding hills Sulla looks down on the city's great crenellated walls punctuated by mighty stone towers, plotting the quickest method to bring it back under the Roman yoke. He is feeling confident, nearby Herculaneum having already fallen to him. But intelligence reaches him that the enemy have sent a relief force under the leadership of a man named Lucius Cluentius. There is a skirmish in which Sulla's men come off second best, but the Roman refuses to take the reverse lying down. Galvanizing his men, he leads them into a second engagement and this time they get the upper hand. Their cause is bolstered when one of Cluentius's men, a giant Gaul, offers to fight any Roman in single combat. He is defeated by a much smaller opponent, and Cluentius and his troops go on the run. On their way to the *socii*-held city of Nola, Sulla picks off 3,000 of the rebels, but the greatest bloodshed is still to come. At the city walls, the rebel Cluentius and his army find only one gate open. With Sulla breathing down their necks, they can get only a trickle of their troops through. By the day's end, the land outside Nola's walls is a blood bath, the earth covered with the bodies of 20,000 men. Almost none are Roman, but Cluentius is among the slain.

More victories follow, including the capture of Bovianum Undecimanorum, the de facto capital of the *socii* forces. It sets Sulla up for a successful run at the consulship for 88 BC, by which time the war with the anti-Roman allies is drawing to a finish. Rome has asserted its dominion, but has also made concessions on citizenship rights. The Italian allies, who have repeatedly demonstrated their loyalty over previous centuries and played such a crucial part in Rome's growth, now have the chance of a louder voice in Rome's decision-making processes. In other words, the *socii* have the opportunity they have craved – to be more Roman!

The consulship, meanwhile, carries the promise of command of a lucrative military campaign against King Mithridates of Pontus, who is threatening Rome's authority in Greece and its eastern territories. The command sets Sulla on a collision course with Marius (who wants it for himself) and his tribune ally, Sulpicius. This pair use the power of the popular assemblies to remove the command the Senate has bestowed on Sulla and transfer it to Marius. Sulla's response is his landmark march on Rome itself. He convinces himself he has no other option. Either he accepts humiliation and eviction from public life or he takes their challenge head on.

## THE FIGHT FOR SUPREMACY

The assault on Rome may have restored his authority in the short term, but Sulla continues to face powerful opposition amid a fervid atmosphere of violence. Marius, meanwhile, has managed to squirrel himself away from immediate danger, exiling himself in Africa. But within a year he is plotting his revenge. Allying himself with an anti-Sulla consul, Cinna, in 87 BC he launches his own attack on Rome while Sulla is away, campaigning against Mithridates. Marius sets about purging his rivals, humiliating his foes in a series of show trials and filling the Forum with the grisly spectacle of their heads displayed on spikes. In 86 BC – the year in which Sulla leads a glorious siege of Athens – Marius declares himself consul for a seventh time. A reign of terror beckons, but after a matter of mere weeks he dies, seemingly after a medical episode. Cinna is now the one pulling the strings of power.

By 83 BC Sulla has reached a peace with Mithridates and looks out across the Adriatic as he at last sails back to Italian lands. He docks at Brundisium, terminus of the Via Appia, along with five legions of grizzled veterans. But as he travels northwards to Rome, his return is met with a mixture of animosity and fear among a population who remember the blood-letting of his consulship. The peninsula is in a state of upheaval, sceptical of the regime Cinna has imposed these last few years even as they worry over the alternatives.

Sulla does little to assuage such concerns as he makes his way home, looting as he goes. He needs all the resources he can lay his hands on as he fights what is once again effectively a civil war. In 82 BC Marius the younger – son of Sulla's old nemesis, Marius – takes up one of the consulships, and the pair clash at the battle of Sacriportus, where Sulla calls on all his experience to engineer a decisive win. Now he picks off the rest of his enemies until he is ready to lead a second march on Rome.

At the beginning of November Sulla arrives at the walls of the city. He surveys his men, exhausted from the forced march he has imposed to get them here before the enemy – a combination of supporters of Marius and an allied force of Samnites and Lucanians. Formidable opponents. Sulla's senior officers plead with him to allow his men to rest, but their leader urges them to seize the moment.

He looks up to the sky. It is four o'clock in the afternoon and the sun is already beginning to set when he hollers the command to assume battle lines. Their pursuers have arrived and his men are soon forced back against Rome's walls. With the city gates closed they have no choice but to stand and fight. When Sulla spies a group of men who seem to have lost their stomach for the struggle, he manhandles them back into the fray. After a long night of hand-to-hand combat, the crashing of blade against blade subsides as the enemy are at last broken. As many as 50,000 have lost their lives during these few dark hours. When Sulla sends the heads of some of the vanquished to Marius the younger, Marius takes his own life. Italy is indisputably Sulla's.

## THE DICTATOR

Back in Rome, Sulla summons the Senate to the temple of Bellona, goddess of war, and executes thousands of prisoners of war. It is a signal of the ruthlessness with which he intends to wield power henceforth. He embarks on a programme of proscription, in which he identifies his opponents as enemies of the state, leaving them liable to execution and their property subject to confiscation. With rewards for those who dispatch the proscribed, close to 10,000 perish during the opening months of 81 BC. Husbands are butchered in front of their wives, sons put to death in their mothers' embraces. Their dispossessed sons and grandsons are in turn banned from holding public office. Among those who escape despite being on Sulla's list is a young man from a high-ranking family named Julius Caesar – nephew of the widow of Marius.

As for Sulla, the Senate appoints him dictator (hardly daring to do anything else), a position that has not been held for over a century. He is granted it not for the six months of tradition, but without time limit, and with the widest of remits: 'for the making of laws and for the settling of the constitution'. Without any practical curbs on his power, Sulla consolidates the position of the old senatorial class, expanding membership of the Senate and legislating that the Plebeian Council must have senatorial approval ahead of passing any bill. He forbids tribunes to hold any other political office, removing its allure for aspiring politicos, and ends the tribunate veto over the Senate. Knock-out blows for the *optimates* against the *populares*.

In 80 BC Sulla resigns his dictatorship. So confident is he of his achievements that he is said to later walk unprotected through the Forum, offering to justify his tenure to any citizen. At last ready for a quieter life, he now retires to a peaceful country villa to drink, hunt and write his memoirs. But his time is short, and in 78 BC he dies, probably of alcohol-related disease. In Rome, he is accorded the grandest of funerals. His body processes into the city on a golden bier, war veterans posting a guard of honour. Senators rise to their feet to praise his memory before his body is cremated, the ashes deposited in a tomb said to be inscribed with the words 'No better friend, no worse enemy'.

In life, he awarded himself the cognomen Felix, meaning 'Lucky'. In many ways, he has been. But he leaves behind a republic still wrought with tension. He has helped pave the way for the dominance of 'strong men' rulers, prepared to use whatever strategy (violent and otherwise) to achieve their goals. The end of the era of the kings was meant to signal the decline of the over-mighty ruler, but with individual generals now commanding such vast personal armies, the cycle of history has swung back in that direction. The Roman Republic faces an existential crisis.

# 7

# SPARTACUS: THE SLAVE REVOLT

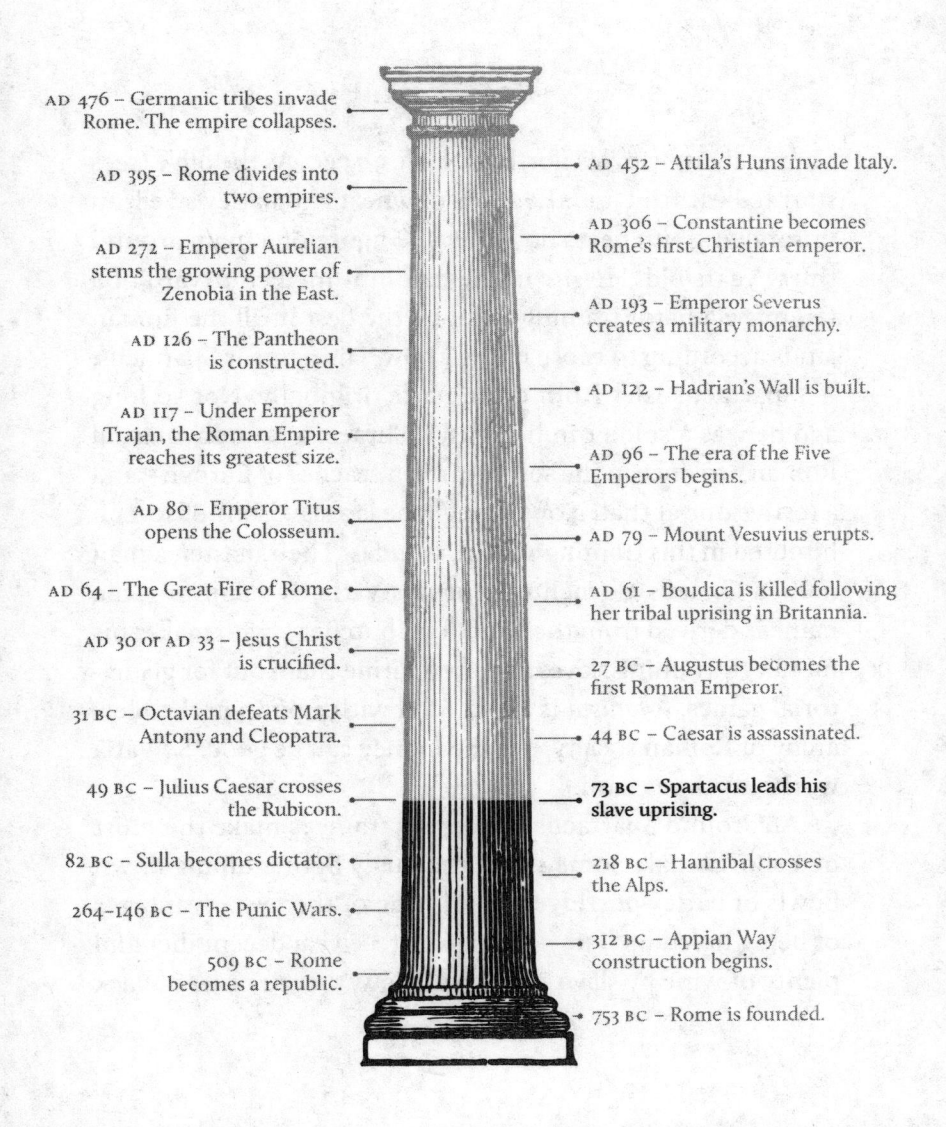

- AD 476 – Germanic tribes invade Rome. The empire collapses.
- AD 395 – Rome divides into two empires.
- AD 272 – Emperor Aurelian stems the growing power of Zenobia in the East.
- AD 126 – The Pantheon is constructed.
- AD 117 – Under Emperor Trajan, the Roman Empire reaches its greatest size.
- AD 80 – Emperor Titus opens the Colosseum.
- AD 64 – The Great Fire of Rome.
- AD 30 or AD 33 – Jesus Christ is crucified.
- 31 BC – Octavian defeats Mark Antony and Cleopatra.
- 49 BC – Julius Caesar crosses the Rubicon.
- 82 BC – Sulla becomes dictator.
- 264–146 BC – The Punic Wars.
- 509 BC – Rome becomes a republic.

- AD 452 – Attila's Huns invade Italy.
- AD 306 – Constantine becomes Rome's first Christian emperor.
- AD 193 – Emperor Severus creates a military monarchy.
- AD 122 – Hadrian's Wall is built.
- AD 96 – The era of the Five Emperors begins.
- AD 79 – Mount Vesuvius erupts.
- AD 61 – Boudica is killed following her tribal uprising in Britannia.
- 27 BC – Augustus becomes the first Roman Emperor.
- 44 BC – Caesar is assassinated.
- **73 BC – Spartacus leads his slave uprising.**
- 218 BC – Hannibal crosses the Alps.
- 312 BC – Appian Way construction begins.
- 753 BC – Rome is founded.

Capua, about 15 miles north of Naples, 73 BC. As the olive trees start to bear fruit and the fields of wheat and barley swell, an unforgiving sun beats down on the figure of a man, around thirty years old. He sits in the column-lined courtyard of a famous gladiator training school – the best in all the Roman lands according to those in the know. His name is Spartacus.

Spartacus isn't from these parts originally. Not so long ago he was a soldier in his native Thrace, a proudly martial Roman province in the south-eastern reaches of Europe – and a restive one at that. Now, though, he is a slave, one of several hundred in this training school, or *ludus*. Their master, a man named Gnaeus Cornelius Lentulus Vatia, is a *lanista* – the name is derived from the word for a butcher – who makes his money by training slaves and then hiring them out for gladiatorial games. A *lanista* is about level with a pimp in the hierarchy of Roman society, but the money can be good. So Vatia works his slaves hard.

All around Spartacus, his fellow trainees make the most of a short break. Some sit on the dusty floor, gulping down bowls of barley porridge. That is one of the few advantages of being holed up here – gladiators receive a decent diet and plenty of wine by slave standards. Now, they're ordered back to training – it's time to get ready to spar. After putting on heavy bronze helmets, and leg and arm guards, they pick up the shields and wooden weapons lying at their feet, training swords that serve as a stand-in for the metal broadswords and daggers used in competition. Fully kitted up, they walk reluctantly to the training arena, sweat glistening on their naked torsos. One of the trainers, himself a retired gladiator, barks out orders. The men advance on a row of six-foot-high wooden stakes driven into the ground, lunging their weapons at these would-be foes. The work is exhausting, relentless and geared to achieve a single objective – the death of one's opponent.

It would be easy, therefore, to imagine that friendships are scarce here. A gladiator can't afford to get attached to his comrades if he might have to slay them tomorrow: this is an 'every-man-for-himself' business, after all. But now, when a German slave launches his spear and loses his balance, falling hard, two other men immediately hurry over to help him up. Spartacus allows himself a small smile. The truth about the connections between these men is a little more nuanced than Vatia would like to believe.

That's not to say the competition between them isn't fierce. There are spectacular rewards for the most successful: glory, celebrity, money, women and – for those who survive long enough – the prospect of eventual freedom. But for almost all, the ultimate destiny is death in combat, sooner or later.

Spartacus and his fellow trainees hardly need reminding of this, but the brutal reality confronts them now. Drifting on the breeze come the roars of the crowd a short distance away in the squat, rugged stone amphitheatre that sits just outside the city walls. The rising clamour indicates that the gladiators have entered the arena. The amphitheatre is full today with those lucky enough to get their hands on one of the clay slab tickets issued for the event. The cacophony lasts for several minutes, their shouts and cat-calls floating across the roofs of the city's sumptuous homes, over the bronze foundries and grain stores upon which Capua's wealth is based.

Suddenly, there is a change in the crowd noise. Bloodthirsty cheers are exchanged for thundering, menacing boos. One of the fighters, facing defeat, must have made a bid for mercy, and now it falls to the game organizer, or *editor* as he is known, to decide whether the man lives or dies. The spectators are letting the *editor* know they have little appetite for clemency. Just a few must be holding out their clenched fists to indicate the gladiator should live. The vast majority clearly have their thumbs extended – the sign that they want him killed.

Merely hearing the all-too-familiar sounds of the arena is enough to make the hairs stand up on the trainees' necks. Just along from Spartacus, the German slave tenses, the muscles in his broad shoulders tightening like a dog's hackles. The Celt behind him, fear writ large across his face, looks nervously about. As their trainer orders them back to work, one of Spartacus's fellow Thracians kicks up the dust with his sandals, while an Italian walks past and squeezes his shoulder. There is something unspoken among them.

Spartacus has a plan.

*Destined to become the most famous gladiator of them all, Spartacus's story has resonated down the millennia, a classic tale of the weak against the powerful, of us versus them. But just how does an uprising that begins with a few dozen slaves turn into one of the most fabled challenges ever posed to Roman authority? Was it unique to Roman history? And how close did Spartacus come to success?*

## POWER BUILT ON SLAVERY

By the time of Spartacus, slavery has long been a foundation stone of the Roman Republic, providing the cheap labour on which it is reliant. The roads upon which Rome's armies march, the aqueducts that bring water for the city folk to drink, the sewers, much of the production of food and other goods – all depend on slave labour. Not to mention the domestic services slaves provide to keep wealthy Romans in the comfort to which they've become accustomed.

As Spartacus sits in his *ludus*, there are over a million slaves in Rome's Italian lands – a quarter of the population or more. Some have been bought from foreign merchants, others taken by military conquest, or enslaved as a punishment for criminality. Then there are the unfortunates who are born into bondage, or who are the victims of kidnap by slavers, or who could see no other option in life than to sell themselves into servitude.

In spite of the numbers of slaves, major uprisings have been few and far between. The fear of brutal repercussions is a powerful deterrent, but it is also hard for slaves to organize themselves in any meaningful way. Nonetheless, there have been a couple in living memory. Both erupted out of Sicily, the island off the toe of Italy, the first in 135 BC and the second in 104 BC. Known as the First and Second Servile Wars, each was eventually defeated, but the scars remain on the psyche of the ruling elite – and perhaps also serve as a reminder to slaves that resistance at scale is possible.

## WHO WAS SPARTACUS?

Little is known of Spartacus's early life, though it seems likely he served as an auxiliary in Thrace in a military unit allied to, but not part of, a Roman legion, since only Roman citizens can serve as legionaries. Some sources speculate that he deserted from his unit, perhaps to become a guerrilla fighter against the Romans. What is certain is that he was eventually captured and enslaved.

Offered for sale in one of the Roman slave markets, clad only in a loin cloth, Spartacus would not have cut the mightiest figure. He is certainly not the largest specimen among the gladiators of Capua. But with a physique honed in the army and trained in Roman fighting ways, he was an obvious target for a man like Vatia. Spartacus's wife, a prophetess who was enslaved alongside him, said he even slept in the market with a snake coiled on his head – a sign of greatness to come, but of misfortune too. Vatia might have interpreted that as indicative of the perfect gladiator, but destiny will prove otherwise.

## THE GLADIATOR LIFE

The first recorded gladiator match took place at the funeral of Roman politician and aristocrat Junius Brutus Pera back in 264 BC, when his sons arranged for three pairs of gladiators to fight at his grave. Possibly the spilling of blood functioned as a sacrifice to the dead. But over the years since, gladiatorial combat has evolved from funerary rite to public spectacle.

The Romans love their entertainment, from theatrical performances to chariot racing, but there is something especially visceral about gladiatorial battles, which are usually presented with animal hunts. By the first century BC, religious festivals and celebrations see gladiators pitted against each other for at least a few days each year all over the republic.

The public's appetite for the contests is extraordinary, and while they can be merciless – like the crowd in Capua – they worship the best fighters as heroes. However, the status of a gladiator is a curious thing. The adulation of the crowds and the promises of fame and riches are a paradox for the likes of Spartacus, who knows first-hand that, collectively, gladiators are treated as the lowest of the low in society. He has had plenty of time to dwell on his fate in his cramped cell, and the oath he swore when he joined the *ludus* tells its own story. 'I will endure,' he was forced to vow, 'to be burned, to be bound, to be beaten, and to be killed by the sword.'

It's no wonder that Spartacus, like so many of his colleagues, craves escape from the *ludus*, and the chance to be free.

### TYPES OF GLADIATOR

There were many different classes of gladiator who faced up to each other in the arena. Each fighter class had their different strengths and weaknesses, and every fan had their favourite. Here are the four traditional types:

- The *murmillo* ('fish man') – Spartacus fought as a *murmillo*. These heavyweight gladiators wore a helmet of bronze adorned with a fish fin at the top and feathers on the side, a belted loin cloth and guards on their arms and legs, but with their feet and chest bare. They fought with a *gladius*, a straight broadsword a foot and a half in length, and carried a large oblong shield called a *scutum*, similar to those of the Roman army. All told, their kit weighed about 40lb. This gave them great protection, but made them slow, while the helmet restricted vision.

- The *retiarius* ('net man') – his weapons were a fishing net and trident. He wore very little armour, if any. Known for speed and agility.

- The Samnite – named after the league of Campanian tribes who warred with the Romans in the fourth and third centuries BC. He fought with a short sword and a long rectangular shield, and wore a plumed helmet. He could be susceptible to attacks to the torso and legs, which went unprotected by any covering.

- The Thraex – he fought with lighter armour, a small square shield and a *sica* (a short, curved dagger). He was celebrated for his agility but needed to be in close range, so was susceptible to attacks from distance.

## THE BREAKOUT

Spartacus may not be the most fearsome gladiator in the *ludus*, but he is intelligent and persuasive. Through careful, secretive networking he has brought together some 200 men from disparate backgrounds into an alliance committed to breaking out. It is likely that he relies on lieutenants to marshal the various ethnic groups, but he stands as their figurehead. Over the spring of 73 BC they have been devising a scheme to overwhelm the guards by sheer strength of numbers and make a dash for freedom. Their time is coming.

But one afternoon a little before the plans have been finalized, as the slaves train on into the afternoon, the large wooden gates to the *ludus* swing open – a battalion of new guards has arrived. Soon it becomes clear why they're there: more security is being deployed around the possible exits from the compound, and around the slave quarters. The guards are making it clear to Spartacus and his fellow slaves that somewhere along the line the plot has been leaked. Vatia knows, and he will do what it takes to put paid to any escape plans.

As the sun descends and the gladiators put their training weapons away, there are hushed, urgent discussions, like the hissing of a wasps' nest. What should they do? For many, the hope of escape has ended. But Spartacus is nothing if not agile. He knows it is now or never. His word is whispered from man to man and seventy or so agree to take their chances and strike.

They swarm through the barracks' kitchens, grabbing cleavers and skewers, the only weapons available to them. Now they must rely on their fighting skills. Thundering out to take on the guards, their weapons clash with those of their oppressors, the gladiators roaring their battle cries as loud as caged lions. By the time they finally outmuscle the guards, the courtyard is marbled with blood. With Spartacus at the forefront, those who've survived make their break for freedom and escape beyond the barracks' walls.

By chance, they spy some passing carts filled with gladiatorial swords and shields on their way to a contest in some other city. They seize the bounty, these very symbols of their enslavement now their greatest hope of freedom. So begins what is destined to be known as the Third Servile War.

## TO VESUVIUS

The first decision Spartacus must make is where to lead his men now they are out in the open. He opts to go southwards, some 30 miles in the direction of Mount Vesuvius on the Bay of Naples. A volcano that has been inactive for as long as anyone can remember, its slopes are known for their fertile soil, and are dotted with farms and vineyards. Moreover, the mountain offers brilliant natural defences.

On their way, the rebels raid towns and wealthy estates for supplies. Their numbers swell with rescued slaves and other social discontents – there are many in the strict hierarchical Roman system. By the time he reaches Vesuvius, Spartacus finds himself leading not merely a motley rabble but a small force with genuine fighting capabilities.

Word of their uprising has by now reached Rome, 100 or so miles up the coast to the north-west, not least because a number of the city's most powerful people have estates in this part of the world. For now, though, they regard the gladiators as a horde of criminals rather than a military entity. Besides, there are bigger, proper battles to focus on, with the bulk of the regular army engaged in Hispania, south-east Europe and Crete.

A militia force of 3,000 under General Gaius Claudius Glaber makes its way to Vesuvius to deal with what the authorities believe is a minor irritation. Glaber's troops are not highly trained legionaries but rather a band of semi-professionals thrown together in haste. Nonetheless, it should be a straightforward job. Spartacus is both outnumbered and trapped on the mountain: there is only one route down Vesuvius, which Glaber has more than covered. The Roman commander is quite happy to wait things out in the foothills, confident that hunger will soon force Spartacus's hand and bring about surrender.

It does not pay to underestimate the slave. Spartacus calls on his reserves of leadership and initiative, setting his men to adapting the vines that cover swathes of Vesuvius into makeshift ropes. In a bravura counter-attack, they abseil down the mountainside, leaving Glaber's unsuspecting troops in their wake. Now Spartacus doubles back on himself, launching an attack on the enemy from behind and annihilating them. Winning against the odds is turning into a habit.

Come the autumn, a new army is dispatched by Rome, this one under the command of the praetor Publius Varinius. He splits his forces into two, one marshalled by a man called Lucius Cossinius and the other by Lucius Furius. Spartacus quickly routs Furius's contingent and then sets about humiliating Cossinius. The Roman is resting up at a villa not far from the nearby town of Pompeii as Spartacus and his slave force catch up with him. It's said that Cossinius is in a state of undress, about to take a dip in the baths, when Spartacus launches an ambush and pursues him all the way back to his camp. There ensues a game of cat-and-mouse, but with Spartacus always managing to stay a step ahead, launching daring raids on the enemy. By now he commands a force of perhaps 10,000.

At one point the Romans are sure they have him besieged, and Spartacus is only too aware of the problems he faces: food is short and his troops have run out of metal for their spearheads. Then, one night, Spartacus utterly outwits his opposite number yet again. In the darkness before midnight he leads a mass exodus of his camp, but before he goes he makes sure that the campfires are fed, and leaves dressed corpses propped up on stakes at the camp gates to look like guards. It is not until the next morning, by which time Spartacus and his followers are long gone, that Varinius has any clue that the enemy have escaped.

## TROUBLE BREWING

As word spreads of Spartacus's successes, so his support grows. More and more slaves join up, and members of the free population, including women and children, also swell his numbers. The winter months are spent training the new recruits, who soon number 70,000 or more. The list of major towns they invade grows too – Nola, Nuceria, Thurii and Metapontum. There are of course some setbacks along the way, and a growing list of casualties. But Spartacus and his army continue to maraud throughout 72 BC, with some sources suggesting he eventually commands as many as 120,000 men. Such is the chaotic nature of the stand-off that exists between him and Rome that it is difficult to track the exact itinerary of his campaigns, but he notches up victories against assorted Roman commanders, his legend growing all the time.

There is, though, trouble afoot. The larger his army grows, the more difficult it is for Spartacus to control. It has always been a multinational force, but now it includes people from all sorts of walks of life, with differing ambitions. For all that he has worked wonders in regimenting them, they are not a professionally trained army. The first signs of a split emerge. There are those who embarked on this adventure with the dream of making their way northwards, to cross the Alps and return to their homelands. But others have grown rather fond of life in this ad hoc rebel movement. It is easy to become a little tipsy on the newly acquired riches and power that come from military conquest. What will they do once they are away from the grasp of Rome anyway? How do you follow an act like this? Having proved themselves against the might of the Roman Republic, there is even talk that they should make a move on Rome itself. By the end of 72 BC Spartacus has led his forces north, to the brink of the Alps and potential escape beyond. But now they turn round and come back south to continue their raiding.

In Rome, no one now is under any illusion that Spartacus is anything but a major threat to the status quo. The time has come to do whatever it takes to bring him and his army down.

## THE BATTLE WITH CRASSUS

The job falls to perhaps Rome's richest man. In Marcus Licinius Crassus, Spartacus faces a formidable opponent, ruthless in pursuit of his ends. A veteran commander under Sulla during the civil war of the previous decade, Crassus rose up the economic and social ranks during Sulla's subsequent dictatorship and in the years since. He has earned a fortune from silver mines, slave-trafficking and through property deals, showing little constraint in his business dealings. He even founded the first Roman fire brigade, though it routinely refuses to help those in direst need until the owner of the blazing property agrees to sell it to Crassus at a knockdown price.

In response to the threat from Spartacus's army, the Senate now gives Crassus the command of eight legions – an army of between 30,000 and 50,000 trained infantry and auxiliaries. There are a number of skirmishes in which both sides manage to land blows. Crassus punishes perceived weaknesses among his men after one particular defeat by reimposing the long-abandoned practice of decimation – the execution of one in ten of his troops by their comrades on the basis of selection by drawing lots. It instils fear in his army but also a determination to fight to the last. Better to die in honour on the field than in ignominy by decimation. Gradually Crassus seems to be gaining the upper hand.

With the stakes raised, Spartacus's job is harder than ever. His forces now number just 30,000 or 40,000 – factions have broken off and there have been many casualties. He leads them south, to Bruttium in the toe of Italy. He's in a tight spot, there's no doubt about that, but he's wriggled his way out of worse before now. Across the Strait of Messina lies Sicily, scene of those great slave uprisings of yesteryear. Spartacus plans to take his followers there – a safe haven over the water. A base too, perhaps, from which he can launch raids on the mainland coast from a position of relative safety.

The question is, how to get his forces across the water?

There is only one possibility. The strait is frequented by pirates, whose boats are speedy and whose knowledge of the area is unrivalled. He is wary of them but, pragmatically, negotiates a deal. After handing over money and other assets on the promise that they will transport his men, he sets off to prepare his troops for the mass evacuation. But when he arrives back at port, the pirates are nowhere to be seen. At his moment of greatest need, he has been double-crossed.

Ever the improviser, he leads an attempt to fashion makeshift rafts, but to no avail. Behind him, Crassus has ordered the construction of a walled ditch that stretches 40 miles from the Tyrrhenian Sea to the Ionian Sea, penning Spartacus on the peninsula. With nowhere left to go, Spartacus determines to break through these defences. It seems an impossible job, but one night in winter, with the snow falling around them, his army steals through the enemy lines and constructs a bridge across the ditch from mud-packed tree branches. His enemies once more outwitted, Spartacus heads north.

## ENDGAME

There can be few who doubt that he has fulfilled his wife's coiled-snake prophecy about greatness, but with it comes the persistent shadow of misfortune too. Though he has overcome daunting odds so many times, he now has not only Crassus in hot pursuit but two more mighty armies, those of Pompey and Varro Lucullus, sent by Rome to help Crassus finish the job. Seemingly doomed to be caught in a pincer movement, Spartacus seeks a truce, but it's declined. Instead, he prepares his troops for one more showdown, at the mouth of the Silarius river. With his army arrayed before him, he calls for his horse. Then he draws his sword and slays the noble beast. If we beat the Romans, he tells his fighters, we will have plenty of horses to choose from. If we lose, then I won't be needing a horse at all.

Spartacus leads from the front, charging at the Roman ranks, smashing into a wall of shields and slashing swords. It has all come down to this. According to some sources he almost breaks their lines and Crassus is in his sights when he is at last cut down by centurions. Others say he is struck by a javelin. However it happens, Spartacus is just one of many thousands who perish on both sides. Those who can get away from the battlefield make a break for the mountains. But the day belongs to Crassus, who takes some 6,000 captives. In the days to come, he will crucify them at regular intervals along the Appian Way, the road that connects Rome with Capua where Spartacus's rebellion began. It is a gruesome reminder of Rome's power – a warning to all slaves, including gladiators, that resistance is futile.

## THE START OF A LEGEND

Spartacus's body, clad neither in distinctive armour nor uniform, goes unrecovered from the field as far as anyone knows. Just as he rose from anonymity two years ago, so he disappears now. Gone, but decidedly not forgotten. His disappearance only adds to the mythology that builds around him, his legendary exploits set to be passed down through the generations – along with the rumour that, just maybe, he survived.

To think that his army of slaves and malcontents could overcome the might of Rome was perhaps never realistic, but he has given the authorities a mighty fright, leading them on a merry dance across Italy. There will never be another slave revolt comparable to that led by Spartacus. It seems the logistical challenges of coordinating such an act are too formidable, and the cost of failure too high. That's not to say that low-level resistance disappears altogether. It's not uncommon for a slave to make an individual bid for freedom, or to steal additional rations or even money from their master. There are even instances of disgruntled slaves murdering their owners, although the price for such defiance can be fantastically high: even fellow slaves who fail to intervene to protect their master are subject to various punishments up to execution.

Tragically for the unwilling fighters involved, rather than the rebellion prompting a decline in support for gladiatorial games, they now achieve new levels of popularity. In the years following the Third Servile War, a great purpose-built amphitheatre is commissioned at Capua. Only the Roman Colosseum, itself built in large part by slave labour between AD 72 and 80, will beat it for size. But though Spartacus's bid for freedom does not spark the sea-change in the Roman Republic he might have hoped for, it does leave a legacy in another, less expected way.

Crassus makes some political capital from his part in the defeat of the slave army. Even so, it is Pompey, who some argue merely mopped up those fleeing the reckoning meted out by Crassus, who gets the true glory of a triumph. The two generals are already rivals, but the resentment Crassus harbours for the slight is a factor in his decision to sponsor another young politician to create a counterbalance to his rival – a young challenger by the name of Gaius Julius Caesar. And though these three – Pompey, Crassus and Caesar – will one day rule together in the First Triumvirate, the enmity between the two older men will become a critical faultline, not just in their rule but in the foundation of Rome as they know it.

The battle against Spartacus's uprising may be won. But the war for the survival of the Roman Republic itself is only just beginning.

# 8

# ALL HAIL CAESAR!: THE EMPEROR WHO WASN'T

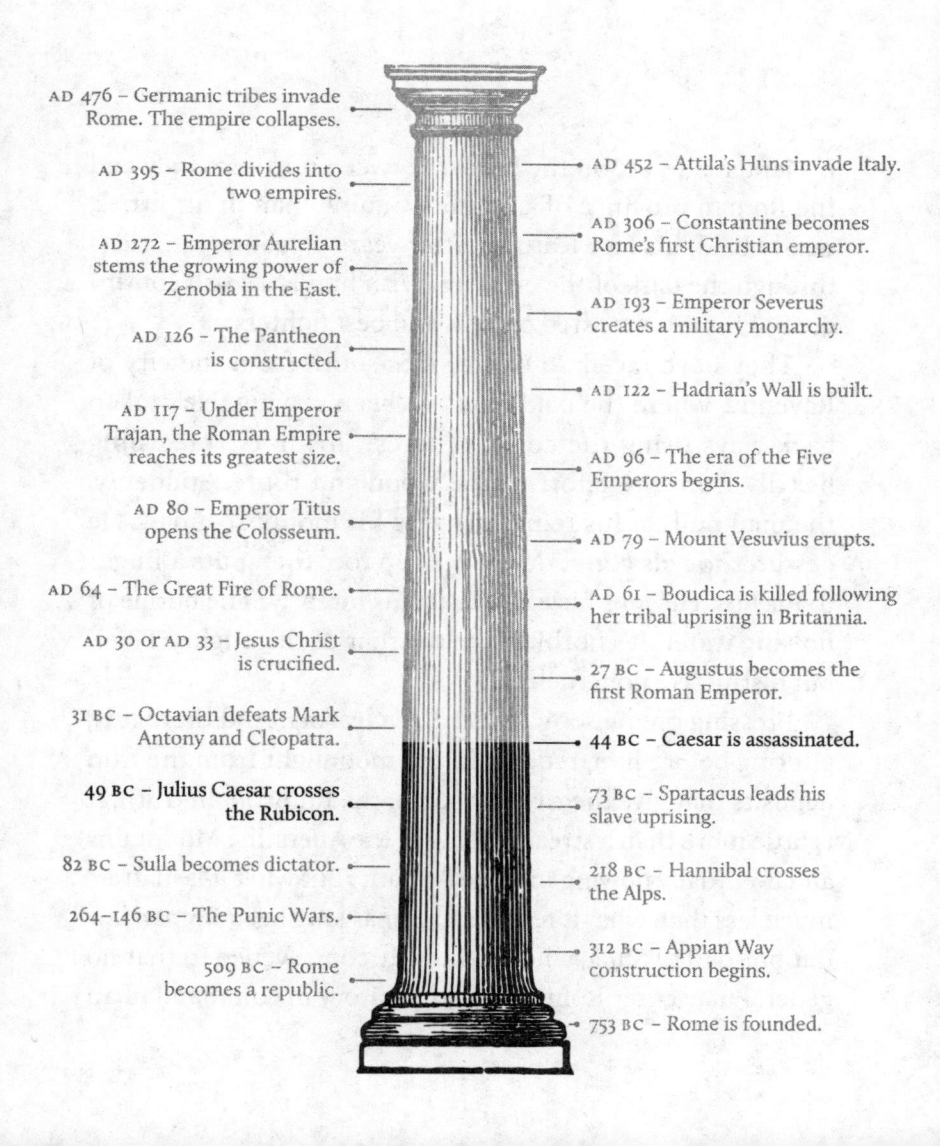

- AD 476 – Germanic tribes invade Rome. The empire collapses.
- AD 452 – Attila's Huns invade Italy.
- AD 395 – Rome divides into two empires.
- AD 306 – Constantine becomes Rome's first Christian emperor.
- AD 272 – Emperor Aurelian stems the growing power of Zenobia in the East.
- AD 193 – Emperor Severus creates a military monarchy.
- AD 126 – The Pantheon is constructed.
- AD 122 – Hadrian's Wall is built.
- AD 117 – Under Emperor Trajan, the Roman Empire reaches its greatest size.
- AD 96 – The era of the Five Emperors begins.
- AD 80 – Emperor Titus opens the Colosseum.
- AD 79 – Mount Vesuvius erupts.
- AD 64 – The Great Fire of Rome.
- AD 61 – Boudica is killed following her tribal uprising in Britannia.
- AD 30 or AD 33 – Jesus Christ is crucified.
- 27 BC – Augustus becomes the first Roman Emperor.
- 31 BC – Octavian defeats Mark Antony and Cleopatra.
- **44 BC – Caesar is assassinated.**
- **49 BC – Julius Caesar crosses the Rubicon.**
- 73 BC – Spartacus leads his slave uprising.
- 82 BC – Sulla becomes dictator.
- 218 BC – Hannibal crosses the Alps.
- 264–146 BC – The Punic Wars.
- 312 BC – Appian Way construction begins.
- 509 BC – Rome becomes a republic.
- 753 BC – Rome is founded.

It's January 49 BC, on the border between northern Italy and the Roman province of Cisalpine Gaul. A man in his fifties, nearly bald, his face leathery after years on campaign, rides through the dark of the evening. With him is a small contingent of his most trusted officers and best fighters.

They have raced 20 or so miles south from the city of Ravenna, where the bald man has been staying. He's taken back ways using the cover of forest, his horse breathing heavily from the effort of the woodland route. Suddenly, the man pulls at his reins, bringing his mount to a halt. He gestures for his comrades to pull up too, then puts a finger to his lips. He cups his ear and listens intently. The burble of flowing water. It's nothing like the roar of the mighty Tiber, but distinctive nonetheless.

Pressing on, he soon comes to a clearing. And there it is, glinting before him, reddish in the moonlight from the iron deposits that give the river its name: the Rubicon. In truth, it is little more than a stream, rising in the Apennine Mountains and eventually flowing into the Adriatic. But what it is matters much less than what it represents. It has long been Roman law (far pre-dating Sulla, who infamously contravened it) that no general may enter Rome's Italian territory in command of an army. To do so renders both the leader and his men outlaws, subject to execution. But the balding general who stands at the Rubicon has a lot on his mind, and he may be about to do what has hitherto been unthinkable.

His name is Julius Caesar, and he has spent the last few years bringing the Gauls under Roman dominion – the latest magnificent triumph in an extraordinary career, both military and political. In Rome, he is a superstar. He has a knack of connecting with the common man. Populism runs through his veins. However, he has also made plenty of powerful enemies.

Caesar is in a fix. There are moves to have him charged with corruption by his adversaries in the Senate. If he can get himself voted consul, which he stands every chance of doing, then he will be protected from legal action. But he can't stand for election unless he gives up his military command. In the time between surrendering his army and winning political office, he would be at his most vulnerable. What to do? Turn his back on his troops and take his chances by going through the established channels in Rome, or face down his enemies in the Senate by breaking Roman custom and marching on the city at the head of his men? Haven't Sulla and Marius set a precedent anyway?

Straightening himself in his saddle, he snaps his reins. 'Alea iacta est,' someone thinks they hear him say. The die is cast.

*Caesar's name is perhaps the most famous in all of ancient Rome's long history, yet his rise to the top was never a certainty. Indeed, his pursuit of power, riches and prestige coincided with a period of intense turbulence in the republic. So, just how did he see off his many rivals for so long? What personal qualities drove his ascent,* and allowed him to become a legend in his own lifetime and a demi-god in death? And why did it end so catastrophically – and at what price to the republic he so dominated?

## A STORMY TIME

We must go back to 12 July 100 BC – the exact date is disputed. Marius is consul yet again, but his frayed relationship with Sulla has not yet descended into armed conflict. In the not entirely salubrious Roman suburb of Subura, a family welcomes a new arrival – a baby, named Gaius Julius Caesar. Although Subura's name becomes synonymous with the underclass that populates many of its corners or 'suburbs', Caesar's family boast a proud heritage. The Julii are one of the city's oldest patriotic families, claiming ancestry all the way back to Aeneas, the ancient Trojan prince who left his homeland to find a new life on the Italian peninsula. Through him, the Julii can be said to be connected to the goddess Venus. However, although the new baby's father has had a decent enough political career, holding magistracies and even a provincial governorship, it's been generations since the clan has been at the very forefront of political life.

By the time the young Caesar turns sixteen, the family's prospects seem bleaker than ever. His father keels over one day when he's doing up his sandals, the victim of a suspected heart attack. Just like that, his teen son becomes the family's breadwinner. He finds a position as a priest of Jupiter, a prestigious role for a young man, but one that suggests he is not marked out for a career in politics. He also breaks off a long-standing engagement he's had with a well-to-do plebeian girl, and instead marries a young woman named Cornelia. It seems like an advantageous union, since she is the daughter of Lucius Cornelius Cinna, four times a consul and a close ally of Marius, who himself was married to Caesar's aunt until his recent death.

Yet any ambitions of promotion that Caesar has quickly fade. Bloody civil discord has been a staple of Roman life these last few years, what with the Social War and the battle for dominance between Sulla and Marius. Recently, Cinna has been keen to carry the war to Sulla, but the hard line he takes with his troops backfires when, in 84 BC, he faces a mutiny and is killed. Sulla duly makes his way home to claim Rome for himself, imposing his dictatorship and enacting his dreaded proscriptions.

Caesar is still only a fairly anonymous eighteen-year-old, but he is nonetheless both the nephew and son-in-law of Sulla's greatest enemies. As such, he is designated an enemy of the state and condemned to death. He goes to ground in the back streets of the city, moving at night from one safe house to another. Eventually he makes it north out of the city and seeks refuge in various villages. But with his dark, piercing eyes and floppy hair, he cuts a distinctive figure – especially with the scarlet red boots and the long-fringed sleeves he wears on his tunic. It's going to be tough to stay hidden for long.

His mother, Aurelia, decides it's time for some parental intervention. She leverages her old family connections and secures a personal audience for the boy with Sulla himself. When Caesar turns up to the meeting he is full of teen attitude, but Sulla is in a merciful mood. Caesar will be allowed to live, just as long as he hands over the dowry he received on getting married. Caesar ruefully accepts, but not before a sneering eye-roll towards those who have been negotiating his redemption. 'Bear in mind,' Sulla is said to comment, 'that the young man you are so eager to save will one day deal the death blow to the cause of the aristocracy.'

## KIDNAP

He may be safe for now, but political life in Rome remains explosive. Caesar is best off out of it, so he does what so many good Romans do and joins the army. He is sent to serve the governor of the province of Asia, analogous to modern-day Turkey. He proves himself a formidable soldier, winning the highest awards for gallantry, but he also becomes embroiled in scandal. It is alleged by some that he has been seduced by King Nicomedes of Bithynia, to whose court he is sent as an emissary. Caesar utterly refutes the claim, but mud like that has a habit of sticking.

When Sulla dies in 78 BC it is at last safe for Caesar to return to Rome, where he trains as a lawyer. Despite a rather pitchy voice, he is a formidable orator and he makes a name for himself, prosecuting corrupt officials. Given that trials play out in the Forum, Caesar earns a reputation as a champion of the common man against the self-serving elite. To further hone his skills, he sets off for the Greek island of Rhodes in 75 BC to study under an eminent orator, Apollonius Molon, whose other students include one of the great men of Roman letters, Cicero. For aspirational young Romans, Greek civilization retains an aura of supreme excellence.

> ## CICERO: THE GREAT ORATOR
>
> Oratory – public speaking – was of great importance in ancient Rome, where it was a prime means of spreading ideas and moulding opinion. It was a key skill for any young man (and it was a predictably male-dominated field). There was perhaps no finer exponent than Cicero (106–43 BC), whose mastery of Latin was also reflected in a body of respected written work, including a famous collection of letters. His powers of communication saw him rise to become a major political figure and a staunch defender of republican ideals. This set him on a collision path with first Julius Caesar and then Mark Antony, eventually resulting in his execution. But his ideas lived on, influencing philosophers through the ages, including major figures of the European Enlightenment, the leaders of the French Revolution and the American Founding Fathers.

Caesar, now in his mid-twenties, finds himself standing on the deck of a galley slicing its way through the cresting waves of the Aegean Sea towards Rhodes. Not so long ago vessels of the Greek navy patrolled these waters, maintaining order in its bustling shipping lanes. But since Rome asserted its dominance over Greece, those patrols have disappeared. So it is with some nervousness that Caesar spots a boat careering towards his own. His trepidation is well justified. It is a pirate ship from Cilicia, the rugged southern coastal region of the province of Asia. Brigands spill on to Caesar's galley, swords drawn as they round up hostages and seize everything of value. This includes Caesar himself, as young Roman noblemen are not ten a denarius out here. The pirates place a ransom of 20 talents on his head – equivalent to about two-thirds of a metric ton of silver. Caesar, though, has a clear idea of his own worth. He tells them to make it 50 talents.

For a month they hold him, as his shipmates sail off in the hope of raising the sum to free him. He charms them over those weeks, sharing jokes and even trying out some of his poetry on them. By the time his shipmates return with the ransom there is a sense of bonhomie between captors and captive. Still, Caesar does not lose sight of the wrong done to him. As his release is negotiated, he reminds them that they are barbarians and that one day he will track them down and kill them.

It does not take him long. Back on dry land, he heads for the nearest port, raises a small fleet and goes off in pursuit of his assailants. He soon overpowers their vessel and hauls them off to the city of Pergamon, where the pirates are sentenced to death by crucifixion. Caesar displays some mercy, though, allowing them to have their throats cut rather than die particularly excruciating deaths on their crosses. By the time Caesar returns to Rome, via Rhodes, word of his exploits against the pirates has spread and he is now something of a hero.

## CAREER-BUILDING

Meanwhile, Caesar's wife Cornelia has given birth to a daughter, Julia, although it does little to bolster her parents' flagging marriage, which has drifted during his long absences.

Caesar has also taken a lover, Servilia. Hardly uncommon for a Roman of noble birth, and only the first of many. But Servilia is an interesting choice of paramour, being the sister of Cato the Younger, a senator constantly in opposition to Caesar. She also happens to be the widow of a man named Brutus, whose ancestor of the same name was instrumental in the fall of the last Roman king. Servilia has a son who also bears the name.

In 70 BC, as he enters his thirties, Caesar wins election to become a quaestor, on the lower level of the magistracy pyramid. It is the same posting his father achieved, and now Caesar is sent to Hispania Ulterior to prove his worth as an administrator. Tragically, as he is preparing to leave, Cornelia dies. Arriving in Hispania as a widower, it is said that he visits a temple in the Spanish city of Gades (modern-day Cádiz) where he sees a crumbling statue of Alexander the Great. A tear wells in his eye as he strains to maintain his composure. He is having some sort of epiphany, comparing his own thus-far meagre achievements against Alexander's, who had already conquered half the world by the same age.

With a new fire in his belly, Caesar returns to Rome, determined to plot a path to the top.

Still only in his early thirties, he must wait at least until he is forty to make a run for the consulship. In the meantime he becomes an aedile, an administrator of public works. This gives him the opportunity to stage fifteen days of games and festivities, during which he showcases his flair for showmanship and his gift for courting popularity. Meanwhile, Crassus – who has been a dominant figure in Rome's political landscape, especially since putting down Spartacus's uprising – is ready to step back from frontline politics to enjoy the fruits of his long career, which include a vast income from his extensive property portfolio. By most reckonings, there is no one in Rome to touch his wealth. And now he is on the lookout for the coming men of the political scene, characters he might bankroll in return for them representing his interests. And if this in time serves to create a counterweight to his hated rival Pompey, then so much the better.

Who better to back, then, than Caesar? At a stroke, Crassus pays off a large part of the younger man's significant debts, since making one's way in Rome is a costly business. Besides, Caesar enjoys the finer things in life, splurging on wine, women and the latest fashions. He likes to feel and look good, even adopting a flamboyant comb-over to hide his rapidly receding hairline.

In 63 BC he is elected *pontifex maximus* ('chief high priest'), a prestigious religious office with responsibility for carrying out important rituals and for overseeing the administration of divine law. Everyone knows that he has bribed his way to the job, but how he got it matters less than the fact that he knows how to win at this game of power politics. The role even comes with a nice big house near the Forum. Caesar also gets married again, to a woman named Pompeia, although the union doesn't last long when she catches on to his loose interpretation of fidelity. All the while he racks up more debt until he owes some 31 million sesterces – about £67 million in today's terms. Caesar conjures up a new plan. He will run for the proconsulship, or governorship, of Hispania. That way he'll be able to attack towns, loot treasures and demand fealty, until his financial worries are a thing of the past.

Not that it will be an easy job. Ruling Hispania never is, with its multitude of tribes ensuring there is never peace for very long. But out there, Caesar proves his mettle as a leader of men. Those under his command respect his willingness to face the same struggles as them. He marches alongside them, eats the same rations, climbs the same hills and swims the same rivers. Most importantly, he stands shoulder to shoulder with them in battle, and they in return will run through walls for him. Though he is ruthless in punishing any hint of insubordination, his men always know where they stand: play fair by him, and he'll play fair by you.

His approach yields fantastic results as he pushes the most troublesome anti-Roman forces in Hispania back to the Atlantic coast. And his successes do not go unnoticed in Rome. People are starting to talk about him in the same breath as Pompey, Crassus's old adversary, the most celebrated general of the age renowned for a series of campaigns in Italy and abroad. When Caesar is offered the honour of his first triumph, it leaves him in a quandary. Such an event will cement his reputation with all Rome, but now he is forty he can run for consul. To do so, he cannot enter Rome as a general but must arrive as a civilian instead, and a civilian certainly can't have a triumph. So, reluctantly, he turns it down, rejecting one huge prize to concentrate on an even bigger one.

## TRIUMVIRATE

Caesar now plays a brilliant political hand. Pompey, already a consul a decade ago, is back in Rome after a stint in the eastern Mediterranean. He wants to enact various reforms, especially around the awarding of land to his men, but he can't get them through the Senate. Crassus is having his own disputes with the same institution. Although Crassus and Pompey are historically enemies, Caesar sees that their interests are starting to align. He suggests that the three of them informally join forces in what will be known as the First Triumvirate. If they help him become consul, he'll look out for their interests.

In 59 BC Caesar duly takes up his first consulship, victor in an election considered spectacularly dirty even by Roman standards, marked by bribery and intimidation from all sides. The republic is now under the de facto rule of these three mighty figures, an alliance further cemented when Pompey, six years Caesar's senior, marries Caesar's daughter Julia – and rumour has it that far from being a marriage of convenience, it's a love match. Caesar himself is back in the market for marriage too, this time with a woman called Calpurnia.

The populist Caesar's nominal co-consul is a man called Bibulus, who along with his ally Cato is a champion of the conservative, traditionalist *optimates* faction. But Caesar has the march on them. On one particularly bleak day for Bibulus, some of Caesar's cronies deposit a bucket of excrement over his head. Meanwhile, Caesar enacts a series of populist measures, including laws concerning land redistribution. It's going swimmingly well, with each member of the triumvirate feathering his nest as the strings of power are pulled. The republic is functioning as an oligarchy. As consul, Caesar is immune from prosecution, but his enemies in the Senate – Cato chief among them – are forming a dim view of his conduct, gathering evidence of his corruption.

Caesar, however, is nothing if not a forward planner. As the end of his tenure hovers into view, he secures for himself lucrative provincial governorships to move on to, including that of Cisalpine Gaul, that region of Gaul south of the Alps in northern Italy. Moreover, he negotiates an additional five years' immunity from prosecution. He seems well set up for the next few years as he relocates to Cisalpine Gaul, where the locals are thoroughly civilized along Roman lines. 'Toga-wearing Gauls', they are affectionately called. But over the frontier lies Transalpine Gaul, and there, conditions are far less amenable. Its many tribes hostile to Rome pose a persistent threat. In this danger, however, Caesar spots opportunity.

## GAUL

Romans have memories as long as those of Hannibal's elephants, and they have not forgotten how the Gauls sacked Rome. Caesar will only add to his legend if he can wreak revenge upon this great adversary – the type best served cold after chilling for three centuries. Still, he needs a good reason to reignite the enmity. In 58 BC it comes. The Helvetii tribe, based in an area that will come to be known as Switzerland, are transplanting themselves westwards to escape a marauding German clan. But their exodus involves cutting across the territory of the Aedui, a client tribe of Rome. It's just the sort of provocation Caesar has been waiting for. He leads 40,000 to 50,000 men on an incursion into Gaul, laying waste to one troublesome tribe after another. Booty and taxes roll into his coffers, and by 56 BC he has brought virtually all of Gaul under his control – an area covering much of what is now France, Belgium, Luxembourg, Switzerland and Germany. There are joyous celebrations in Rome, but Caesar does not return for them. Politics there is more cut-throat than ever and he dare not risk it. Instead, he meets with Crassus and Pompey at Lucca, the southernmost town in Cisalpine Gaul, to re-pledge their allegiance to the triumvirate.

It's now that they hatch a plan to carve up the republic.

Knowing they are currently stronger together than apart despite their long-held rivalry, Pompey and Crassus have already served a term as joint consuls, and will now attempt a re-run. In return for Caesar's endorsement, they will grant him a further five-year extension on his governorship of Gaul. Then later, Pompey will be given command of Hispania, and Crassus, Syria. A win for each of them.

In the meantime, Caesar has a little local trouble to deal with on Gaul's eastern frontier – incessant incursions by Germanic tribes. He drives the raiders back until he reaches the German city of Koblenz, where he orders one of the most spectacular feats of military engineering the world has ever seen – construction of a 400-metre-long bridge over the mighty Rhine river, raised in just ten days. Now he uses it as a launching point for Roman raids deeper into German territory. For two and a half weeks his men indulge in a frenzy of looting and pillaging, before withdrawing and destroying the bridge. In case anyone doubted it, it is an awesome reminder of Caesar's power.

## BRITANNIA

While in Gaul, Caesar has been intrigued by talk of an island over the sea to the north. Inhabited by Celts just as Gaul is, it is said to be rich in precious metals and even pearls. It is late August in 55 BC when he leads a fleet with about 10,000 men across the water to a white-cliffed port called Dubris (modern-day Dover) on the southern coast of what the Romans call Britannia. His vessels plot a cautious path in choppy seas, giving the Britons plenty of time to spy them. Caesar's deep-bottomed galleys are unsuited to landing on Dubris's shallow beaches, so he detours a few miles around the coast. By the time his troops disembark, the Romans face a force of ferocious locals, their bodies painted with blue woad, some of them driving horse-drawn chariots. For the visitors who have had to wade to shore decked out in full armour, it is all too much. They survive a few skirmishes, but a little under three weeks later Caesar decides to turn his back on Britannia ... for now.

The following spring he is back with more men and a larger, better prepared fleet. The squally crossing tests his mettle again, but this time the Romans' sheer force of numbers allows Caesar to advance deep into the island's southern region. He is disappointed not to discover any of the promised gold and pearls, but when he leads his men back across the sea after six months, Rome celebrates what it considers a major triumph. This is, after all, a land where rumour has it the exotic locals are truly beastly, even headless, with faces buried in their chests. Yet brave Caesar has tamed them and raised the prospect that one day Rome might rule there too.

## GAUL 2.0

Caesar's triumphant expedition is, however, marred by devastating personal news. His beloved daughter, Julia, has died in childbirth – a loss that loosens the ties that have bound him to her husband, Pompey. At the same time, Crassus has taken it into his head to seek new riches and glory by leading an army against the Parthians – the civilization that spans modern-day Iran and Iraq. Driven by that deeply held Roman desire for personal glory, each of the three men is hugely competitive.

But Caesar, once reliant on the greater wealth and prestige of his partners in the triumvirate, now threatens to supersede both. Crassus is clearly keen to reassert his credentials by taking on mighty Parthia but he has badly misjudged the mission and is killed on campaign. Back in Rome, a group in the Senate led by Cato is agitating to pull apart what remains of the triumvirate. And they are much keener to work with Pompey, whom they consider more pliant, than the unpredictable Caesar.

Caesar has other problems. While he's been in Britannia, his control of Gaul has weakened. Its people have now mobilized under the inspirational leadership of a chieftain named Vercingetorix. In 52 BC Caesar is forced to dig his way through Alpine snowdrifts to confront the threat. When the two armies meet at Gergovia, in central Gaul, the unthinkable happens: the Romans are defeated. Vercingetorix and 80,000 of his men fall back to Alesia, his fortress perched on top of a steep hill, hoping to tempt Caesar to follow him and lay siege. His plan is that a second, even larger force of Gauls will then attack the Romans from the rear.

When a spy comes to Caesar with the plot, he decides to draw on the elite engineering skills of his military to build a staggering 11-mile wall that will encircle Alesia. With battlements and towers, a 20-foot-wide moat, walls of stakes and hidden pits, it is a fortress outside a fortress. Then he has another wall constructed outside the first – a combined 23 miles of fortifications in two concentric rings – one to keep Vercingetorix in, the other to keep the second Gaul army out. Dominating the middle ground, now all Caesar can do is wait.

Over several weeks Alesia's grain supplies run down, and outside the walls piles of rotting corpses start to mount.

Starvation takes mostly the town's women, children and elderly, but soon Vercingetorix's warriors begin to succumb too.

Then one day the main gate opens and the leader of the Gauls, sporting a long moustache, braided hair and full armour, rides out alone on a white horse. Caesar is sat in a throne-like chair, watching nonchalantly as his enemy threatens to topple over, his body ravaged by malnutrition. The horse halts a few yards away, and Vercingetorix struggles to dismount before laying his sword at Caesar's feet and falling to his knees. The Roman accepts the surrender and Vercingetorix is led away. To all intents and purposes, Gaul is now Caesar's – a conquest years in the making. Rome is transformed from master of the Mediterranean to European superpower.

Caesar, keen to make sure that Rome knows all about his exploits, writes a multi-volume account, *Commentaries on the Gallic War*. Among his observations on logistics and strategy, he recounts his slaughter of 8,000 German civilians at the Rhine, the beheading of the entire ruling council of one of the Gallic tribes, and how all the captured warriors in one unfortunate town had their hands chopped off. Altogether, he estimates enemy deaths at over a million, with a similar number enslaved. Some might call it a genocide, although it is difficult to know how reliable the numbers are and whether that has really been the aim.

## CIVIL WAR

Rome goes wild for these latest triumphs, but not everyone is celebrating. To his enemies in the Senate, which incidentally never sanctioned his incursions into Britannia, Caesar is the ultimate rogue operator. Together with long-standing accusations of corruption, he is now suspected of what would today be considered war crimes; even by the loose rules of Roman warfare, his murdering of tens of thousands of women and children is something of a breach of the moral code. There is also the small matter of exceeding his assigned territory by crossing the Rhine – something that, so his detractors say, violates his proconsular authority.

His relationship with Pompey has collapsed too. Caesar knows he is at risk of prosecution as soon as he becomes a private citizen again – unless he can get himself elected as consul in the meantime. But that is the last thing Pompey wants, given that he has made himself the main man in Rome in Caesar's absence. Now Caesar faces his big decision: does he surrender his command, as the law demands, to return to Rome and contest the consulship, or does he bring his army with him? It is at this point that he crosses the Rubicon, a phrase that becomes synonymous with an act from which there is no return. Caesar navigates the river and sets foot on Roman soil, deciding to maintain his command in defiance of legal custom.

As he rides into Rome for the first time in almost a decade, he is struck by the eerie quietness of the place. There is no opposing force to meet him. Pompey and his allies in the Senate are wise enough to know that they cannot win against Caesar's agile and battle-hardened legions. They have skipped the city instead, marshalling their resources and waiting for the moment to strike. In the meantime, Rome lives under a state of emergency. Caesar pronounces himself dictator for a little over a week, just long enough to put a new, pliant *populares* Senate in place and to assure those left that he intends them no harm. He does, however, have Pompey in his sights.

His old partner in the triumvirate has fled across the sea to Greece, but Caesar does not immediately give chase. He wants to take apart Pompey's forces bit by bit. Leaving Rome under the charge of his deputy, Marcus Aemilius Lepidus, and the rest of Italy under Mark Antony, he heads for Hispania, where Pompey still has armies loyal to him. Only once Caesar has cleaned up there – in a matter of mere weeks – does he make for Greece to undertake what comes to be known as the Macedonian campaign.

Caesar lands on the Illyrian coast, at Dyrrhachium, in what is now Albania, in November 49 BC. He and Pompey play a game of cat-and-mouse until, in early August 48 BC, they meet for a showdown on the plain of Pharsalus. Pompey, nearing sixty, is a shell of the great war leader he once was. It's twelve years since he was last in the field, and a stomach ulcer torments his wearied body. But Caesar is old enough and wise enough to know not to underestimate him. Even as Caesar's men crush their opponents – killing 15,000 and capturing close to 25,000 according to Caesar himself – Pompey escapes and makes for Egypt. It's also during this battle that Caesar encounters the son of his one-time lover Servilia, a man by the name of Brutus. Some say – albeit improbably – that the young man may even be Caesar's own son. Whatever the truth, though Brutus fought on Pompey's side, when he later comes to Caesar's camp to surrender, Caesar spares his life. Had he known how he would one day be repaid for this act of mercy, Caesar may not have been so quick to forgive.

In September 48 BC Pompey arrives in the bustling

metropolis of Alexandria and sends greetings to Egypt's boy-king, Ptolemy XIII. Caesar arrives just three days later, but as he lands he is met by one of Ptolemy's emissaries who presents him with a gift: Pompey's head. A gesture, the Egyptian reckons, to win Caesar's favour. Caesar, however, is appalled. For all their rivalry, he does not want to see a great Roman warrior like Pompey murdered in such tawdry fashion. He is, nonetheless, a guest in a foreign land and calculates that he cannot show Ptolemy his displeasure. For now, he will keep his counsel.

He is resting in his room in the royal palace one evening when a servant arrives with a laundry bag. Caesar suspects nothing as the servant pulls the drawstring and the bag falls open. But inside is a woman, twenty years old and strikingly attractive. Her name is Cleopatra, and she is the king's sister and co-ruler. It just so happens that she would like the throne all for herself, and has engineered a meeting with this great Roman whom she hopes might help her.

Caesar is more than thirty years older than Cleopatra, but he utterly falls for her. She joins the ranks of his many lovers, and he backs her against her brother. As ever, Caesar's small but battle-hardened army proves its worth. Supplemented by reinforcements, the Romans eventually engage Ptolemy's men in battle, during which the young king drowns trying to escape across the Nile. Caesar appoints Cleopatra queen alongside another of her brothers, but as he is just eleven, in effect she rules alone. With little concern for the feelings of his wife, Calpurnia, Caesar makes no secret of his love for his new trophy girlfriend, who soon falls pregnant. She has a son and names him Caesarion, in case there is any doubt as to his parentage.

Caesar's antics, however, are causing ructions back in Rome. How can the leader of the Roman Republic have given himself so entirely not only to a foreigner but to a *royal* foreigner too? Where have his republican principles gone?

### A LOVER AND A FIGHTER

According to the Roman biographer Suetonius, Caesar was 'much addicted to women' and 'debauched many ladies of the highest quality'. Alongside his three marriages (to Cornelia, Pompeia and Calpurnia – or four, if it is to be believed he was also married to a childhood sweetheart named Cossutia), Caesar's list of conquests allegedly included:

- Cleopatra, Queen of Egypt
- Eunoë, wife of King Bogud of Mauretania
- Lollia, wife of long-time Pompey ally Aulus Gabinius
- Mucia, wife of Pompey
- Postumia, wife of Caesar's political ally Servius Sulpicius Rufus
- Servilia, mother of Brutus
- Tertia, daughter of Servilia and wife of Cassius
- Tertulla, wife of Crassus

## HOMEWARD BOUND

It is time for Caesar to head home to smooth things over, but not before a detour to modern-day northern Turkey in August 47 BC to battle the troublesome King Pharnaces II of Pontus, who has attempted a land-grab around the Black Sea while Rome has been wrought by civil discord. Pharnaces is no match for Caesar, who dispatches him in just a few days with victory at the battle of Zela – another milestone in an already extraordinary military career. Caesar's dismissive comment about the campaign – 'Veni, vidi, vici' ('I came, I saw, I conquered') – is carried on placards by his men when a few weeks later they make their triumphal re-entry into Rome.

Reappointed dictator, Rome's leader has been away for over a year and a half, but he has not lost his popular touch. He rewards his veterans with land in Gaul and signs off large-scale civic works in the city. Most spectacularly of all, he begins work on a new Forum, designed to astound. And still he has time to travel to North Africa to put down an incipient uprising there, at the centre of which is his old nemesis, Cato. Realizing that his game is up, Cato disembowels himself rather than entrust his fate to the hands of Caesar.

When he returns to Rome in July 46 BC the city holds a forty-day celebration to mark his many victories over the last few years. Among the festivities, a naked Vercingetorix is freed from his six-year incarceration to be paraded and then delivered for a ritual garrotting. Caesar watches on as his faithful citizens cheer and feast on the gourmet food he has provided for them, laid out on some 22,000 tables. His old legionaries, meanwhile, sing bawdy but affectionate songs about their great commander, and revel in the games during which 400 lions are butchered. A vast parade ground is even flooded to host a re-enactment of Caesar's triumph over Ptolemy on the Nile. There is no party quite like a Roman party.

This year, Caesar is voted consul for a third time, with fourth and fifth terms following – all alongside his dictatorship. He seems unstoppable as he introduces welfare measures for the poor, extends citizenship rights, reduces dependence on slave labour and even reorganizes the calendar, increasing the year from 355 to 365 days and making allowances for leap years. One of the months is even named in his honour. With literal extra time to fill, he ventures to Hispania to defeat the army of two of Pompey's sons, effectively ending the last feasible domestic opposition to him at the gruesomely bloody battle of Munda. He is at the peak of his power.

As proof, he is granted the consulship for ten years and is awarded the honorary titles of *imperator* (until now exclusively used by the military for celebrated commanders) and *liberator*. He encourages the cult of personality that is growing around him, filling temples with statues of himself, and becomes the first Roman ruler to put his own image on the currency. Thanks to his changes in grain allocation, land reforms and policies of debt relief, he's enormously popular with the urban poor – although not to the extent of the godlike status he enjoys within his unstoppably powerful armies. But among the traditionalist *optimates* in the Senate the voices of dissent are growing, especially when Caesar presides over their sessions from a large golden throne. In 44 BC he names himself *dictator perpetuo* ('dictator for life') – the first time such a title has existed.

He's still only fifty-five years old, so that might mean a very long time. How can a republic be a dictatorship? his opponents are left to ponder.

## FALL

It's mid-February, and Rome is in the throes of the Festival of Lupercalia. It's quite a spectacle, in which naked priests smear themselves in the blood of sacrificial animals then run through the city, whipping people with the skins of the dead creatures. But the real talk of the town comes from a moment of political theatre enacted between Caesar and his long-time ally, Mark Antony. Approaching Caesar, who is spectating the day's events, Mark Antony places a diadem on the dictator's head in what appears to be a mock coronation. The crowd falls silent, half in shock, half in expectation. Caesar makes a joke and waves the crown away not once, but twice, as if it is all just a jape. Or has Caesar been testing the public appetite for a real coronation?

For a band of disgruntled opponents in the Senate – a group numbering about sixty – it is a step too far. Their glorious republic was built on its rejection of a monarchy; they're not about to allow that to change on their watch. They galvanize under the leadership of a man named Cassius and another called Brutus – the same Brutus whose life Caesar spared a few years previously, but who is married to the daughter of Caesar's great rival, Cato. Brutus's family reputation for regicide no doubt weighs heavy on him. Cassius's wife, meanwhile, is Tertia, Servilia's daughter, with whom Caesar is also said to have been romantically connected. It's a heady mix of affairs of state and affairs of the heart.

Caesar has been planning a massive campaign against

fearsome Parthia, an attempt to secure a legacy that perhaps even surpasses that of Alexander the Great. He's due to leave on 18 March and doesn't expect to be back for three years. In Rome, his imminent departure focuses his enemies' collective mind.

On the morning of 15 March – the ides, or the midway point of the month – Caesar is in good spirits. He dined out last night and now dresses himself in a toga dyed purple, as denotes elite power. But his wife has had a nightmare in which she cradled her husband in his death throes. She begs him to stay at home today. Caesar recalls he too has recently been warned by a soothsayer to beware the ides of March, and decides that perhaps he should. That is until a messenger turns up at the house, requesting he meet the Senate at the Theatre of Pompey to sign off some minor business.

Reluctantly, he goes, carried half a mile or so in his litter before walking the last stretch past his half-built Forum, a crowd of enthusiastic hangers-on gathering at his heels beneath the morning sun. It's coming up for eleven o'clock as he steps inside the theatre. Brutus wanders over to guide him to his golden throne. Then a senator named Cimber approaches, with a request that his exiled brother be permitted to return to Rome. A throng of senators circle round to hear Caesar's judgement on the matter. Now Cimber leans over and tugs at the robe on Caesar's shoulder. Caesar looks puzzled and hardly notices another senator, Casca, step forward. He has slipped a dagger from the folds of his toga and slashes at Caesar's neck. Maybe he is nervous, but he manages only to graze the leader. When Caesar puts his hand to his neck and sees blood, he lunges for his attacker. This prompts a free-for-all as other senators advance on him, many bearing knives. They slash at him with varying degrees of effectiveness, Caesar's puzzlement giving way to a ferocious will to survive.

A few men loyal to him try to break up the melee but they are beaten back by the majority. Now Brutus steps forward, blade glinting in his hand, and drives it into Caesar's groin. Caesar staggers, his hand failing to stem the fountain of blood. He fixes his gaze on his assailant, reaching for a few words of the Greek favoured by Rome's elite. 'Kai su teknon,' he reportedly mumbles. 'You too, my child?'

Caesar slumps before the statue of his great rival, Pompey. In shame at his miserable end, his body punctured with twenty-three wounds, his final action is to pull his robe up over his face. The man who, albeit briefly, has been the absolute ruler of the Roman universe – from the Atlantic to Asia; from Britain to North Africa – is no more. And now the question is, who will step into the breach? And what will it mean for the republic?

# 9

# OCTAVIAN: BIRTH OF THE EMPIRE

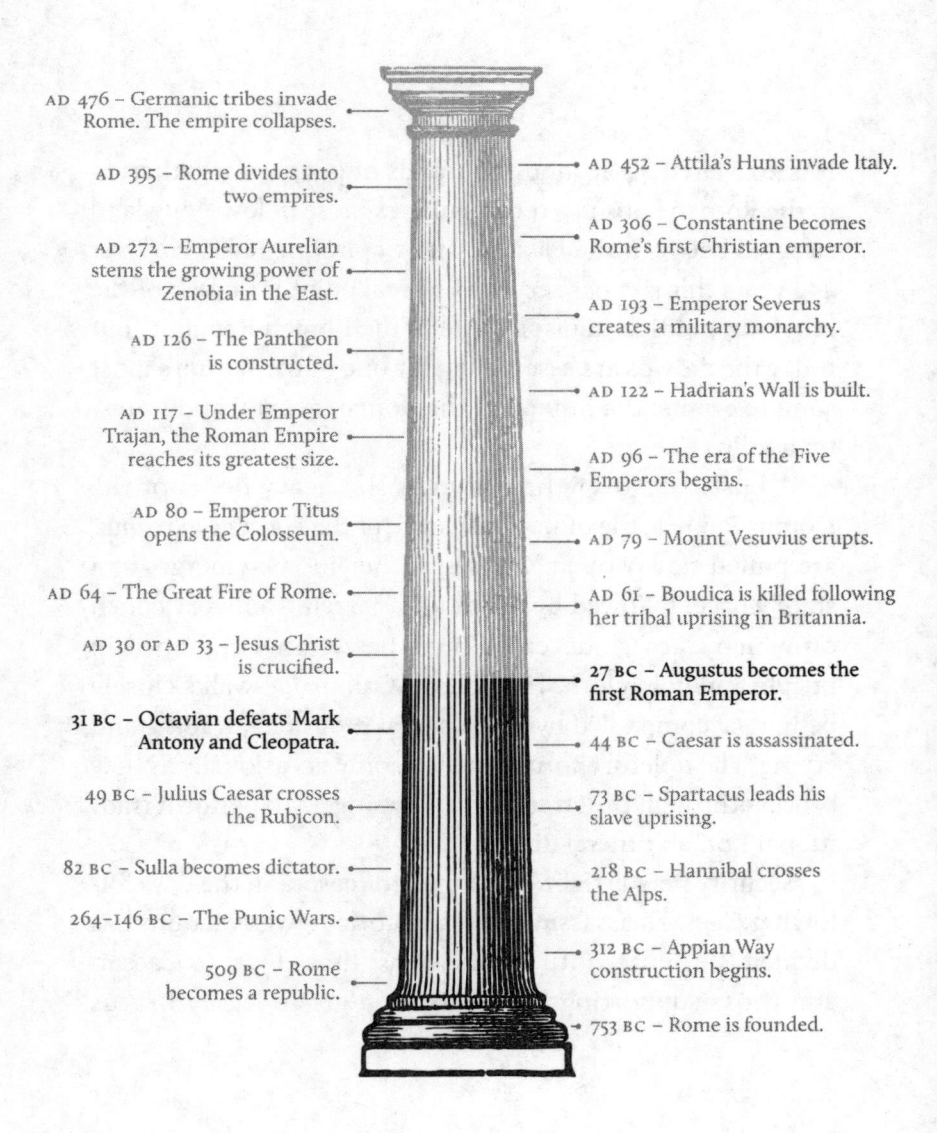

AD 476 – Germanic tribes invade Rome. The empire collapses.

AD 395 – Rome divides into two empires.

AD 272 – Emperor Aurelian stems the growing power of Zenobia in the East.

AD 126 – The Pantheon is constructed.

AD 117 – Under Emperor Trajan, the Roman Empire reaches its greatest size.

AD 80 – Emperor Titus opens the Colosseum.

AD 64 – The Great Fire of Rome.

AD 30 or AD 33 – Jesus Christ is crucified.

31 BC – **Octavian defeats Mark Antony and Cleopatra.**

49 BC – Julius Caesar crosses the Rubicon.

82 BC – Sulla becomes dictator.

264–146 BC – The Punic Wars.

509 BC – Rome becomes a republic.

AD 452 – Attila's Huns invade Italy.

AD 306 – Constantine becomes Rome's first Christian emperor.

AD 193 – Emperor Severus creates a military monarchy.

AD 122 – Hadrian's Wall is built.

AD 96 – The era of the Five Emperors begins.

AD 79 – Mount Vesuvius erupts.

AD 61 – Boudica is killed following her tribal uprising in Britannia.

**27 BC – Augustus becomes the first Roman Emperor.**

44 BC – Caesar is assassinated.

73 BC – Spartacus leads his slave uprising.

218 BC – Hannibal crosses the Alps.

312 BC – Appian Way construction begins.

753 BC – Rome is founded.

It is 20 March 44 BC, and thousands of people are gathering in the Roman Forum, a rectangular expanse of low-lying land situated between the Palatine and Capitoline Hills. For over 450 years this site has served as a focal point for much of the religious, political and social life of the Roman Republic. But today the crowds are assembling for one of the Forum's most sombre events: the funeral of the Roman general and statesman Julius Caesar.

A hush falls over the crowd as the heavy doors of the Domus Publica, the official residence of the *pontifex maximus*, are pulled slowly open. Caesar's father-in-law emerges at a stately pace, followed by pallbearers carrying an ivory couch on which Caesar's deceased body lies arranged, draped in purple and gold cloth. His widow, Calpurnia, walks closely behind, accompanied by professional mourners, wailing and crying. The doleful chorus gives way only occasionally as they process through the streets, to allow singers to perform traditional Roman funeral dirges.

Security here is tight, and for good reason. In the days following Caesar's assassination, a chaotic power vacuum has divided the Senate into two factions: those loyal to Caesar, and those supporting his assassins, a group led by Brutus and Cassius who now refer to themselves as the liberators. In recent days the latter have demanded that Caesar's body be unceremoniously thrown into the Tiber river – a fitting end, they believe, for a man arrogant enough to appoint himself dictator for life. The loyalists, on the other hand, have called for the liberators to be treated as murderers and for Caesar to be given a grand funeral. In the skittish stalemate that followed his death, the Senate mediated a compromise between the opposing sides by granting Caesar today's ceremony while also granting amnesty to his assassins. The fragile truce has done little to lessen tensions within the Senate or outside on the city streets.

The solemn procession continues along the Via Sacra, the city's main road. Mourners lining the route grimace as the fallen leader passes – the perfumes and oils covering Caesar's body do little to mask the pungent stench of the five-day-old corpse. After a short journey, the body is lowered on to the *rostra*, a platform in the centre of the Forum. Mark Antony steps forward. Though relations between him and Caesar have been bumpy in the years preceding his death, he's known as one of the dead man's most loyal allies. He addresses the crowd, a sealed parchment containing Julius Caesar's last will and testament firmly gripped in his hand. With Caesar having no legitimate heir, several of Rome's most influential loyalists have been feuding over which of them will be named his primary beneficiary and take control of his wealth and armies. A hush descends as his lieutenant breaks the parchment's seal and begins to unroll it. As Caesar's right-hand man, many believe Mark Antony himself will be rewarded with Caesar's worldly riches, but there are rumours that Lepidus, Caesar's trusted deputy, could be named.

Few have considered that Caesar may not have chosen any of these Roman elites gathered here today as his heir. Unfortunately for the funeral attendees, Caesar has prepared one final plot twist to be woven into Rome's story. Because the man named on the scroll Mark Antony holds is not involved in today's spectacle; in fact, he's not even in Rome. Known to avoid grandeur and ceremony in favour of modest simplicity, the primary inheritor of Caesar's vast fortune is a little-known youth currently studying in Apollonia, in modern-day Albania. At eighteen years old, he has just been posthumously adopted as a son of his great-uncle Julius Caesar, and will receive around three-quarters of the dead man's fortune. Regaining his composure and, for now at least, putting aside his shock and disappointment, Mark Antony reads the name aloud to his rapt audience. Caesar's heir is Gaius Julius Caesar Octavianus (or Gaius Octavius, as he was prior to his sudden adoption) – known by future scholars as Octavian.

Murmurs of confusion or disapproval ripple through the crowd, but Mark Antony holds up a hand to silence them – there is more to be heard. Though the bulk of Caesar's enormous estate will go to Octavian, the fallen leader has not forgotten the people over whom he ruled. Significant bequests have been left to the city of Rome, and every freeborn citizen of the city – some quarter of a million people – will receive 75 denarii, the equivalent of several months' wages for many. This generosity, rather than cheering the crowd, turns the atmosphere dark. Will they really stand by and allow the murderers of this great man, a *populare* even in death, to walk away unpunished?

Seizing on the shift in atmosphere, Mark Antony now comes to the climax of his speech. He presents a larger-than-life wax effigy of Caesar's mutilated corpse, graphically depicting each of the twenty-three stab wounds inflicted upon his body. Then, to gasps of horror, he raises Caesar's purple toga above his head, torn as it is by the assassins' knives and soaked with blood. Though Shakespeare will famously bring his speech to life in centuries to come, his actual words have been lost to time. But by reminding the crowd of Caesar's standing, his achievements, his love of Rome, and the barbaric nature of his death, Mark Antony transforms the mournful assembly into a baying mob. After summarily cremating Caesar's corpse in the Forum, they turn their fury on the Senate House, setting it ablaze. And amid the full-blown rioting that follows, Caesar's terrified assassins flee.

*After the gruesome death of the most powerful man in Rome, the future of the republic sits on a knife edge. More divided than ever, with its Senate in flames and many of its members on the run, war between the factions seems inevitable.*

*The teenage heir to Caesar's vast resources awaits his baptism by fire in the complex, duplicitous world of Roman politics. Too young to take a seat in the Senate and with powerful enemies ranged against him, how will this newcomer navigate a path to power? And though his predecessor failed at the final hurdle, with the stage now set for a seismic shift in the way power is wielded, will Rome ever be the same again?*

## CAESAR'S HEIR

When Octavian arrives in Rome several days after the funeral, the smell of smoke still hangs in the air. He surveys the streets of the city in which he now holds such a huge stake, but at every turn he sees evidence of the recent disquiet. To the Romans who pass him as he walks, he cuts an unusual figure for a man of such power. With his unkempt golden hair, widely spaced teeth, hooked nose and eyebrows that converge in the centre, he's hardly the image of senatorial power that Caesar was.

> ## EDUCATION AND SCHOOLING
>
> Octavian's childhood was far from typical. But what sort of education might a boy from a well-to-do background usually expect? In the early days of the Republic, children were primarily educated by their fathers, the paterfamilias, who passed down Rome's origin myths, and told stories about its military conquests, gods and heroes. Emphasis was placed on children memorizing texts such as the Twelve Tables, the name given to the legislation underpinning Roman law. Some children were also taught basic martial skills, often through games and role-playing. Over time, children from wealthy families received instruction from Greek educators, often in public squares or on street corners, with teaching emphasizing philosophical debates, logic, oratory, and literature. Exact figures do not exist, but it's estimated that perhaps 10–15 per cent of Rome's citizens were literate. Access to education was overwhelmingly limited to sons of wealthy elites, setting them on the path of the *cursus honorum*, the ladder of public offices held throughout Rome. However, there is evidence that a proportion of girls from high-ranking families

> received some education too, although almost exclusively at home with private tutors. Among the limited evidence (much of it from male writers making barbed observations about the dangers and disadvantages of educated women), an extraordinary fresco has survived in Pompeii. Known as *Woman with a stylus*, it shows a young woman with a writing tablet in one hand and a writing instrument in the other, which she holds contemplatively to her lips. Intended to emphasize the refinement of the family that commissioned it, the piece is a rare example of female education in ancient Rome being celebrated. Julia Felix, the subject of Chapter 12, is a further real-life example of a woman who had the benefit of schooling. Education, then, was mostly a boys' club – but not quite exclusively.

Octavian now travels to meet Mark Antony, who has been safeguarding Caesar's wealth and legions. But to the younger man's surprise, he refuses to relinquish control of the inheritance. And Caesar's former general has good reason to be confident in this power-grab: physically strong, he's a popular veteran with a persuasive personality – an obvious choice of successor, especially compared to Octavian, who in contrast is a mere youth without influence or (notwithstanding his recent windfall) financial backing. But if Mark Antony believes he can disregard him, he may want to consider why Caesar entrusted his legacy to this seemingly unimpressive adolescent. Perhaps Caesar had caught a glimpse of the ruthless and unceasingly determined traits that will one day define him.

Without an army or wealth to his name, Octavian consults Cicero, one of Rome's most influential politicians. The older man is renowned for his loyalty to the republic and his persuasive public speaking. Now Cicero aligns himself with Octavian. Though he frames his allegiance as a moral choice, the correct and legal position a good Roman should take when the contested will was so clear, it's possible he also views the newcomer as a useful, pliable figure – someone he can manipulate to further his own political ambitions. When Mark Antony mocks Octavian's lack of noble lineage, Cicero swiftly defends the young man, declaring, 'we have no more brilliant example of traditional piety among our youth'. Publicly turning against Mark Antony, Cicero eventually delivers fourteen masterful public speeches now known as the Philippics, condemning him as a deceitful and cowardly drunkard who ought to have been assassinated alongside Julius Caesar.

As the attacks on Mark Antony gain momentum, Octavian makes an astute political move. In Caesar's will, the late statesman specified that he wished some of his fortune to be used for public games to entertain the populace. At significant financial risk to himself, Octavian takes out substantial loans in order to fund these games. The message is unimpeachable: even if Mark Antony won't honour Caesar's wishes and pay for the games, then he, Octavian, will do it, out of his own pocket.

His gamble pays off, with many of Caesar's troops as well as the city folk recognizing the considerable financial risk Octavian has taken in the name of righteousness. Consequently, several of Mark Antony's soldiers, who once fought for Caesar, shift their pledge of allegiance to Octavian. And when Mark Antony then opposes a proposal in the Senate to elevate Caesar to divine status, he finds himself even more distanced from the Caesar-loyalists in his army. With Octavian's popularity rising and Mark Antony's in freefall, the Senate inducts the teenager as a senator, waiving the usual age restriction of thirty. Again at his own expense, Octavian starts to gather an army. That early decision to dismiss the youngster as an easy conquest has well and truly come back to haunt Mark Antony.

## THE SECOND TRIUMVIRATE

Cicero's public criticisms of Mark Antony are so effective at undermining his character that Octavian and the Senate hatch a plan to bring him down. Mark Antony has by now made clear his plan to take Gaul, which is currently governed by Brutus Decimus, one of Caesar's assassins. The Senate wait for him to begin what they see as an illegal march on its territory, then declare him an enemy of the people. With a combination of the Senate's own forces and those of Octavian, in late 44 BC both consuls are dispatched to confront him in what will eventually be known as the War of Mutina. Despite being overrun by the superior force, Mark Antony showcases the military prowess that once saw him become Caesar's right-hand man. His soldiers kill both consuls before retreating to Gaul, where Lepidus offers them sanctuary.

Following the battle, Octavian urges the Senate to reward his men for their success and requests to be given one of the now vacant consulships. But though it's one thing to bend the rules to allow a man of his age to become a senator, it's quite another to give him a consulship when he's more than twenty years short of the official minimum age. His request is duly denied, but by this point Octavian has come to enjoy what he's tasted of power, and he's not above switching sides entirely to get his hands on more. So it is that he now proposes an alliance with Mark Antony to seize control of Rome.

In late 43 BC the three rivals for Caesar's legacy – Mark Antony, Lepidus and Octavian – form a coalition known as the Second Triumvirate. Soon after joining forces, they revive Sulla's practice of proscription. Almost overnight, lists are posted around the Forum detailing the names of 2,000 of Rome's most notable citizens, including half of the Senate, who are to be executed for any alleged sympathy towards the liberators. In truth, for Octavian at least, this has already gone far beyond any thought of justice and retribution for Caesar's murder. Instead, he's simply orchestrating this brutal purge to upend the social fabric of Rome and seize power for himself.

The proscription lists seem deliberately crafted to instil fear, distrust and confusion. Those named are often killed in the streets as soon as their names appear. Worse still, families and friends are incentivized to betray their loved ones in exchange for a share of land and wealth that will be confiscated from the victims. It seems that great Roman virtue of *fidelis*, or loyalty, is perhaps more flexible than it once was – something Cicero will now have to come to terms with. Despite being key to Octavian's rise, in December 43 BC Cicero discovers his name has been put on the proscription list. The man who perhaps best represents the traditional values of the Senate is caught and murdered as he attempts to flee the city. When the famed orator's lifeless body is returned to Rome, Mark Antony makes a macabre display of his head and hands on the *rostra*, where Cicero had once led his tirades against him. And as if that were not indignity enough, one account also details how, upon seeing the decapitated head, Mark Antony's wife Fulvia spits in Cicero's face and stabs his tongue with her golden hairpin.

Though they're certainly barbaric, inhumane and underhand, the proscriptions do also serve their purpose. Those senators who aren't simply slaughtered are terrified into submission, and the seized estates help finance the armies of Mark Antony, Lepidus and Octavian. Amid the bloodshed, several of those on the list manage to escape the city and travel to Greece, where they recount the recent events to the liberators' leaders, Brutus and Cassius. Knowing that Mark Antony will not stop until he has wiped out his enemies, the generals ready their troops. The fight for the future of the republic is coming.

In October 42 BC the Second Triumvirate clashes with the forces of Brutus and Cassius in two fierce battles near Philippi in Macedonia. Octavian's army is defeated in the confrontation, but Mark Antony's emerges victorious. Knowing what likely awaits them if they are captured, both Brutus and Cassius take their own lives.

With the liberators no longer posing a threat, the members of the triumvirate divide Roman territory among themselves. Octavian takes Hispania and Italy, while Mark Antony claims the entirety of the eastern Mediterranean. Lepidus, who was tasked with staying behind to keep an eye on things at home, didn't personally take part in the fight. Unable to claim the military victory as his own, he is effectively sidelined, and with his influence diminished is allocated a section of less desirable land along the North African coast. And though Lepidus then volunteers his troops to assist Octavian in capturing Sicily and Sardinia, in a demonstration of stunning disloyalty to the weakest link in the triumvirate Octavian seizes the moment to incentivize Lepidus's troops to switch their allegiances to him. Left without an army, Lepidus is forced into retirement. Now, only Mark Antony stands in the way of Octavian's domination of the Roman world.

## ANTONY AND CLEOPATRA

It is 41 BC, and Mark Antony is stationed in Tarsus, around 10 miles inland from the Mediterranean, in present-day Turkey. It's a beautiful morning, but as he strides through the grand stone archway of the city's port gate, he's got important business on his mind. Several weeks ago he requested the presence of an extraordinary foreign leader, someone to whom his late, great ally Caesar was very close. He'd begun to lose hope that his invitation would be accepted, but news has just reached him of a procession of ships heading upstream from the sea towards Tarsus along the Cydnus river. And according to the messenger, they're no ordinary boats.

Arriving at the riverbank, he has to shield his eyes as he sees the scene for himself. A flotilla of smaller vessels surrounds an astonishing sight – a gold-plated barge, propelled by silvery oars. A massive purple sail flutters in the gentle breeze, and as it pulls closer he catches sight of the passengers on board, resplendent in fine linens, elaborate jewellery and headdresses. By the time the boat docks, Mark Antony has assembled his finest soldiers to welcome the party from overseas, but as he steps on board, military matters are all of a sudden the furthest thing from his mind.

Its polished surfaces almost too dazzling to behold, the boat is also adorned with hundreds of flowers, their rich, fragrant perfume filling the air. All around Mark Antony are women dressed as nymphs and boys as Cupids, many of them playing flutes and harps. And now, as he is led to a golden canopy at the centre of the deck, he sees her – Cleopatra, Queen of the Ptolemaic Kingdom of Egypt. Reclining while she is gently fanned by her attendants, she appears exactly like Aphrodite, the Greek goddess of love. For Mark Antony, she may as well be the deity herself. As he fumbles over his words, it is clear that the great Roman general has met his match, in more ways than one.

Though Antony and Cleopatra crossed paths in Rome several years earlier when Cleopatra was the youthful mistress of Julius Caesar, with the ill-fated leader now long dead they are free to make the most of their mutual attraction. Before long they become embroiled in an affair that appears motivated as much by genuine love as political convenience. Even so, the political aspect is not insignificant, with Mark Antony seeking Egypt's financial and military support to launch an invasion of the Parthian Empire, and Cleopatra after Mark Antony's assistance in ensuring that her son is officially recognized as Caesar's rightful heir. With what's left of the triumvirate still technically standing, this latter is no meagre task. Should Mark Antony convince the Senate of Caesarion's legitimacy, it could supersede Octavian's claim to Caesar's estate.

Cleopatra and Antony become parents to twins, a daughter named Cleopatra Selene and a son named Alexander Helios. After divorcing his Roman wife Octavia (Octavian's sister), Mark Antony formalizes his relationship with the Egyptian queen, who is now assisting his invasion of the Parthian Empire to the east of Roman territory. When news of Mark Antony's new romance reaches Octavian, he promptly sets out to exploit it. Capitalizing on the Roman Senate's fear and disdain for monarchs, he openly questions whether Mark Antony's connection to a queen is indicative of a covert desire to become a king. With Egyptian customs appearing rather peculiar to the Romans, Octavian insinuates that Mark Antony could somehow be under a spell cast by a seductive foreign temptress, leaving him bewitched. The racist and sexist attacks on Cleopatra effectively transform a bitter quarrel between rival Roman generals into a clash of civilizations: Octavian's Rome versus Antony and Cleopatra's Egypt.

In the autumn of 32 BC a golden opportunity arises to slander Mark Antony so decisively that he will be ruined, once and for all. Octavian is visited by two soldiers, Plancus and Titius, who have recently defected from Mark Antony's army. The two men claim that Mark Antony's last will and testament, stored in the Temple of Vesta at the heart of Rome's Forum, contains several explosive revelations about him. It's too good a prospect to miss, and although entering the Temple of Vesta is deeply sacrilegious, Octavian orders his men to retrieve the document for him. Forcing their way past the Vestal Virgins residing in the temple, the soldiers do as they're told and seize Mark Antony's will from their protection. With his rival still none the wiser in Egypt, Octavian proceeds to read the deed aloud to the Roman Senate. Though the behaviour is scandalous, the secrets it reveals are so shocking that many now believe the end justifies the means. Mark Antony's will names his children with Cleopatra as legitimate heirs and states that Caesarion should be considered Julius Caesar's true heir. The will also asserts that Mark Antony wishes to be buried beside his love, Cleopatra, in the beautiful Egyptian city of Alexandria rather than in Rome. The damning revelations confirm that the once-loyal Mark Antony has succumbed to the allures of Egypt, and the Senate now officially declares Cleopatra an enemy of Rome. In the wake of Octavian's political masterstroke, Mark Antony is forced to choose between severing ties with his beloved wife, not to mention her military and financial support, or committing to her and becoming an enemy of Rome himself. As the father of Cleopatra's children, Mark Antony appears genuinely in love with her and decides to stand by her side. And so, war is declared, and Mark Antony and Octavian prepare for a final showdown.

## ACTIUM

In the summer of 31 BC Octavian's forces march to confront Antony and Cleopatra's troops. Conceding that Mark Antony is a far superior military general, Octavian recruits his friend Agrippa to take charge on his behalf, on the understanding that Octavian will take all credit for any successes. It is a masterstroke by Octavian, who compensates for his own lack of natural military talent (a significant shortcoming in a society that prizes martial glory) by appointing perhaps the single greatest general in Roman history after Julius Caesar. What he lacks in battlefield acumen, Octavian makes up for in talent-spotting.

With Octavian's army outnumbered and lacking resources, Agrippa launches a series of raids on Mark Antony's supply lines – small victories that boost morale among his men and frustrate Mark Antony and his forces. Over time, these minor successes lead to significant food shortages and reports of starvation and disease among Mark Antony's soldiers.

To make matters worse for Mark Antony, his men are reluctant to fight their fellow Romans, and many now risk perilous escapes to join Octavian's forces. Particularly embarrassing is the defection of one formidable soldier to whom

Mark Antony has just awarded a gold-plated helmet and breastplate to inspire loyalty.

On 2 September 31 BC the two forces meet off the west coast of mainland Greece for the battle of Actium. To Mark Antony's further humiliation, several of his ships switch allegiance mid-battle. Finding themselves outmanoeuvred, he and Cleopatra flee the scene, only to be relentlessly pursued back to Alexandria by Octavian and the Senate's forces.

In late July the following year, with Octavian's army closing in, Cleopatra enters her mausoleum with her two maidservants. Believing that she has done so with a plan to end her life, Mark Antony subsequently instructs a servant to kill him. What follows is a chaotic, undignified end for the great general. Stabbing himself instead, the servant leaves Mark Antony to fall on his own sword. Critically injured, he is painfully carried by his soldiers to Cleopatra. Though he finds her alive, he dies in her embrace. According to Roman historians, when Octavian's forces finally breach the mausoleum door, they discover Cleopatra lifeless on a golden couch with her two servants lying dead beside her. However, theories persist that Octavian's men may have killed the Egyptian queen and framed it as a suicide. Either way, Cleopatra dies aged thirty-nine having ruled Egypt for over two decades. Octavian's soldiers continue to hunt down and eliminate Cleopatra's inner circle, and in late August they find and kill Caesarion, who is now around sixteen years old. With the biological son of Julius Caesar slain, along with Mark Antony, Octavian is now in sole control of the Roman world.

He visits the tomb of Alexander the Great in his great city of Alexandria. Almost three centuries previously, the Macedonian conqueror had seized control of much of the known world by the time he died aged thirty-three. The Roman biographer Suetonius documents that Octavian, thirty-three himself, orders the sarcophagus to be unsealed so he can scatter flowers on Alexander's corpse and place a golden crown upon his head. Later still, another chronicler adds that Octavian accidentally knocks part of Alexander's nose off while touching the centuries-old body. Whether the account is based on historical records lost to time or merely conjured from folklore remains unknown, but the story at least reflects Octavian's admiration for a leader who shared his unrelenting pursuit of territory and power.

## A NEW MODEL

A little after his pilgrimage, Octavian makes his jubilant return to Rome. His triumphal procession snakes through the city, showcasing the exotic Egyptian treasures his soldiers seized during their campaign, and even an effigy of the demonized Egyptian queen Cleopatra. To symbolize the stability he claims to have brought his people, Octavian declares that the doors of the Temple of Janus should be closed – a rare event that occurs only when Rome is at peace. He also cements the adulation of the crowds by announcing the distribution of parcels of land to veterans across Rome's sprawling territory. There are beast hunts featuring exotic animals, gladiatorial games, feasts, and sacrifices to the gods. He decrees that every citizen be given 400 sesterces, equivalent to approximately £3,000 today – even more than that distributed by his late, great adoptive father, Julius Caesar.

With his army's loyalty assured, a devoted public and wealth beyond his dreams (especially given that Egypt has been taken as his personal possession), it seems as if Octavian can do virtually whatever he wants. But he is wiser than that. He remembers all too vividly the brutal slaying of Julius Caesar, and he recognizes Rome's loathing of autocracy. Rather than assume the mantle of a dictator, he instead sets about meticulously building a different sort of rule, one in which he is effectively all-powerful but which maintains the outward appearance of republicanism – a form of government known as the *principate*. He assiduously consults with the Senate and the institutions of the people, deriving his legitimacy from them and adopting the title of *princeps*, 'first citizen', suggestive of a position as first among equals. The Senate awards him another title – Augustus, meaning 'the revered one' – as well as naming the eighth month of the year after him.

In practice, his decision-making is most influenced by the Consilium Principis ('Privy Council'), which Augustus (as he is now commonly known) gradually moulds in his own image. Despite his apparent deference to the Senate, that institution correspondingly declines in influence. Augustus fills many prominent public positions not with members of the senatorial class but with *equites* who are, he finds, generally so grateful for their elevation that they are more pliable to his will. His power is vast but, crucially, he has not openly grabbed it. He has instead assimilated it without, it might be said, scaring the horses. How you appear to hold power, he realizes, can be just as important as what you do with it.

Having thus established his authority, he is well placed to pursue his principal goal: to usher in a Golden Age of Rome. Militarily, he expands Rome's territories in all directions, almost doubling its extent. Just as importantly, he stabilizes its frontiers, prizing security over expansion for its own sake, and prioritizing negotiation over military engagement where he can.

The empire will grow more in the future, but only rarely from this point on. Augustus seeks closer integration of the existing territories, for example through the astute granting of citizenship to important figures beyond Italy's borders, fostering a sense of unity that ensures Rome will not be greatly plagued by revolts or secession movements in the centuries to come.

There are new laws against demonstrations of excessive luxury, and Augustus himself cultivates a reputation for frugality in his everyday life. Senators are compelled to follow dress codes, and women are banned from spectating at athletic contests in which there is nudity. There are also legislative efforts to promote marriage and child-bearing (a sign of concern that Rome's population is in decline), while adulterers face strict punishments – even his own daughter, Julia, who suffers exile. Alongside a dedicated pursuit of traditional Roman notions of *virtus*, there is also a push for greater religious observance. After all, how can Rome reach its peak if it does not have the gods onside?

Augustus oversees a cultural blossoming, too. New temples, theatres and baths are built in Rome, as well as a new forum named after him. His reign coincides with one of the richest eras of Roman literature, headlined by such famous names as Virgil, Livy, Horace and Ovid. Meanwhile, statues of himself, magnificent in their artistry, spring up throughout the city, delighting those who set eyes upon them even as they serve as propaganda to extol the virtue of the *princeps*. (By contrast, all the statues of Mark Antony are destroyed and his birthday declared a day of ill fortune.) It all contributes to the glorification of Augustus's rule.

His last great achievement is to secure the succession. He has no natural heir, and in any case, the position of *princeps* cannot simply be inherited. Instead, he works hard to mark out a suitable successor with the right titles and sufficient prestige. When Augustus dies peacefully in his mid-seventies in his villa on the slopes of Mount Vesuvius after forty-four years in power, there is no descent into civil war, nor attempt to reimpose the old republican ways. His chosen one, Tiberius, simply takes over, the *principate* secure.

Augustus's reign is the first and longest imperial tenure in Roman history. He has dismantled the existing political structure, replacing it with an imperial system that grants individuals almost absolute authority, with few checks and balances, as long as they respect the image of the *princeps*. In words he has prepared for his own funerary inscription, the *Res Gestae*, he sums up his legacy as follows: 'I excelled all in influence, although I possessed no more official power than others who were my colleagues in the several magistracies.'

With its core value of shared, temporary power now fully undermined, the Roman Republic is no more. The Roman Empire has arrived – and its future looks well set.

# 10

# NERO: LUST FOR POWER

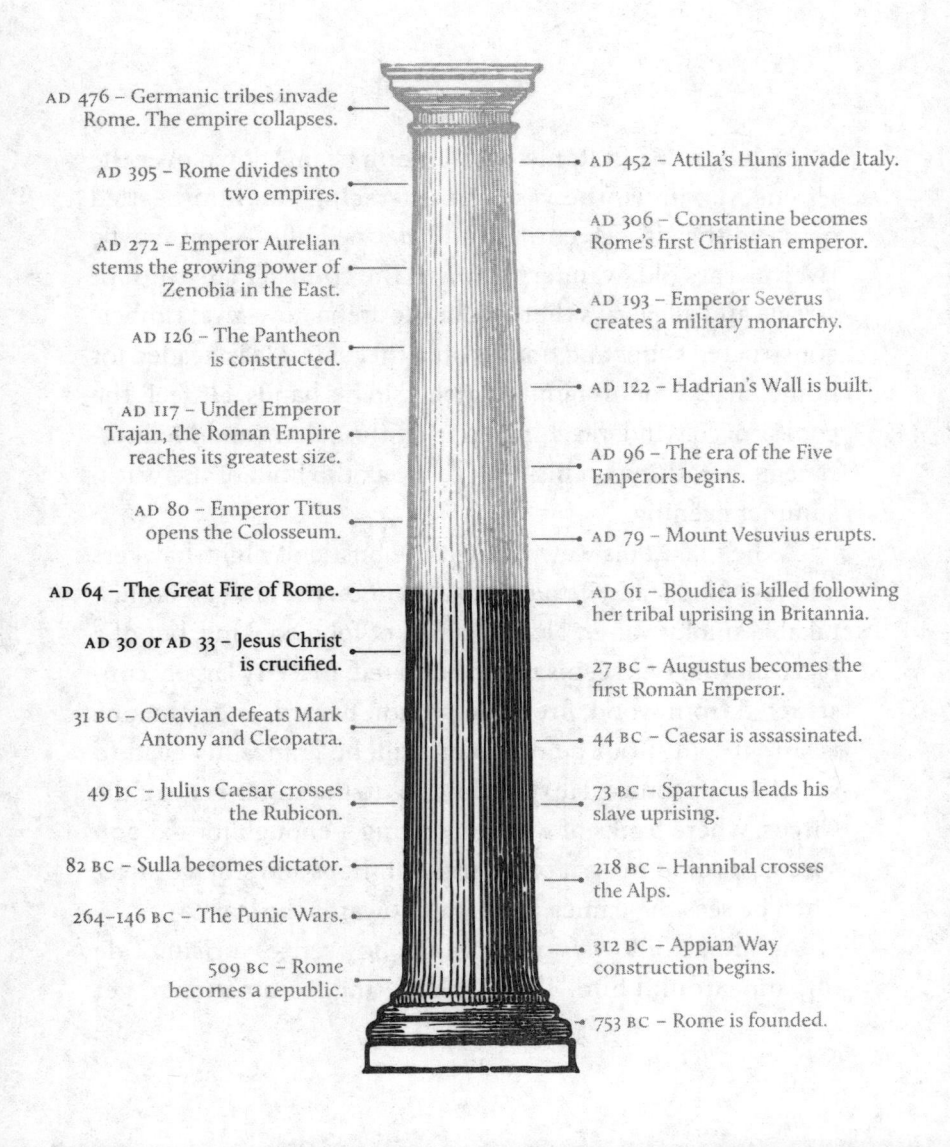

- AD 476 – Germanic tribes invade Rome. The empire collapses.
- AD 395 – Rome divides into two empires.
- AD 272 – Emperor Aurelian stems the growing power of Zenobia in the East.
- AD 126 – The Pantheon is constructed.
- AD 117 – Under Emperor Trajan, the Roman Empire reaches its greatest size.
- AD 80 – Emperor Titus opens the Colosseum.
- **AD 64 – The Great Fire of Rome.**
- **AD 30 or AD 33 – Jesus Christ is crucified.**
- 31 BC – Octavian defeats Mark Antony and Cleopatra.
- 49 BC – Julius Caesar crosses the Rubicon.
- 82 BC – Sulla becomes dictator.
- 264–146 BC – The Punic Wars.
- 509 BC – Rome becomes a republic.

- AD 452 – Attila's Huns invade Italy.
- AD 306 – Constantine becomes Rome's first Christian emperor.
- AD 193 – Emperor Severus creates a military monarchy.
- AD 122 – Hadrian's Wall is built.
- AD 96 – The era of the Five Emperors begins.
- AD 79 – Mount Vesuvius erupts.
- AD 61 – Boudica is killed following her tribal uprising in Britannia.
- 27 BC – Augustus becomes the first Roman Emperor.
- 44 BC – Caesar is assassinated.
- 73 BC – Spartacus leads his slave uprising.
- 218 BC – Hannibal crosses the Alps.
- 312 BC – Appian Way construction begins.
- 753 BC – Rome is founded.

It's 18 July AD 64 in Rome. A full moon beams down over the Circus Maximus, the vast chariot-racing stadium nestled between the city's Aventine and Palatine Hills. A boy, maybe twelve years old, wanders through the compact labyrinth of streets and alleyways that adjoin the arena, low-level timber-constructed shops and houses on either side. He is headed for home, snacks for his family clutched in his hands. He feels the cool sirocco wind, reaching up from the Sahara and Mediterranean, breathing on his neck to break the hold of the warm summer evening.

As he makes his way through the bustle of night-hawkers and fast-food stalls, he picks up a scent on the air – an unmistakable smoky odour. Not the smell of food cooking, but of a blaze. But no one seems much bothered: in a city largely constructed from wood, fire is a common hazard, and someone is sure to put it out before long. Still, he cranes his head to search for its source. He turns his eyes to the eastern end of the Circus, where banks of wooden seating – enough for 150,000 spectators or more – sit on a parade of shops and storage areas. Then he sees the flames, licking up towards the stars.

As smoke billows skywards, the boy senses a rising tide of panic around him. There is shouting, commands to get supplies of water over to the conflagration, people bellowing for the fire brigade. The boy cannot take his eyes off the cinders flickering and dancing on the breeze, spreading the flames higher and further. People begin running for their lives, and he joins the melee. Even if the fire brigade does eventually arrive, their blankets and buckets of water and vinegar will be no match for this inferno.

As the boy runs, he discovers a similar scene in other parts of the city. Building after building, street after street go up. Thousands abandon their homes to race for open ground. Only a few bands of looters seem intent on staying put, taking their chance to profit from the mayhem.

After several terrifying hours, the boy is at last reunited with his parents in the crowd, who fled their home while he was out buying provisions. Tonight, they will sleep out in one of the city's public areas, which the fire has been unable to touch.

As the blaze runs out of fuel to burn and the smoke eventually clears, it isn't long before the first whispers of rumour swirl around Rome's citizens. What if the fire was not an accident? Somebody will say they think they saw the emperor, Nero, watching the disaster unfold from high up on the surrounding hills. Playing his beloved lyre, no less. Where the story originates is unclear, but Nero's opponents in the Senate are happy to see it fly. For years the emperor has been at the centre of lurid stories concerning his private life. For a society that prides itself on military prowess, his preference for the arts and sport has raised questions too. Just how good a Roman is he? Might he have had something to do with this? Did he, perhaps, see an opportunity to rebuild this great city in his own image?

The boy refuses to believe such stories. Instead, he clings

to the reports of Nero turning out to dig through the rubble himself, searching for survivors, and giving food and shelter to the newly homeless. That is his emperor. But for others, the niggling doubts are hard to shift.

*No one knows for sure how the Great Fire of Rome began, but it marks a downturn in the relationship between the city and Nero, destined to be one of the most reviled and controversial leaders in Rome's fabled history. Immersed in rumours concerning his sexual predilections, debauched behaviour and, most seriously, his appetite for murder, he will be accused of killing children and loved ones, engaging in incestuous relationships, and demonstrating negligence and barbarism. Sorting the fact from the fiction is a treacherous task. Many of the stories seem to emanate from his political opponents, while the main records come from historians writing many decades after Nero's rule, each of whom is an upper-class Roman with a particular angle to adopt, their works full of contradictory material. Though Nero is undoubtedly guilty of many extravagant crimes, determining precisely which accusations are fair and which unfounded is, ultimately, a game of best guesses in a time of Roman fake news and post-truth.*

*Though initially well liked by his people, his rule would prove a turning point for imperial Rome, marking the end of its first major phase, under the Julio-Claudian dynasty. His story is a parable of a polity dogged by instability. Here is a global power at the mercy of personal ambition and deadly rivalry, still negotiating the troublesome terms of the relationship between emperor and Senate. So, what happened to ensure Nero's downfall and the rapid ruination of his reputation? And how did his personal passions prompt a series of incredible lapses in judgement that would bring about this downfall?*

## THE JULIO-CLAUDIAN DYNASTY

The Julio-Claudian dynasty was made up of the four successors to rule Rome after the death of Augustus in AD 14. Each of these rulers was descended from one or both of two ancient and celebrated Roman family lines:

- Tiberius (14–37) – descended from the Claudian line and the adopted son of Augustus, an able ruler who maintained his imperial provinces well and kept a tight eye on finances. However, his taste for tyranny made him increasingly unpopular.

- Caligula (37–41) – the great-grandson of Augustus, as well as great-nephew and adopted son of Tiberius, Caligula was initially welcomed by the Roman people. But his profligacy, intense paranoia and stories of his cruelty made him loathsome to the ruling class, who engineered his assassination.

- Claudius (41–54) – Caligula's uncle, who oversaw imperial expansion (including the conquering of Britannia), an impressive programme of public building works and relative stability across the empire, even if Rome itself was a hotbed of intrigue.

- . . . and Nero (54–68).

## EARLY LIFE

Nero is born Lucius Domitius Ahenobarbus on 15 December AD 37 in the well-to-do town of Antium, on the coast about 40 miles south of Rome. His family have impeccable connections. An only child, his father is a great-nephew of the old emperor Augustus who has enjoyed his own good career in public office, including a stint as consul. Lucius's mother, Agrippina – much younger than her husband – is the daughter of the heralded general Germanicus, who had once been expected to take over as emperor. But she's also the sister of the current emperor, Caligula, who has a reputation for fearsome cruelty.

Lucius, then, has a prestigious family line and looks well placed to enjoy a fruitful life, but his seemingly idyllic childhood is soon turned on its head. First, his uncle Caligula accuses his mother, Agrippina, of infidelity with her brother-in-law and involvement in a plot to overthrow the emperor. She is cast into exile, prompting Lucius's father to flee Rome with their young son. This husband of hers, though, is a difficult man with a reputation for violence and an over-fondness for drink, who has never much taken to his boy. Within the year he is dead anyway, and three-year-old Lucius is made the ward of his paternal aunt, his once glittering future thrown into doubt.

Then, in the year 41, events overtake him once more. Caligula is assassinated after a plot by members of the Senate and the Praetorian Guard, his personal bodyguard. Caligula's own uncle, Claudius, is chosen by the Senate to succeed him, possibly because he is considered something of a soft touch who might be controlled, but he soon proves far more decisive a ruler – not to mention more ruthless – than expected. Though his intellectualism and tendency to rule from his palace leaves him a remote figure to the populace, the new regime is a blessing to Agrippina. She returns from her banishment, fuelled by natural ambition and the sense that an opportunity has opened up to restore some of the family's former fortunes.

Reclaiming Lucius from his aunt, she takes a new husband, who happens to be her brother-in-law via her first husband (and a different brother-in-law from the one with whom she was earlier accused of having an affair). He is a rich and powerful figure in Rome, but before the decade is out he dies, likely the victim of poisoning. There are whispers that Agrippina is involved, but nothing sticks. She has other things on her mind anyway.

The position of women of all classes in imperial society is precarious. It is not that there is a lack of roles for them, whether that be slave, shop trader, prostitute, priestess, mother, wife, daughter or one of many others besides. No woman, though, has the legal right to vote nor entitlement to a voice in public affairs. They tend to be judged in terms of how highly regarded they are in any specific field by men, and rely on those same men to make representations for them in the forums of power.

Agrippina realizes that her family connections put her in a situation at once precarious and advantageous, since she knows how power can be exercised from behind the throne, as a wife and as a mother. Take, for example, Livia, wife of the first emperor, Augustus, who wielded enormous influence on Roman affairs several decades ago, to the extent that her enemies portrayed her as some sort of monster.

Having already seen hard times, Agrippina is determined to do whatever it takes to secure a seat at Rome's top table for herself and her son. She sets her sights on the emperor himself.

Despite being his niece, she marries Claudius on 1 January 49, with the Senate leaned on to pass a law normalizing such relations. Another legislative sleight of hand allows Lucius to officially come of age when he is just thirteen. Now adopted by Claudius, the teenager changes his name to Nero Claudius Caesar Drusus Germanicus. Nero becomes the emperor's designated heir, usurping Claudius's own natural son, the younger Britannicus. Britannicus's mother, Messalina, had been involved in a long battle with Agrippina in which both women sought to firm up their son's grip on power. But now Messalina has been executed by her husband for allegedly attempting to overthrow him. To shore up Nero's claim on the imperial corona, Agrippina next arranges his marriage to Claudius's daughter, Octavia – who also happens to be both the groom's cousin and stepsister – when he reaches fifteen. The political and dynastic machinations of the Roman Empire are rarely straightforward.

In October 54, when Nero is sixteen, Claudius dies. It's said he has fallen ill after a dinner of bad mushrooms. Another rumour declares that he has had his throat tickled with a poisoned feather to induce vomiting. Many in Rome, once again, suspect Agrippina's hand in it all, with Claudius just the latest in a long line of those she is alleged to have had murdered or executed. It is no secret that their marriage has been testy for some months, and there have been whispers that, after all, Claudius was looking towards the maturing Britannicus, not Nero, to succeed him. Agrippina has now seen two husbands expire at some convenience to herself, but nothing is proven. What matters is that Nero, thanks to the wily manoeuvrings of his mother, is now ruler of the Mediterranean world.

## A PROMISING START

The young emperor hits the ground running. His mother has seen to it that he has a good team around him. The head of the Praetorian Guard is a man called Burrus, with personal loyalty to Nero and his mother, and she has also secured the brilliant, liberal-minded Stoic philosopher Seneca as the emperor's tutor-cum-adviser. Under his guidance, Nero grants greater powers to the Senate, begins to tackle corruption and introduces a slew of liberally progressive laws around crime and punishment, and the rights of slaves. He reduces the tax burden on Rome's poorest too, and opens new gymnasiums and bath houses. Moreover, he happily acknowledges his debt to his mother, making sure that her image is equal with his on newly minted coins – the first time a woman has appeared on Rome's currency. He seems like the new broom Rome has been crying out for.

There are seeds of trouble, however. Nero has other interests besides ruling. He is utterly convinced of his preternatural abilities as a musician, poet and actor, and is equally confident as a chariot racer. There is no doubt he has talent, especially as a musician, but whether his skills quite justify his extreme self-assurance is less clear. Certainly no one is in a rush to criticize him regardless of his level of performance. But unlike his predecessors, he shows little inclination to prove himself as a military leader. For now, the people do not seem to mind.

When he goes to the races, he chats to them like any other knowledgeable punter. He focuses on providing them with 'bread and sport', as the Roman poet Juvenal famously terms the people's prerequisites for contentment: in other words, enough to eat, and entertainments to distract them. It makes for what seems like harmony between ruler and ruled.

## SCHISM

In public, Nero might be Rome's young darling, but privately there is a very different side to him. He has decadent tastes and spends his evenings carousing with friends, stumbling from drinking den to brothel. He makes sure to disguise himself, but this brings its own problems. His unruly behaviour is regularly confronted by fellow revellers, and he is forever getting caught up in brawls with young men who have no idea who it is they are fighting. On one occasion a man of senatorial rank bests the emperor in a fistfight before he recognizes who his opponent is; he's then rewarded for his victory by being forced to commit suicide.

Then Nero falls for a girl, a Greek slave by the name of Acte. He entertains the idea of marrying her, even having a genealogy fabricated to suggest the girl is linked to the royal line. Though he has never felt much in the way of chemistry with his wife, Octavia, as far as Agrippina is concerned he could hardly have found a more unsuitable candidate to whom to give his heart.

Barely a year into his reign, Nero and his mother are rowing ferociously. He is growing tired of her interference, and her criticism of his romance with Acte, while she can feel her influence giving way to that of Burrus and Seneca. To make matters worse, he has inherited his mother's ruthless streak. It is coming up to the fourteenth birthday of Britannicus, his most obvious rival for power, and he is paranoid that Agrippina will transfer her support to him. At his own celebration banquet, Britannicus falls ill and dies. It is said that he has suffered from epilepsy, but others are not so sure. Suspicion falls on Nero, with the suggestion that he has resorted to that old family favourite, poison.

Over the next few years Agrippina continues her vocal criticism of her son, but she is increasingly peripheral and eventually moves out of the imperial palace. By the year 59 Nero is in his early twenties and he wants a more permanent solution. Inspiration strikes one night at the theatre as he watches a drama involving a memorable boat scene.

It's a balmy evening a little after mid-March in the prosperous resort town of Baiae on the Bay of Naples. The air is pungent with sulphur from the local hot springs. Starlight dapples the pristine water of the bay while its golden beaches pulsate with music and dance as well-oiled revellers celebrate the festival of Quinquatria, dedicated to the goddess Minerva. A roar goes up as a group of party-goers rip off their togas and launch themselves into the sea. Tonight, nothing is out of bounds.

Agrippina and Nero are walking down to the shore from his villa, their bellies tight from feasting. It has been a happy evening. After all the bad blood between them, a chance to reconnect. They share an easy embrace, then Nero helps her on to the compact wooden ferry boat that will take her home. As the captain sets sail, she looks back at her son one last time and waves. Minutes later she is thrown out of her contemplations by the roar of wood cracking and splitting. The boat is falling apart, having been booby-trapped, just like the one Nero saw in that show. As passengers and crew are thrown overboard, Agrippina is as quick-witted as ever, sensing this is all meant for her. Anonymity is now her best chance. Though she manages to swim to safety, it is only a brief reprieve. Nero sends assassins to her villa to see the job through. Ambushed, it is said that she stares at her sword-wielding attackers and points to her belly, telling them, 'Strike here, for this bore Nero.'

## THE DESPOT

Shed of his mother's influence, in 62 Nero also loses that of Burrus, who dies, and Seneca, who retires. He is suddenly without the two men who have kept his rule on track, at least in the public sphere. By now he is in a new relationship too, with the widely acclaimed beauty Poppaea Sabina. She is already married to an aristocratic friend of Nero, but she is keen for the emperor to divorce Octavia and take her as his new wife. When Poppaea falls pregnant by Nero, he seizes his opportunity. His eight years with Octavia have been childless, so he divorces her on the grounds of barrenness and sends her into exile. Just twelve days later he marries Poppaea. But he is not done. Aware that his ex carries the sympathy of the Roman populace, he further defames Octavia on trumped-up allegations of adultery, has her executed and delivers her head to Poppaea. In January 63 his daughter Claudia is born, although the child survives only four months.

Nero is becoming increasingly temperamental, egged on by Burrus's successor as head of the Praetorian Guard, Tigellinus. In 64, for example, at the festival of Saturnalia – already infamous for its ribald merrymaking – Nero takes part in a wedding ceremony with a freedman called Pythagoras, during which he wears a bridal veil. To Rome's conservative elite, such behaviour is not merely unbecoming, it is scandalous. This is the year, too, of the devastating Great Fire.

## THE TORMENTING OF THE CHRISTIANS

For six long days Rome burns, and then just as it seems to be subsiding, it catches again for three more. By its finish, much of the city lies in ashes. Only four of its fourteen districts have escaped altogether, and three have been completely razed. Hundreds are dead and some 200,000 rendered homeless. In its immediate aftermath, Nero displays the same sure touch he had at the start of his reign. He pumps plenty of his own money into rescue operations and rebuilding projects. The plans for redevelopment are encouraging, including building in brick rather than wood and incorporating lots of firebreaks to avoid such a disaster ever again befalling the imperial capital.

And though Nero was miles away when the fire broke out, rumours grow of his possible involvement, or at least of his disregard. Some witnesses tell of how they encountered looters that first night who said they had been paid to obstruct the rescue efforts. It is the sort of mud that sticks. Nor does Nero much help matters when he begins to build on vast swathes of the land cleared by the conflagration. He spends huge sums on an extraordinary new palace complex known as the Domus Aurea, or Golden House, covering hundreds of acres. His decadence is encapsulated in plans for its vast banqueting hall, with a revolving rotunda from which guests will be showered with perfume and flower petals, while outside stands a 100-foot-high statue of himself, the Colossus of Nero.

To fund his grandiosity he imposes higher taxes and claims the valuables of the city's many temples as his own. When that does not prove sufficient, he devalues the currency. It is too much for the citizenry to take. Aware of popular opinion turning against him, Nero searches for someone else to take the heat. He alights on a small community within Rome, already unpopular for its denial of Rome's traditional religious beliefs and regarded by some as a potential danger to the empire itself: the Christians.

Blaming them for somehow starting the fire, Nero exacts savage revenge. Some, like their leader Peter, are crucified. Others are forced to wear animal skins before being set upon by dogs and torn apart. Still others he keeps back for soirees at his palace, where, to the delight of his guests, he ties them to stakes in the garden, covers them in pitch and tar, and sets them ablaze as human candles.

## OUT OF CONTROL

As the year 65 dawns, there is no sign that Nero is reining in his increasingly tyrannical ways. This year he hosts the second edition of the Neronian Games, having debuted the Olympics-style event five years ago. Its mixture of competitions – equestrian, musical and gymnastic – has been a smash hit, and this time he is determined to put himself centre stage. He has been training hard for years, sometimes consuming nothing but oil-soaked chives for the good of his vocal cords, or drinking boar dung diluted with water to build up his physical strength. His performances, sporting and artistic, are now met with fervent acclaim by spectators, even if the more traditional elements of Rome's establishment are less impressed. To them, his love of performance is unsuitable for a man of his position, lacking dignity and disrespectful to the good, martial name of Rome.

His compulsion to attend sporting events is not going down well at home either, with Poppaea, pregnant once again, reportedly scolding him for spending too much time at the races. Then suddenly she miscarries, and dies. There is speculation that Nero has kicked her in the stomach during a fit of pique at one of her tirades. Whatever the truth, he is utterly inconsolable at the lavish funeral he puts on for her, where incense equivalent to a year's worth of importations is burned. Soon afterwards, he hits upon a truly peculiar way of paying tribute to his dead wife. After falling for a servant boy, Sporus, who bears an uncanny resemblance to Poppaea, Nero has the lad castrated and then marries him, issuing strict instructions that Sporus from now on should be known as his empress.

With Nero increasingly erratic and his Golden House draining Rome's coffers, a cabal of high-ranking officials plot his assassination, to be enacted one day during the races at the Circus Maximus. But their conspiracy is given away to the emperor and its ringleaders are executed. His old mentor, Seneca, is among those caught up in the scandal, although the extent of the philosopher's involvement is hotly disputed. Nonetheless, Nero compels him to commit suicide, the old man who had once coached him in ruling for the good of the people another victim of his protégé's propensity for extreme behaviour.

## CIRCUS MAXIMUS

The Circus Maximus, Rome's oldest and biggest public space, was built during the sixth century BC and was in active use until the sixth century AD, variously hosting charioteering, the Roman Games in honour of Jupiter, gladiatorial contests, hunts, public executions and other entertainments. It reached its greatest extent in the rebuild after the Great Fire, when capacity increased to 250,000 and its track stretched for 540 metres. Generally regarded as the most successful charioteer of them all was Diocles (AD 104–after 146), whose career earnings equated to the annual salaries of 30,000 Roman legionaries.

In 66 Nero marries once more, this time to Statilia Messalina. A relatively low-profile character by the standards of his previous wives, her consul husband has been forced to commit suicide in order for her to be free to marry. Then almost immediately, Nero takes his leave of Rome for a prolonged tour of Greece. It is as if he has tired of ruling altogether. Instead, he becomes an itinerant performer, persuading the Greek authorities to postpone the Olympic Games so that he can take part. In festivals across Greece he is victorious in every competition, artistic and sporting, that he enters – over 1,800 'first prizes' in all. The thought seems never to occur to him that his success is based on anything but merit, even when he wins a ten-horse chariot race despite being thrown from his chariot and having to quit the contest.

## DECLINE

Meanwhile, in Rome, his absence of over a year consolidates the growing resentment against him, especially when news arrives from Greece that he has been performing a poem celebrating the burning of Troy, which seems incredibly insensitive given Rome's own recent devastating experiences with fire.

Although Nero has shown precious little interest in its concerns, the wider empire has been getting restive too. There has been rebellion in Britannia, headed by the troublesome Boudica, conflict with the Parthian Empire, and disturbances in Judaea too. There is also growing disquiet among Nero's own officials. In Gaul, the Roman governor Vindex rebels at Nero's demands for increased taxation. He is followed in short order by Galba, governor in Hispania, who declares himself emperor in Nero's long absence. Nero's house of cards looks poised to tumble.

By the time he returns to Rome in 68, he can no longer rely on the support of the Praetorian Guard. In June, the Senate formally declares him an enemy of the state. Holed up in his imperial palace, Nero ponders his options. He considers making a break for Alexandria in the distant Roman province of Egypt. It is just the sort of cosmopolitan, cultural hub that appeals to his artistic side. But as he steals downstairs in the middle of the night, he finds he has been abandoned by his guards and palace servants. Believing the Senate intends to execute him, he knows the moment has come to flee.

It is said that he disguises himself as a beggar and makes for the villa of a still-loyal freedman. According to legend, at this point even his horse deserts him, throwing him off and leaving him in the dust. Somehow he makes it to his refuge, but the Senate's horsemen are not far behind. Convinced that death is inevitable, despite evidence that the Senate in fact intends to spare him, Nero orders the few people who have stayed with him – a handful of servants and Sporus among them – to dig his grave.

With his pursuers arriving at the villa, he declares, 'Like an artist, I die,' and attempts to stab himself in the throat. According to some reports, however, he is incapable of inflicting a fatal wound, and calls on a companion to do the job instead. One of the newly arrived horsemen kneels beside him, trying to stem the flow of blood, but it is to no avail. The emperor bleeds out. 'Too late! But ah – what fidelity,' he is supposed to proclaim as his life ebbs away. It is a suitably confused, violent, messy end to the tumultuous reign of one of Rome's most chaotic rulers.

## AFTERMATH

While the emperor's death is greeted joyously by many in the political class, among the Roman populace and eastwards across the empire the mood is more restrained. For most ordinary people Nero is still the man who gave them bread and sport, who showed up for them after the fire, who wowed the crowds with his musical and theatrical performances. To them, the intrigues of the ruling elite are a mere footnote.

But Nero's fall bookmarks a period of intense instability. Galba is his immediate successor, but the following year, 69, goes down in history as the Year of the Four Emperors. After Galba's brief rule ends in assassination, the next two emperors die by suicide and bloody execution before the throne comes to Vespasian, who successfully founds a new dynasty.

Nero's rise to power has been a study in political cunning and ruthlessness, and had he been able to curb the more extreme traits of his personality, he might have enjoyed a long and celebrated reign. Instead, his egoism, lack of political acumen and incurable cruelty leave the empire in short-term turmoil and condemn his name to the annals of the despised. It may be that some of the blackening of his reputation is overly harsh, and that his successors are keen to sully his name because his popularity with the masses is a lingering inconvenience for the dynasties that follow. Regardless, just as his rule has ended in the sort of chaos that has characterized large stretches of the Julio-Claudian era, it will not be long before a period of relative stability takes its place – the calm that follows the storm.

# 11

# BOUDICA AND THE ROMANS IN BRITAIN: THE EDGE OF THE WORLD

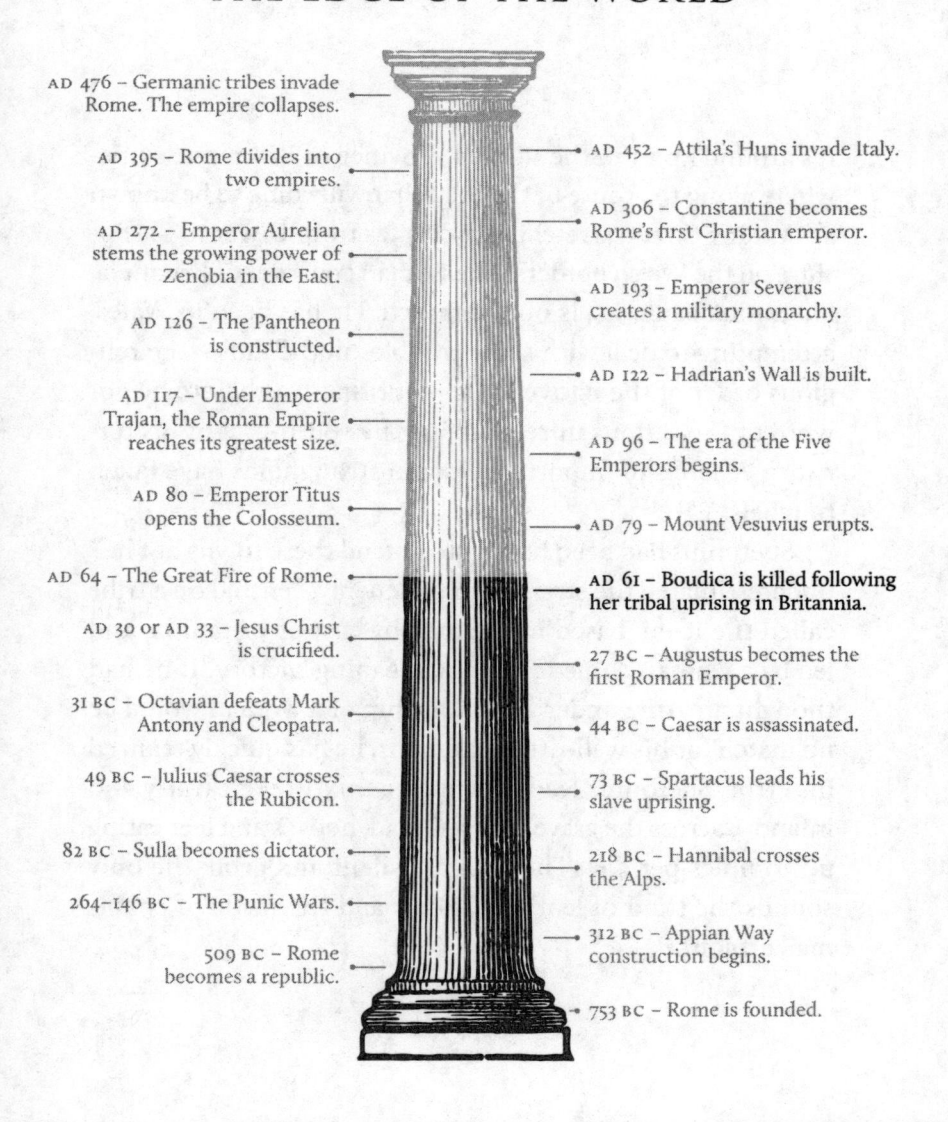

AD 476 – Germanic tribes invade Rome. The empire collapses.

AD 395 – Rome divides into two empires.

AD 272 – Emperor Aurelian stems the growing power of Zenobia in the East.

AD 126 – The Pantheon is constructed.

AD 117 – Under Emperor Trajan, the Roman Empire reaches its greatest size.

AD 80 – Emperor Titus opens the Colosseum.

AD 64 – The Great Fire of Rome.

AD 30 or AD 33 – Jesus Christ is crucified.

31 BC – Octavian defeats Mark Antony and Cleopatra.

49 BC – Julius Caesar crosses the Rubicon.

82 BC – Sulla becomes dictator.

264–146 BC – The Punic Wars.

509 BC – Rome becomes a republic.

AD 452 – Attila's Huns invade Italy.

AD 306 – Constantine becomes Rome's first Christian emperor.

AD 193 – Emperor Severus creates a military monarchy.

AD 122 – Hadrian's Wall is built.

AD 96 – The era of the Five Emperors begins.

AD 79 – Mount Vesuvius erupts.

**AD 61 – Boudica is killed following her tribal uprising in Britannia.**

27 BC – Augustus becomes the first Roman Emperor.

44 BC – Caesar is assassinated.

73 BC – Spartacus leads his slave uprising.

218 BC – Hannibal crosses the Alps.

312 BC – Appian Way construction begins.

753 BC – Rome is founded.

It's around AD 61 in the Roman province of Britannia, somewhere along the route of the road that will come to be known as Watling Street, stretching 250 miles from Dover to Shropshire on the Welsh borders. The Roman governor of Britannia, Suetonius Paulinus, is on the march. He has been in Wales, attempting to deal with some troublesome druids – the religious order of the native Celts – but that was before he got word of the serious unrest seizing the south-east of his territory. A series of important Roman strongholds have fallen to rebels.

Suetonius had been hoping to defend these towns but he's underestimated the strength of the enemy, centred on a tribe called the Iceni, based in the marshy east of Britannia, and led by a woman named Boudica, meaning 'victory'. If he had thought an army under the leadership of a woman would be no match for his well-drilled Romans, he has quickly realized his error. Suetonius leads his men, a mixture of cavalry and infantry, across the gravel-topped road, hooves and feet eating up 30 miles per day. The men are silent and grim, the only sounds the thud of leather sandals and the rattle of chainmail armour.

From horseback, Suetonius scans the land in every direction. Just now there is nothing but flat countryside, but his time in the province has taught him that the landscape never stays the same for long. Soon enough he'll be in forest, or amid rolling hills, or riding into another town. He's not exactly sure what he's hoping to see but he's on the lookout for a suitable site to engage Boudica and her troops, somewhere his 10,000-odd men will stand a chance against her militia, rumoured to be ten or even twenty times stronger. When he sees it, he'll know the spot.

It is not long before he's having to urge his horse up a steep incline, and wondering whether Boudica's army will suddenly rear up over the crest of the hill. They cannot be far away now. He is struck by the rich verdant hues, so different from the landscape of his coastal home in Italy. But the sudden undulation here gives him an idea. Commanding his legion to halt, he leads a small team off on a scouting mission. They follow a path through a thicket of trees, branches claustrophobically bearing down on them. As he emerges from the vegetation, there in front of Suetonius is a rugged, craggy valley. When he finally reaches the floor of the basin, he gallops for a flat mile between rocky outcrops until the ravine opens on to a wide plain.

This is what he has been searching for. It's what military commanders call a 'defile', a narrow pass that can act as a chokepoint, a bottleneck. He can tuck his troops deep in the gorge, where the steep sides and trees will prevent an ambush from Boudica's horsemen. Then they can level the playing field against their much larger enemy. He sends messengers back to Watling Street to call for the legions to descend into the gorge and meet him here. When they are in place, he orders his men to adopt a close formation, ready to burst out of the mouth of the valley.

Soon, the enemy start to assemble on the plain, a sea of foot soldiers and cavalry as far as the eye can see, along with fighters in chariots – a vehicle the Romans are really only familiar with in a sporting context. Most are clad in pelts, their fearsome faces smeared with a blue dye derived from the woad plant. A few carry swords and shields decorated with red enamel so it looks from a distance that they are already coated in blood. Many, though, have only makeshift weapons and rudimentary armour, presumably relying on the volume of numbers for their protection. Beyond them, women and children, many having travelled in carts with their pack animals, take up position to watch the battle, seemingly assured that victory is guaranteed. Suetonius scans the throng, trying to catch a glimpse of Boudica. Intelligence reports suggest she is an unusually tall woman, with a spectacular head of hair and a distinctive multicoloured woollen cloak. For now, he cannot spot her. But it will not be long before the two rivals are in the thick of the action – the small Roman contingent fighting for their lives, the Britons for the future of their homeland.

For Suetonius, this is by no means just another day, but he takes it all in his stride. When you have an empire as large as the Romans have built, a little local trouble is to be expected. And here in Britannia, at the very western reaches of the Roman realms, there is a clash of cultures that it seems only violence can decide.

*Boudica's rebellion at the edges of the empire is reported in several ancient histories, most notably by Tacitus and Cassius Dio.*

*Both wrote at a time substantially after the events and employed aspects of fiction, not least in relating speeches that Boudica almost certainly didn't give. However, there is general consensus that Boudica (also known by several variations, including Boadicea) was real, and that her uprising caused the Romans in Britannia significant difficulties. Indeed, Tacitus's father-in-law, Gnaeus Julius Agricola, was serving as a tribune to Suetonius at the time, so would have been an eyewitness to the events his son-in-law then put down in writing. So, while we may assume that Boudica has been mythologized, what can we really know about her? And what does the story – told by the Romans – tell us about the problems Rome faced in administering such a vast empire, encompassing people with world views entirely different from their own?*

## INVASION

It's AD 43 when the seeds of Boudica's uprising are sown – nearly a century since Caesar ventured across the sea to this strange, unfamiliar island. There have been several schemes for renewed Roman incursions in the years since. None of Augustus's planned expeditions came to fruition, and as recently as three years ago Caligula assembled an attacking force across the sea from Britannia, only for the invasion to be aborted for reasons lost to time. His work, though, helped pave the way for the current plans developed under the new emperor, Claudius.

Likely drawing heavily on the army put together by Caligula, Claudius has assembled four legions of around 5,000 to 6,000 men each, and some 20,000 auxiliaries. The pretext for invasion is to restore to power Verica, the leader of a British tribe allied to Rome who has been exiled by more bellicose local rivals. But for Claudius, it also offers the enticing prospect of mineral wealth, along with the reflected glory of victory on the battlefield and the expansion of the imperial territories.

The expeditionary force sets off from northern France and lands in Kent on the south coast of Britannia. It meets fierce resistance, most notably from an army under the leadership of two high-ranking tribal figures, Togodumnus and Caratacus, but the well-prepared Romans make steady progress. When the army is ready for a triumphant march on Camulodunum (modern-day Colchester in Essex), a *colonia* or military stronghold that the Romans intend to make their provincial capital, even Emperor Claudius makes an appearance. He arrives in high summer at the head of a force complete with war elephants – almost certainly the first time native Britons have seen such a creature – to accept the surrenders of eleven tribal leaders. Such overseas exploits do an emperor's reputation the power of good back in Rome.

Next, it's westwards for the Romans, eventually into Devon. While Britannia's northern reaches remain in native hands, Rome gradually brings much of the south under its control – at least, seemingly so. It's an impressive expansion that Nero is keen to continue when he comes to power in AD 54. But six years later the druids of North Wales are still proving a tough nut to crack. Suetonius, by now the provincial governor, is doing his best to tame local dissent, leading his troops on an invasion of the island of Mona, off the northeast coast of Wales.

## THE SCOTTISH PROBLEM

While the Romans were eventually successful in subduing much of what we now call England and Wales, they never managed to take Caledonia (roughly equivalent to Scotland) for any length of time. In the AD 80s Roman forces advanced as far as north-east Caledonia and won a major victory at the battle of Mons Graupius, but demands for manpower elsewhere meant a withdrawal in just a few years. In 122 Emperor Hadrian ordered the construction of the wall that carries his name, stretching from the north-west to the north-east coasts of England, effectively marking the northern boundary of Roman power in Britannia. His successor, Antoninus Pius, built a wall of his own further into Scotland in the 140s, but within two decades it was abandoned and Hadrian's Wall restored as the border. It was not until the third century that Rome made any further serious incursions, but these too were soon repelled by local tribes.

## THE ICENI

Among the tribes that have already come to an agreement with the Roman authorities is the Iceni, based 100 or so miles north-east of London. With their home among the waterlogged fens, they are more insular than many of their neighbours and bound to their traditional ways. They live in small communities on farmsteads, in large roundhouses constructed from wicker walls plastered with mud and dung. Smoke billows through high thatched roofs from the fires essential to fend off the worst of the British weather. They cultivate fields of barley and wheat, and tend their flocks of sheep. There's good money to be made from selling the wool and there are thriving local trades in both pottery and salt, which is essential for food preservation. The Iceni might lead a simple life as far as the Romans are concerned, but they've accumulated stocks of silver and gold to make anyone take notice. They take great pride in their horsemanship too, and boast admirable skill as chariot-drivers.

Their chieftain is a man named Prasutagus, husband to Boudica who, for the time being, remains in his shadow. Though Prasutagus's precise heritage is unclear, it is possible he is one of the tribal leaders who surrendered to Claudius in return for some level of independence. Alternatively, he may have been installed by the Romans following their suppression of a rebellion by the Iceni a few years back, when they came out in defiance of Roman plans to disarm the tribes. Whatever the case, by AD 60 he has managed to navigate peaceful co-existence with the occupiers for well over a decade, the very model of a good client-king. His preference for keeping the imperial overlords sweet is even reflected in his will, which promises Emperor Nero half of everything he holds, his daughters inheriting the other half. So, as Suetonius goes off to deal with the druids at Mona, the Iceni are low down his list of concerns.

## TROUBLE BREWING

When Prasutagus dies shortly afterwards from natural causes, there is trouble in the air. The chieftain's decision to leave half his estate to Nero is received not as a compliment but an insult. Besides, Roman law does not acknowledge the right of women to inherit a man's estate, so as far as the emperor is concerned Prasutagus's daughters have no claim on what their mother Boudica regards as their birthright. Nero instructs Decianus Catus, recently appointed to look after Rome's financial affairs in Britannia, to put all the Iceni lands directly under imperial control.

Decianus Catus is already unpopular in these parts. Having imposed new taxes, he is also demanding the prompt repayment of what he is now calling loans from Rome, but which have not necessarily been understood as such, and which the tribes argue have already been paid in kind. Boudica coordinates organized resistance along with other disgruntled neighbouring tribes, convinced that having to pay tariffs and cede land to the occupiers is scarcely different from being enslaved. She may have kept a low profile through her husband's reign, but now that the futures of her girls and her people are under threat, she is ready to fight their corner. However, she is about to encounter a side to the Romans more brutal than anything she has yet experienced.

Wearing leather leggings and with her long hair hanging loosely around her shoulders, Boudica makes her way between thatched Iceni roundhouses, their conical roofs rising to twice her height. The smell of roasting meat kindles her hunger. She has been working all day with her horses and chariots, and is still carrying her metal-tipped javelin, when she hears a scream coming from one of the huts. She goes to investigate, and finds an old man being soothed by his family as he drags his fingers through his hair, his face in a rictus of anguish. A girl in her teens, his granddaughter, takes Boudica aside to explain that he has been like this since returning from his day's work in the fields. As the sun dipped in the sky, he claims the clouds burned red and the marsh waters turned to blood. The old man whispers that it is an omen.

It's been like this since Boudica's husband's death, when the Romans started throwing their weight around – the whole village is on edge. Boudica says her rueful goodbyes and returns to her own roundhouse, where her adolescent daughters have just finished preparing mutton stew. The family eat together, then settle down for the night. But when the girls are safely in their beds, Boudica hears a noise that makes her snatch up her javelin again. A steady tramp of leather-clad feet. A rattle of metal helmets. Shouts in a strange language.

Romans. And they're coming this way.

She wakes her daughters and orders them to hide in a store cupboard, before slamming the door firmly behind them. Then she rushes outside and sounds the alarm by banging her spear tip against a metal pot. The villagers emerge, and some decide to flee for the moonlit marshes, hopeful their local knowledge will keep them safe from the sinking mud and the goblins said to lurk out there. Better those dangers than the Romans.

Boudica tells those who remain to arm themselves. They do not have long to wait. The soldiers soon arrive, fanning out to swamp the settlement. Some start fights with the locals; others duck into huts. There are screams, dogs barking, the clash of blades as Boudica's people make a stand. She runs to defend her girls, but the Roman commander cuts her off before she reaches her home, pointing a sword at her throat. His eyes gleam between the metal panels of a helmet that covers most of his face. He says he knows who she is and he has come to teach her a lesson.

Boudica is surrounded. She's dragged away by a posse of troops who manhandle her and tie her to a post. Her shirt is ripped from her back and she gasps as a whip lashes her bare skin – a symbolic punishment usually reserved for slaves. She vows to herself to hide the pain she is feeling, but when she sees other soldiers rush into the roundhouse where her girls are hiding she lets out a blood-curdling scream. She knows what's coming next. Amid the din of her home being ransacked, all Boudica hears are her girls' cries for help. But however hard she struggles against her bonds, she cannot save them. As the Roman commander continues to flog her, his men violate her daughters, and Boudica vows to have her revenge.

## FURY UNLEASHED

Boudica finds herself at the heart of a complex culture clash. The Romans see the Britons as barbarians, subjects ripe to be taxed and stripped of their lands. One need only watch Suetonius waging war against the Welsh druids, destroying their holy sites, to realize that. Meanwhile, the Britons, epitomized by Boudica, see the Romans as immoral intruders who will stop at nothing in their lust for wealth.

That Suetonius has taken the majority of the Roman army west to deal with the druids provides the vengeful Boudica with a window of opportunity. She makes a call to arms to her own tribe and to the neighbouring Trinovantes. Soon she commands a force in the tens of thousands. They are not professional soldiers, but given that this is a time of perpetual conflict between tribes, they're already armed and dangerous. She leads them on a march on Camulodunum, which has been the territory of the Trinovantes until recently. Now it is the closest Britannia has to a Roman town, full of soldiers and veterans living in relative comfort on appropriated land, demanding taxes and supplies from local farmers, bleeding them dry until the peasants suffer famines. To make matters worse, the Romans have been conscripting local youths and forcing them to fight against their own people. A final insult comes when the Trinovantes are obliged to construct at their own cost a temple to Emperor Claudius, who is worshipped like a god.

It is the middle of the day and a grey-haired sentry, a retired legionary, keeps guard high on the red-brick town wall, his woollen cloak heavy with accumulated drizzle. He hears a whistle from further along the wall. It's one of his fellow soldiers pointing towards the local river, the Colne. There is a sound drifting on the wind – a mass of shouting and clattering. A rag-tag army on the march. The legionary climbs down from the wall and hurries to the barracks to raise the alarm. Soon, a few hundred soldiers are snatching up their shields and swords, and the sentry dispatches a rider to the nearby settlement of Londinium (modern-day London) to call for reinforcements. But he knows it's a vain plea, as most of the troops normally stationed there are currently in distant Wales.

Now he can see the approaching horde in more detail. At the front, in a chariot, is a tall woman wielding a spear and chanting a war cry echoed by drummers and warriors. Clad in skins and furs, they carry axes and cudgels, terrifying in their primitiveness. The column of barbarians stretches as far as the sentry can see.

When they reach the city gates, they break through with a battering ram and begin spilling through the streets. Hurrying over to the tall woman, the old legionary tries to reason with her, but she silences him with a blow to the head. He slumps, mortally wounded, and watches as she spears another legionary, then turns her wrath on a Roman woman.

All around, barbarians set fire to wattle-and-daub buildings. Even beneath the pounding rain, the city is soon aflame. Through the swirling smoke, the dying legionary sees Iceni warriors pour into the Temple of Claudius, where the residents of Camulodunum have rushed to seek refuge. Inside the sanctuary, their prayers for salvation turn to screams as they are cut down in a blood bath.

When at last Roman reinforcements arrive in the form of the 9th Legion, an elite squad of 5,000 soldiers, Boudica routs them in a day of infamy for the occupiers. She simply has too many fighters at her disposal for them to stand a chance, and 80 per cent of the legion is killed. Then, over two agonizing days, she and her army slaughter whoever else they find – not just Romans but anybody they deem to have cooperated with the enemy. Boudica refuses to loot the town – better to burn it than profit from the Romans in any way.

## LONDON AND ST ALBANS

It is this attack that lures Suetonius from his war against the Welsh druids. He hopes to intercept Boudica before she can wreak similar violence on her next target – the burgeoning settlement of Londinium, a 50-mile march south from Camulodunum. Londinium is a *colonia* unique in the Roman Empire, established by the invaders as a new town rather than by occupying an existing settlement. From humble beginnings seventeen years ago as a small encampment around a pontoon bridge over the Thames, these days Londinium is home to 10,000 residents with shops and offices, a forum (or marketplace) and a *basilica* (or public hall). But as it stands, there are only about 200 auxiliaries to defend it. Nowhere near enough for them to stand a chance.

Suetonius manages to arrive a little before Boudica, but he quickly makes the decision that even with his additional numbers they cannot take on her vast army. So he orders Londinium to be abandoned to the rebels, who attack it with similar or perhaps even greater severity than Camulodunum. Still, Boudica is not satisfied. She marches another 25 miles north-west to Verulamium (modern-day St Albans) and sacks that too. According to the sources, her troops kill some 80,000 people in all, committing acts of atrocity in the name of vengeance, including impaling women on spikes and defiling their bodies in other appalling ways.

While military might was fundamental to the expansion of Rome's territories, assimilation as epitomized by Romanization – making sure subjects felt some benefits of Roman hegemony – was vital to maintaining those territories over many centuries with remarkably little serious resistance.

## ROMANIZATION

Boudica's rebellion was one of a relatively small number of uprisings designed to shake off Roman rule where it had already been established. This was in part due to the success of Rome's ability to impose its authority and culture on the existing culture and customs of conquered peoples – a process sometimes known as 'Romanization'. Although an amorphous term, in essence it refers to the creation of a state of mind that ensures conquered peoples see themselves as an integrated part of the Roman Empire, rather than unwilling subjects of a foreign power. Though in the eastern regions of the empire, where Greek civilization was so deeply embedded, there was a much more equal interaction between Greek and Roman culture, in the west, Romanization flourished. Its core aspects included:

- *Government* – With Roman administrators in limited supply, it was vital to work with local elites to impose the Roman model of governance. This was done, for instance, by granting citizenship to local leaders and providing their children with a Roman education.

- *The army* – Garrisons were a crucial early point of contact between victor and vanquished. Local communities provided goods and services in return for payment, and some were directly employed by the army, starting a process of economic and social integration.

- *Urbanization* – Rome established large numbers of new towns and cities, drawing on a distinct Roman pattern that typically included a central forum, colonnaded streets, bath houses, temples, theatres and the like – key to building a uniform culture.

- *The economy* – Rome conquered to get resources – taxes, tribute, produce, manpower. But it offered a good deal in return. Though not everyone in subject territories felt the material benefits, many found themselves with access to vast new markets, as well as new technologies.

- *Language* – For efficient administration, a single language was essential. Latin was the unifying medium through which disparate communities were able to communicate. (In the east, in contrast, Greek long remained the lingua franca of administration.)

- *Religion* – The Romans looked to impose their own religious beliefs but did so strategically, marrying their own faith to local religious traditions wherever they could.

While military might was fundamental to the expansion of Rome's territories, assimilation as epitomized by Romanization – making sure subjects felt some benefits of Roman hegemony – was vital to maintaining those territories over many centuries with remarkably little serious resistance.

## THE BATTLE OF WATLING STREET

Suetonius's planned retreat buys him time. His force regroups, readying themselves for what he plans to be a decisive confrontation at the location with the defile that he has discovered. When Boudica's army arrives and begins its confident charge, her chariot as ever in the front and her troops filling the valley with war cries, the heavily outnumbered Romans are ready. They hold their line in the face of the terrifying onslaught, allowing the enemy to funnel deep into the gorge until they run out of space. With the Britons crushed into the bottleneck, the Romans launch a storm of spears through the air, the javelins producing a dismal whistle on their destructive arc.

One by one, Boudica's people fall. They are immediately replaced by reinforcements streaming up the gorge, only for them to meet another deadly wave of spears. Having got themselves on to the front foot, the Romans now advance in a wedge shape. Their superior training and small weapons prove lethal in the tightly packed melee, and their cavalry brings chaos to Boudica's ranks. As the Britons realize they are losing, they try to retreat back to the plain, but find themselves hemmed in by their own carts and the crowds of onlookers they have brought with them. It is only a matter of time until the battle of Watling Street is over, and with it, Boudica's revolt.

According to Roman reports, Boudica loses 80,000 soldiers on this day alone, against Roman losses of just 400 – although it is likely there is exaggeration in the disparity. As for Boudica, the details of her fate are disputed. Cassius

Dio will report that she dies of a sickness – presumably from injuries sustained in battle – and is accorded a lavish funeral by her supporters in an unknown location. Tacitus, meanwhile, claims she poisons herself rather than be taken prisoner of war. What is certain is that the cold professionalism of the Roman military has ultimately triumphed over the mighty but more haphazard ad hoc rebel army. The machine has won.

Any survivors from Boudica's uprising return to East Anglia, but the Iceni face stern punishment for their rebellion. Rome attacks their settlements, burning down homes and taking people into slavery. Meanwhile, the towns brought low by Boudica are rebuilt with organized streets and modern conveniences such as baths and heating. So successful is the reconstruction of Londinium that the Romans move their capital here.

Boudica may have been unsuccessful in the end, but she has given the Romans an almighty scare. That a woman should have come so close to crushing the eternally patriarchal Roman system in Britannia is an extraordinary tale that scars the Roman psyche. For a while Nero seriously considers abandoning the province as unmanageable, but he perseveres, and by the end of the century Rome has grasped control of most of England and Wales.

There are no further significant revolts in Britannia, which becomes an integral part of the empire for centuries to come. Once the scars of invasion begin to heal, the population are able to enjoy the many benefits of Roman dominion, from strong central government and improvements to the physical infrastructure to prosperous trade and upgrades in agricultural production. For many people, whether living in the thriving cities established by the Romans or scraping a subsistence living in the countryside, arguably life improves. The introduction of Roman husbandry skills, as well as superior agricultural techniques leading to larger yields of feed, mean that even the size of livestock significantly increases over the period of Roman occupation – a development with real-world impact. So, there is no great clamour to try again to remove the imperial overlords.

Boudica's rebellion, though, remains a stark reminder: nobody said ruling a great empire would be easy. Ancient Rome has not yet enjoyed its heyday but it has perhaps glimpsed the seeds of its eventual demise.

# 12

# JULIA FELIX:
# A TIME CAPSULE OF LIFE
# UNDER THE ROMANS

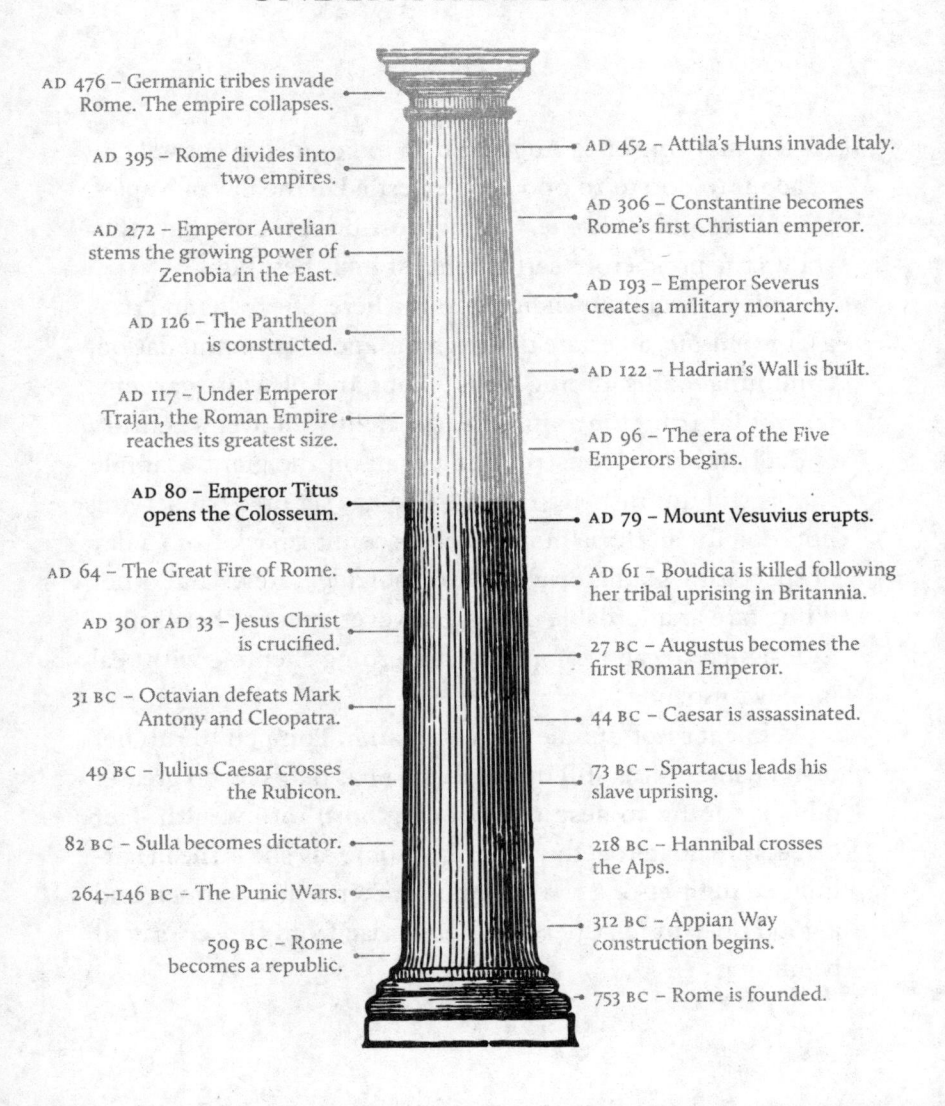

AD 476 – Germanic tribes invade Rome. The empire collapses.

AD 395 – Rome divides into two empires.

AD 272 – Emperor Aurelian stems the growing power of Zenobia in the East.

AD 126 – The Pantheon is constructed.

AD 117 – Under Emperor Trajan, the Roman Empire reaches its greatest size.

**AD 80 – Emperor Titus opens the Colosseum.**

AD 64 – The Great Fire of Rome.

AD 30 or AD 33 – Jesus Christ is crucified.

31 BC – Octavian defeats Mark Antony and Cleopatra.

49 BC – Julius Caesar crosses the Rubicon.

82 BC – Sulla becomes dictator.

264–146 BC – The Punic Wars.

509 BC – Rome becomes a republic.

AD 452 – Attila's Huns invade Italy.

AD 306 – Constantine becomes Rome's first Christian emperor.

AD 193 – Emperor Severus creates a military monarchy.

AD 122 – Hadrian's Wall is built.

AD 96 – The era of the Five Emperors begins.

**AD 79 – Mount Vesuvius erupts.**

AD 61 – Boudica is killed following her tribal uprising in Britannia.

27 BC – Augustus becomes the first Roman Emperor.

44 BC – Caesar is assassinated.

73 BC – Spartacus leads his slave uprising.

218 BC – Hannibal crosses the Alps.

312 BC – Appian Way construction begins.

753 BC – Rome is founded.

It's the morning of 24 August AD 79 in Pompeii, a coastal city of about 10,000 to 20,000 people nestled in the Bay of Naples, 150 miles south of Rome. One of those bright sunny days that shows the prosperous settlement off in its best light.

Julia is a well-known figure round here. She owns and runs a large *praedia*, an estate that includes rental accommodation, communal baths, dining areas, shops and pleasure gardens. It's not far from the amphitheatre, built well over a century and a half before construction began on the giant example that is still unfinished in Rome. She has set up a bar serving hot food for all those hungry bellies coming back from a day of spectating gladiatorial games – porridge, stews and other filling fare at affordable prices. However, most of her facility is designed to cater for a more discerning clientele with real money to spend.

While it's not unique for a woman in Pompeii to run her own business, it is still unusual. Julia has defied even greater odds by doing so despite not being born into wealth. Her origins are not altogether clear, but some say she is the illegitimate daughter of a freedman. It's taken some acumen and a good dose of feistiness for her to rise from those sorts of beginnings.

She stands in a room that serves as her office, its walls adorned with vibrant paintings of food and money – an insight perhaps into her fondness for the finer things in life. Over a customary ankle-length white tunic she wears an elegant sleeveless silk robe draped from the shoulder. She has applied some make-up too: powdered chalk to give her a fashionably pale complexion, some red ochre to give her cheeks and lips a blush, and an ash-based concoction to accentuate her eyes. Next she puts on hemispherical gold earrings and a gold and pearl necklace, then slips on to her finger a gold ring adorned with a large reddish-brown carnelian stone. Ready for whatever the day might throw at her, she begins an inspection of the estate.

It's a labyrinthine property, one of the largest in all of Pompeii. Julia, now perhaps in middle age, has owned it for maybe sixteen or seventeen years. In fact she talked the local authorities into letting her merge two properties together, which meant removing a road that had run in between. Considering how busy it is around this neighbourhood, she had to leverage a lot of influence to get permission. Over half the footprint of the complex is given over to astonishing gardens, including a tranquil orchard bordered by low wooden fences. Then there's a spectacular ornamental garden, complete with marble-edged canal, artificial waterfall, several miniature bridges, shaded pergolas and a grotto complete with statues of nymphs. She loves to walk out here when all the customers are gone – a perfect oasis amid the urban sprawl, the trickle of running water soothing away her worries.

But for now it's business, and she moves from one airy room to another via a series of atria and open courtyards. Everywhere, beautiful artwork adorns the walls, and marble pillars add to the sense of grandeur. She steps into the *triclinium*, a dining area with long couches extending along three sides so that guests might recline as they eat, looking on to the gardens outside. No porridge or stew here, but sophisticated plates of tender meat and delicious fresh produce, from artichokes and mushrooms to figs and grapes grown on the local mountainsides. The room is painted in rich blue lapis paint, depicting scenes of life by the exotic Nile which, along with the grand centrepiece water fountain, transport visitors to faraway lands. Julia wipes a finger along the top of one of the couches, satisfying herself that it is dust-free. Next on her list for inspection are the baths, dedicated to Venus and decorated with strikingly beautiful mosaics. Since the city's main public baths have long been out of service and in need of renovation, hers are a big draw. Large enough to accommodate only eight bathers at a time, they maintain the complex's sense of exclusiveness and indulgence.

Julia soon hopes to hand over some of the day-to-day hassle of managing the complex. She is advertising for someone to take over a long lease. But it is not yet time for her to rest. She summons a servant and gives him a long list of errands to run at the forum. As he is about to leave, she flings out a hand, and the pair lock eyes momentarily – the ground beneath them is shaking. It's over in a moment, but they're both certain they haven't just imagined it: that was a rumble all right, somewhere from deep within the earth. They have been happening for four days now. And though at first Julia ignored them – the people of Pompeii have experienced much worse in recent years – she'll soon understand that these are no minor tremors.

\*

Pompeii is about to find itself at the centre of an existential event – one that incidentally leaves the modern world with a wholly unique insight into daily life in the Roman Empire. Pompeii as it is on 24 August AD 79 is about to be preserved as if in a time capsule. But what transpired on this fateful summer day to ensure the name of Pompeii resonates so powerfully down the centuries? And what can it tell us about daily life in ancient Rome?

## GETAWAY ON THE BAY

Pompeii is a well-to-do sort of place. It sits a few miles up the road from another, smaller resort town called Herculaneum, whose streets and squares are abuzz with officials from the empire and their families who choose the Bay of Naples for their holidays. Pompeii's own location near to the bay ensures it's also popular with wealthy Romans keen for an attractive bolt-hole. However, it is not solely reliant on tourism. Lying at the heart of a rich agricultural region, it is also a trading centre, with goods arriving here by sea before making their way to Rome and other major population hubs via the nearby Appian Way.

Back in the last century, Pompeii stood against Rome during the Social War before eventually falling to Sulla. It was designated a Roman colony in 80 BC and Roman veterans were rewarded with land and property here in a classic example of Roman conquest-and-assimilation. Prior to that it had been inhabited by, variously, the Greeks, the Samnites, the Etruscans and assorted local Oscan-speaking peoples from central Italy.

That is not to say that it doesn't have a strong sense of its own identity, nor that it has ceased to be an occasional thorn in Rome's side. Less than a decade after being subsumed into the Roman sphere, it was the setting for part of Spartacus's famous slave revolt. More recently, twenty years ago in AD 59, gladiatorial games hosted in the amphitheatre saw high spirits fuelled by the Neapolitan sun and the local wine descend into riotous violence that resulted in many fatalities. The authorities in Rome issued an edict that the city could not hold gladiatorial games for ten years, although the ban was lifted early by Emperor Nero. His decision was in part an empathetic response to the disaster that befell Pompeii in AD 62, when a devastating earthquake destroyed homes and businesses, knocking the city back on its heels. Even today, seventeen years on, there is evidence of its impact in the forum, where teams of sweaty workmen lug heavy stones as they slowly erect new temples and civic buildings out of the wreckage. Other ruins lie untouched, or serve as storage depots, the workmen piling stones and other architectural debris within them until they can be used in some new project.

For those with memories going back to those days, the recent tremors are at once a little triggering but also minor by comparison. No one really believes that anything similar could ever happen again. Especially as so much work has gone into getting Pompeii back on its feet. Indeed, Julia Felix is one of those entrepreneurial spirits who set up their business in the aftermath of the earthquake and has helped return prosperity to the community, as well as to herself.

## A JOURNEY TO THE FORUM

Her servant makes his way to the forum, reciting his list of errands so he does not forget anything. It's only a short walk, but with the sun beating down, he's already wiping sweat from his brow. Turning a corner, he sees Vesuvius in the distance, the great mountain that dominates the skyline, looming 4,000 feet above Pompeii some 6 miles beyond the city walls. On its mountainsides, farmers tend their crops and nurse bountiful orchards and vineyards that thrive in the rich soil. Someone has to provide all the food and wine for the city's couple of hundred cafes after all, and there are the dice bars too – not to mention the brothels.

Nearing the marketplace, he smells the delicious aroma of baking bread, as well as the distinctively pungent smell of garum, the fermented fish sauce common to so much cuisine in these parts. Soon he's among the stalls, where Pompeians buy and sell not just agricultural produce but local pottery and textiles, and fish straight from the nets pulled in by the boats bobbing around in the bay.

The servant has to repeat his list louder now to hear himself over the noise. A gang of children fly past him, chasing a pair of yapping dogs, while around the corner another crowd roars excitedly at a game of marbles. There's the whinnying of horses and braying of donkeys somewhere nearby, almost drowning out a hopeful poet he passes, seeking an audience for his verse which he recites while standing on top of a box.

Just another regular day in Pompeii. Except, as the time nears midday, the servant cannot shake off a strange sense of foreboding. He looks up at the sky, which is darkening quickly. Over all the hustle and bustle down on the ground, he hears the raucous squawking of seagulls, flying inland from the sea. Then there is another of those tremors – except now, with buildings starting to shudder, their stone creaking under the pressure, there's no denying the frightening truth: they're getting bigger.

## ERUPTION

The fear is, naturally, that the earth is quaking once more. There has been a rumour doing the rounds recently that sheep have been dropping dead on the mountainsides of Vesuvius, as if poisoned. The servant has heard the stories, but he, like everyone else, sees no connection between these tales and the earth tremors. As far as the locals are concerned, Vesuvius is just an ordinary mountain, albeit one with particularly bountiful soil.

Nervousness, if not yet full panic, is overtaking the forum. Stallholders pack up their wares and children run back to their homes, seeking the reassurance of their parents. The servant, meanwhile, gives up on his list of tasks and rushes back to his employer's estate. On his way he passes city folk with carts and wheelbarrows, loaded up with prized possessions to be taken with them as they head down to the harbour and evacuate across the sea. Many will try to flee inland on foot or in wagons, hoping for refuge in towns and cities they hope are far enough away.

The air is noticeably hotter by the time the servant is safely back at Julia's, sometime between midday and one o'clock. But he's barely started to explain what he's seen when they hear a distant boom. Rushing to the north-facing terrace, they finally understand: their life-giving mountain is a volcano, and it's erupting.

Ash and pumice – light, porous rock formed from rapidly cooling lava – are now raining down on the city. But, though the city folk don't know it yet, the more significant danger is the enormous cloud rising from the peak, ascending into the sky like a long trunk and then branching out miles and miles above the earth. Soon, this lethal combination of carbon dioxide, chlorides and burning particles of ash and volcanic glass will be rolling down the mountainside at speeds of over 100 miles an hour. And once it reaches them, there will be no escape.

Watching on in horror, Julia, the servant and the rest of her staff contemplate their next move. Is it better to run or to stay indoors and hope that the danger quickly passes? But it does not pass. Instead, Vesuvius continues to spit out its combustible mix, until it forms a plume that extends for miles into the atmosphere, causing the sky to darken further. The deadly shower of volcanic matter begins to fall. Pompeii will lie under half a foot of debris in just an hour, and it keeps coming, faster and thicker. Soon, the cloud has so comprehensively blocked out the sun that it appears as if night has descended.

The streets fill with screaming, terrified residents, running for their lives from what seems like nothing less than an airborne assault from the gods. Most, though, lock themselves inside their homes or in public buildings, hoping they can withstand the bombardment.

## STARING INTO THE VOIDS

Synonymous with Pompeii are the haunting casts of many of Vesuvius's victims – men, women and children preserved just as they were when the pyroclastic flow surged over them. It was in 1863 that Italian archaeologist Giuseppe Fiorelli, then in charge of the Pompeii excavations, first decided to inject plaster into some of the many voids his team had discovered, all containing human remains. He had a hunch that they would reveal the form of the people who had perished in those spots, their decomposed bodies leaving behind cavities in the volcanic rock. The results proved more stunning and breathtaking than he could have imagined. In the years since, over a hundred casts have been taken from among the thousand-plus sets of remains that have been identified at what has proved to be one of the world's most extraordinary archaeological sites.

Researchers and tourists alike continue to be fascinated by the time-capsule insights offered by what was preserved. As well as providing a perfect snapshot of Roman life – how the people of Pompeii lived, worked, ate and loved – it also demonstrates how fragile even the most sophisticated of ancient civilizations could be.

## PLINY

Further across the bay from Pompeii is Misenum. Inside one of its attractive villas, a family are having lunch. The property belongs to Pliny the Elder, a big man in his mid-fifties, and a figure of power and startling intellect. He is the author of a landmark encyclopedia on natural history and, as a friend of the recently deceased Emperor Vespasian, he is also a senior Roman official. In Misenum, he enjoys the position of commander of the imperial navy.

His sister is staying with him along with his nephew (and adopted son), Pliny the Younger, whose account of today's events will become an invaluable and famous record. As the cloud, reminiscent of an umbrella pine tree, grows above Vesuvius, the elder Pliny's sister beckons him over to the window. His curiosity is piqued by the spectacle. It might even make for an interesting chapter in his next book. So he decides to take a boat out to inspect the phenomenon more closely. He is just about to leave when an exhausted messenger arrives at the house. He has been sent by Rectina, a friend of Pliny's who lives at the foot of the mountain. The messenger passes on her plea that Pliny send a boat to help her escape. With a navy at his command, Pliny changes his plans and orders a fleet of huge galleys to take to the water.

It's getting towards evening as the fleet approaches the shore at Pompeii, powered by hundreds of oarsmen fighting with every sinew against the volatile sea. It's been dark for some time, and the rain of ash and stone is only growing denser. Though the Romans have no way of knowing it, activity in Vesuvius's magma chamber is causing the sea first to pull away from the shore and then crash back towards it in a series of mini tsunamis. Pliny's navigators fear their ships will be stranded by waters that can shallow beneath them in a moment, and which are topped by growing islands of floating debris. One of his most senior officers tries to persuade Pliny to turn back, but he is adamant. 'Fortune favours the brave,' he says stoically. But even he must know the chances of success are tiny.

Rather than dock at Pompeii, Pliny redirects his fleet to Stabiae, 3 miles further along the bay, where he has a friend with a large property. Once on dry land, Pliny decides to rest here for the night and see what tomorrow brings. But as night draws in, and the slopes of Vesuvius blaze with fire, even the courtyard here fills with volcanic ash and debris, and the buildings rock as more tremors strike. Pliny and his companions consider whether it is safer to be inside, in an unstable building, or outside under a shower of rocks.

## NO ESCAPE

In Pompeii, meanwhile, the streets are becoming impassable, covered in up to 20 feet of debris. Though half the population or more has managed to flee, for those who have gambled on staying behind, the option of running is all but gone. A few brave souls make a last bid to escape, desperately trying to navigate their way over the ash. Some die as a result of injuries caused by the collapse of the city's once proud buildings, the masonry disappearing instantly into the deep banks of Vesuvius's ash and rock.

By one o'clock in the morning the cloud above the volcano stretches for over 20 miles. The only light comes from the fires raging on the mountainside. Eventually, the cloud is visible

150 miles away in Rome, and it is now too big to support itself. When it collapses, a pyroclastic surge begins, in which a mass of ash and superhot gas reaching temperatures of over 250°C rushes down Vesuvius and overwhelms everything in front of it. It pours through the streets and into homes, the stranded citizens powerless to fight it. Herculaneum succumbs first during the early hours of the morning. Pompeii just about stands firm a little longer, but yet another surge at six thirty a.m. proves too much.

In through Julia's complex it gushes. Lead-tin silverware melts before it, while wood, leather and food all instantly carbonize. The servant, unsure what has become of his mistress, tries to run, but in no time at all even the prospect of fleeing becomes a thing of the past. With the toxic, black, blistering-hot mist now billowing through the streets, the men, women and children of Pompeii start expiring where they stand. The young man's eyes and throat are suddenly red-raw and his skin tingles, then it begins to blister and burn. The ash and gas coat his moist lung walls like plaster, until he passes out and stops breathing. Most of those not already killed by the onslaught of debris will suffocate within minutes. It is as if the entire city has been swallowed up into the infernal dungeons of Tartarus. No one knows exactly how many people die tonight, but the total is into multiple four figures.

Over in Stabiae, Pliny weighs up his options in the light of a new day, and then collapses. The smell of sulphur is thick in the air, and there is the singeing heat of approaching fire. His friends are convinced he is overcome by fumes, but just as likely, perhaps, his ageing heart has given up under the stress. Regardless, Vesuvius has claimed perhaps its most famous victim, a giant of the empire. Stabiae itself survives not much longer, destroyed along with Pompeii and Herculaneum. A great many smaller settlements, farms and villas also perish on the Vesuvian plain.

## LEGACY

Pompeii lies beneath a sea of ash and pumice, a volcanic mausoleum. When a drip-feed of people start to return in the weeks after the disaster, they discover not a ruined city but an unearthly ashen landscape from which only the upper parts of some taller buildings now protrude – taunting relics of the life that so recently thrived here.

A few opportunists carry off anything of use or value that has been left exposed, or which can be got at with a little quarrying, until even the last vestiges of Pompeii are gone. The presence of Vesuvius ensures no one quite forgets about the eruption, but within a generation, Pompeii as an inhabited location falls out of the collective memory.

It is over a millennium and a half later, in 1599, that a team of Italian canal diggers hit a massive underground wall, then another and another. However, although the discovery is registered, no further investigations ensue. Not until the first half of the eighteenth century, during construction of a palace for the King of Naples, do the remains of both Herculaneum and Pompeii begin to come to light, from grand public buildings to loaves of bread carbonized as they sat baking in ovens. Ancient Roman life preserved for the ages.

As to what befell Julia Felix, we will never know. Perhaps she was one of the lucky ones to make it out alive. However, in the 1950s a skeleton is dug up in the grounds of the buildings she once owned and ruled. It is the body of a woman,

## JULIA FELIX

complete with elegant jewellery. Is this Julia Felix, a woman who had made a life for herself in Pompeii and perhaps could not bring herself to leave it, even in its darkest hour? Pompeii has surrendered many of its secrets, but some it will keep for ever.

# 13

# TRAJAN: GOOD TIMES IN THE PAX ROMANA

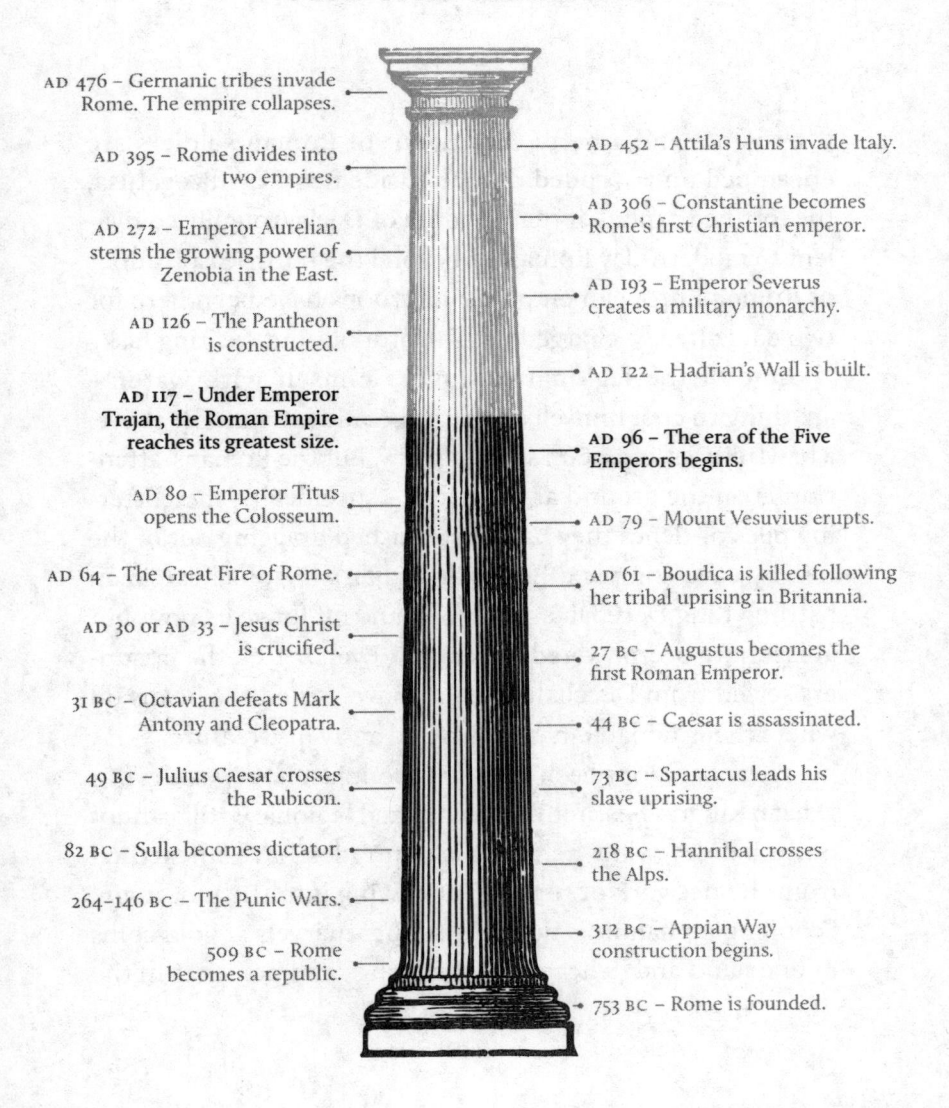

AD 476 – Germanic tribes invade Rome. The empire collapses.

AD 395 – Rome divides into two empires.

AD 272 – Emperor Aurelian stems the growing power of Zenobia in the East.

AD 126 – The Pantheon is constructed.

**AD 117 – Under Emperor Trajan, the Roman Empire reaches its greatest size.**

AD 80 – Emperor Titus opens the Colosseum.

AD 64 – The Great Fire of Rome.

AD 30 or AD 33 – Jesus Christ is crucified.

31 BC – Octavian defeats Mark Antony and Cleopatra.

49 BC – Julius Caesar crosses the Rubicon.

82 BC – Sulla becomes dictator.

264–146 BC – The Punic Wars.

509 BC – Rome becomes a republic.

AD 452 – Attila's Huns invade Italy.

AD 306 – Constantine becomes Rome's first Christian emperor.

AD 193 – Emperor Severus creates a military monarchy.

AD 122 – Hadrian's Wall is built.

**AD 96 – The era of the Five Emperors begins.**

AD 79 – Mount Vesuvius erupts.

AD 61 – Boudica is killed following her tribal uprising in Britannia.

27 BC – Augustus becomes the first Roman Emperor.

44 BC – Caesar is assassinated.

73 BC – Spartacus leads his slave uprising.

218 BC – Hannibal crosses the Alps.

312 BC – Appian Way construction begins.

753 BC – Rome is founded.

It's AD 106, and a hefty contingent of Roman soldiers are encamped on a wooded mountainside near Sarmizegetusa, the fortified capital of the kingdom of Dacia (roughly equivalent to modern-day Romania), beyond the north-east frontier of Rome's European empire. The troops have been here for two days already, charged with an arduous but exciting task.

One of the legionaries douses himself with water – anything to cool himself beneath the midday sun. Up above, a hawk circles, intent on spotting prey. But the Romans' attention is on the ground at their feet – specifically, the glittering piles of riches they have just finished dragging out of the nearby cave complex. Emperor Trajan's legions have been battling King Decebalus's forces on and off for years now, but at last have overpowered the enemy. Even better, the prisoners seized from Decebalus's court have spilled the beans on where their monarch has squirrelled away his treasure.

There have long been rumours about just how wealthy this Dacian kingdom is. Yet the overheated legionary still cannot quite believe what he and his comrades have unearthed from the network of tunnels burrowing into the mountain. Scooping up handfuls now, the soldier marvels at gold coins in one hand and delicately crafted rings and bracelets in the other, before unceremoniously stuffing them into saddle bags draped over a horse. The beast neighs its mild displeasure. No one knows just how much gold and silver there is in the king's treasury in total, but it is tons, tens of tons, perhaps even hundreds. Enough to provide a massive boost to Rome's coffers and to spend on adventures in hostile lands, not to mention the emperor's penchant for spectacular public works.

When the soldier is content that the horse can carry no more, he nods to a colleague who takes the animal's reins and leads it off on its journey back down the mountain and westwards towards the imperial capital. Another pack animal arrives to take its place and the soldier begins the work of loading up once more. It is now that he spots an item that momentarily distracts him from the blistering heat burning his arms and neck. A bangle, hewn from gold into the shape of a coiled snake – most likely an offering to the Dacian gods. The kaleidoscopic golden band culminates with a flattened serpent's head that glints deliciously in the light. Weighing it in his hand, he struggles to drag his gaze from its enthralling beauty. The pride in claiming such treasures for Rome almost makes him feel light-headed – though perhaps it is simply dehydration.

It has not been an easy campaign out here. The Dacians are tough opponents, and the legionary misses his wife and baby boy back home. But the effort and sacrifice are worth it. To be able to say he has been part of the first major expansion of the empire in decades (save for the long-running forays into the outer reaches of Britannia) is achievement enough in itself. But to have had a hand in the discovery of this vast hoard of treasure is more than he ever dreamed when he began his career in the army. Under Trajan's guiding hand, the empire is on the cusp of achieving its greatest extent. What a time to be a Roman!

*Ruling from* AD *98 to 117, Trajan will become one of the most beloved of all the Roman emperors. A man who conquered new territories, grew the empire as far as anyone would and enriched Rome with awe-inspiring building projects. Indeed, the Senate will welcome future emperors with the wish that they be* melior Traiano *('better than Trajan') – evidence that he is to be the benchmark for all who follow. Historians often consider his reign to be the pinnacle of the Pax Romana – the 'Roman Peace' – a feted era of prosperity and relative peace across the imperial lands. But what are the conditions that allow for Trajan's celebrated rule, and why did the empire go into almost instant retreat afterwards? What problems could Trajan's success be concealing? Is he extending Roman power too far, and what new challenges might arise?*

## THE PAX ROMANA

It is the middle of the first century AD when Seneca the Younger makes the first known use of the term Pax Romana. The consensus is that this perceived Golden Age begins in 31 BC, during Octavian's ascent to become Augustus, Rome's uncontested 'first citizen'. His rise seemed to usher in a period of sustained stability after the internecine conflicts that had dominated Roman politics for so long by then. Fending off the threat of further civil war and holding the provinces in imperfect concord, Augustus would three times close the gates of the Temple of Janus in the Roman Forum – long a symbol, though unused for great stretches of time, that Rome was at peace and free from war.

Key to the development of this peace is, perversely, the existence of an all-powerful emperor. Back in the days of the republic, the competition between powerful senators for *gloria* and *dignitas* through military success saw Rome locked into a near-constant state of war. But since Augustus's consolidation of power – the 'Augustan Settlement' as it becomes known – the armies now essentially answer to the emperor alone. As a result, there's much less reason for individual generals to seek out war or expansion with their private troops in the pursuit of glory. By following the advice Augustus left in his political will to be satisfied with Rome's existing borders and put aside desires to expand further, the need for military engagement also decreases. Yet while peace may seem desirous, it requires a conceptual shift for a population used to war and familiar with the glory and riches it potentially offers. It takes a while to convince everybody that peacetime can offer comparable rewards, so great emphasis is placed on the advantages of expanding trade, especially in the east, unencumbered by conflict. Even the topsy-turvy reigns of the Julio-Claudian dynasty – culminating in the Senate trying to expunge all public memory of Nero amid the domestic instability that followed his death – don't significantly challenge the firm foundations of the Pax Romana. After the calamitous Year of the Four Emperors has passed and Vespasian eventually gets his hands on the levers of power in 69, he introduces sensible political and military reforms and firms up the existing imperial boundaries to reinforce the sense that all is well with Rome. His good work is carried on by his son Titus, until his death after just two years. He is replaced by his brother, Domitian, whose run-ins with the city's elite over money see his rule descend into increasing autocracy, but whose skills as an administrator leave the empire still in a generally healthy state even as he is dispatched by that familiar Roman method – assassination by a band of courtly conspirators.

The next man to take on the top job, in the year 96, is Nerva, already in his late sixties and with decades of imperial service to his name. It's hoped by the Senate that he'll restore some of the liberties curtailed by his predecessor, but he runs into problems with the military who were rather keen on the hard-line rule of Domitian. Among the demands they place upon him is that, being childless, he should adopt an heir to ensure no succession crisis. As events unfold, it proves a prescient stipulation.

## ENTER TRAJAN

It's the year 97 on Rome's Rhine frontier. A young up-and-coming military tribune by the name of Hadrian hurries to a meeting with the recently appointed governor of the province of Upper Germany, his cousin and legal guardian, Trajan. He has important news to deliver – word from Rome itself. Nerva, under pressure from the army, has named the individual he will adopt and make heir to the imperial throne. And the man he has chosen is Trajan himself.

It confirms an impressive rise up the social ladder for Trajan, born Marcus Ulpius Traianus forty-plus years ago in what is now Andalusia in southern Spain. His childhood was divided between the family home on Rome's Aventine Hill and various provinces where his father held senior postings, including as governor. The family had strong social connections too, with Trajan's aunt married to Emperor Titus. But any thoughts that Trajan himself might actually become emperor seemed fanciful.

In the customary way, he had joined the army as a young man and found himself serving along various stretches of the empire's most disputed borders. He was in Syria in the east, where his father for a while was governor, and later moved to the frontier with Germania, where it is reported he saw fighting first-hand. Then, in the mid-80s, he became the guardian for two of his cousins – including Hadrian – after their father died. Before the decade was out he turned up in Hispania as a military legate, and then made for the Rhineland to support the then emperor, Domitian, in the suppression of an attempted coup. In 91, when he was still not yet forty, Trajan became consul for the first time, as well as getting married to a noblewoman, Pompeia Plotina. It seems a very happy marriage, albeit a childless one – although the adoption of the cousins perhaps makes this less of an issue. There are even rumours that Trajan's preference is for male physical companionship. It is not so unusual for Rome's menfolk to conduct relationships with both men and women, but an exclusive attachment to men does raise eyebrows. According to some, Trajan has the perfect model of a marriage of convenience.

All things considered, he already has a strong track record of imperial service when Hadrian breaks the news of his adoption by Nerva. In fact, his steady handling of his German governorship has won him the honorary title 'Germanicus'. So, when Nerva dies after a bout of ill health in late January 98, Trajan succeeds him without challenge. That the new emperor opts not to immediately rush to Rome may be a sign of the confidence he has in his new position, or conversely indicative of uncertainty about quite how he will be received in the capital. Whatever the reason, he undertakes a long detour to inspect outposts along the Danube and Rhine.

He is an emperor keen, it seems, to make sure he is across all the potential impediments to further expansion (territorial enlargement being an ambition that never quite leaves the Roman psyche), as well as to impose his authority on a military that had so strongarmed Nerva before him.

When he finally makes it back to Rome in 99, his entry is not the orgy of self-glorification that some of his predecessors have enjoyed. Instead, Trajan focuses on making friends and pursuing stability. He gives generous financial gifts to the people, introduces welfare schemes for the poor and is respectful in his dealings with the Senate. On New Year's Day of 100 Trajan takes the opportunity of his inauguration to invite the Senate into a partnership with him, as joint caretakers of the empire. After the excesses of, say, Domitian, Trajan seems positively understated. It hardly seems to matter whether or not he really intends to put into action his warm words of cooperation.

## EYES ON DACIA

Domitian went to war with the Dacians in the late 80s in response to incursions into Roman territory, culminating in a fragile peace being agreed. But the Dacian king, Decebalus, continues to trouble Rome, and has the resources to launch a full-scale invasion if he chooses. So Trajan decides to tackle the threat head on – encouraged, no doubt, by the rumours of the rich mines Decebalus has at his disposal. By contrast, Rome's finances have been strained by the demands of running a vast empire in almost perpetual conflict somewhere or other, regardless of the Pax Romana. Some Dacian gold might come in very handy.

By 101 Trajan gets the backing of the Senate for a military assault. Rome sends some 80,000 men across the Danube, who then cut through Dacia like a knife through butter left out under the Carpathian sun. Within weeks they are at Tapae, a mountain pass a short distance from Dacia's capital Sarmizegetusa, where the Romans and Dacians have fought twice before. Decebalus summons a force of several tens of thousands to meet Trajan's even bigger army, and the casualties quickly mount on both sides as the sky begins to roar and darken on the first day of fighting. Now come the first drops of rain, quickly turning into a deluge. Blood puddles on the ground as troops blinded by the downpour engage in hand-to-hand conflict. With the Dacian commanders wondering if this is not some kind of sign from the gods, Decebalus makes the decision to withdraw, taking refuge in a local network of forts. He has not suffered a decisive blow, but Trajan has the upper hand. He holds out for as long as he can, but when the tide fails to turn he eventually decides to make a new peace. Dacia becomes a client-state of Rome, with the Romans establishing a garrison and putting in a governor at Sarmizegetusa. For a while Decebalus seems resigned to his fate, playing nice with his new overlords. But subservience does not suit him. His men begin to raid Roman territory again, and he incites other tribes to rise up against the occupier.

In 105, at a gorge on the Danube river between modern-day Serbia and Romania, a man in his thirties surveys the scene. Named Apollodorus, originally from Damascus in Roman Syria, he is an architect by trade, and a favourite of the emperor since Trajan encountered him during his own time in Syria a decade and a half ago. He has been in charge of a large team of engineers and labourers for getting on two years now, building a bridge. A bridge quite unlike any other. Just now, his carpenters are putting the final touches to a wooden arch, one that completes the bridge's span. Despite the occasional shouts and curses of workers catching a thumb with a hammer strike or straining themselves heaving some great weight, it's a scene which fills Apollodorus with contentment. He knows how extraordinary their collective accomplishment is. It began with diverting the course of the river over a mile, then driving enormous masonry pillars into the ground, strong enough to support the arches, each of which spans 125 feet. Now the bridge, 50 feet wide and rising 60 feet above the water, stretches almost three-quarters of a mile. It is the longest arch bridge anyone has ever seen, and ranks among the greatest engineering achievements Rome has yet conjured. Most importantly for now, it serves as the means by which Trajan can move new troops at speed into Dacia to finish off Decebalus's resistance once and for all.

The Dacians, with the support of allied tribes, remain a formidable enemy but gradually Trajan's forces make headway. By 106 they reach the fortress walls of Sarmizegetusa, which has fallen back under Dacian control. The defenders repel the first Roman attack, but when Trajan's men discover the location of the city's water pipes, they smash them to pieces. With no water and food stocks diminishing, it's just a matter of waiting now. When Sarmizegetusa is on its knees, the Roman legionaries raze it to the ground – but not before Decebalus manages to flee. It is only a brief reprieve, though. With the Roman cavalry in pursuit, he opts to die by his own hand, slashing his throat. His body likely still warm, he is discovered by a Roman cavalry scout, who sees to it that the vanquished king's head and right hand are sent to Trajan, encamped in a nearby village, as evidence that the mission has been accomplished. With Decebalus's death comes the intelligence about where he has hidden his gold and silver.

Trajan's victory is marked by 123 days of official celebration back in Rome, during which over 10,000 gladiators fight it out, along with thousands of wild and domestic animals. Chariot racing, meanwhile, draws in the crowds at the Circus Maximus, which Trajan has expanded and improved, replacing with stone tiers the wooden seating that not so long ago had been reduced to ashes. Since Augustus's admonition not to expand the imperial boundaries, Rome has forgotten the thrill of conquest. And with *princeps*, or 'first citizen', being the preferred term for emperor, the Senate now bestows upon Trajan the title *optimus princeps* – in other words, best emperor.

## THE PEERLESS ROMAN MILITARY

By no stretch has it been an easy path to victory against the Dacians, whose mineral resources have provided them with weaponry far in excess of the Celtic and Germanic tribes. They have been great in number too – likely over 200,000. Yet still they have proved no match for the Roman legions. What is it that makes Rome's military so consistently effective?

Back in Dacia, a Roman soldier wakes up to a new morning. He is a legionary (a citizen-soldier) rather than an auxiliary (a soldier from a social group allied to or under the control of Rome, but not himself a Roman citizen). This does not necessarily mean that he will face a different frontline experience, but it does ensure he earns three times or so the wage of his auxiliary comrades. Because – unlike so many of the armies

Rome has faced over the years, such as those of the Celtic and Germanic tribes, as well as here in Dacia – Rome's army is professional. The military life is hard, but it offers rewards too, including prestige. If you're a high-born Roman and want to make your way in politics, a strong military record is essential to support your claims for office. And when this legionary in Dacia eventually retires, he can look forward to receiving land where he can farm and make a life for himself. The auxiliaries, meanwhile, are offered the prospect of being granted full Roman citizenship and all that brings. No wonder there is, by and large, a steady supply of willing new recruits.

While there is no minimum age requirement, soldiers must sign up before they're thirty-five and typically commit themselves to twenty-five years' service. They need to be in decent shape too, and at least 5 feet 7 inches tall. As the soldier in Dacia prepares his morning porridge in a pot that forms part of his regulation kit, he can be confident that the training he has received is superior to anything the enemy will have experienced. While that does not guarantee victory at every battle – and by Jupiter, he has suffered some brutal reversals already in his career – he never doubts that Rome will triumph ultimately.

Heating his porridge over an open fire, he chats away with the seven other men who share his tent, who together form a unit known as a *contubernium* – literally, those who tent together. Each Roman century consists of ten *contubernia*, or eighty active servicemen (an additional twenty support staff swelling the ranks to a hundred personnel), under the command of a centurion. Six centuries, or 480 servicemen, make up a cohort, and ten cohorts make a legion, although the single cohort charged with bearing the legion's standards has five double-strength centuries, totalling 800 men. With each legion also boasting 120 cavalry, in total a legion comprises 5,240 active servicemen. But it is the tightly bonded, basic unit of the *contubernium* on which the military is built, and which ensures the army's adaptability and responsiveness. It is nothing for entire city-like military encampments to spring up overnight, every soldier aware of his precise role.

The legionary's stamina has been honed by countless 20-mile marches in full armour. Then there are the strategies he has drilled into him, readying him for whatever each military encounter might throw at him. He knows defensive drills like the back of his hand. For instance, the tortoise-like *testudo* formation, in which a phalanx of soldiers defends itself by the outer soldiers carrying their shields in front of them, while those on the inside of the phalanx raise them skywards to fend off aerial assaults. When on the front foot, they learn how to strike in tight formations, throwing their spears from distance to weaken the enemy before marching slowly and purposefully towards them to carry on the fighting at close quarters, while the cavalry perhaps takes its opportunity to land the crushing blow.

The soldier is also benefiting from Rome's unrivalled infrastructure. He is amply fed this morning because the army maintains excellent supply routes, using the road network they have so expertly developed for centuries, and taking advantage of trade throughout the provinces and with client-states. Not to mention the extraordinary weapons that travel with them, including giant catapults and *ballista* that rain down flurries of giant arrows.

His belly full, the legionary readies himself for another day of toil in foreign lands, consoled not just by the numerous and extensive benefits of his work, but also by the certainty that he is a cog in the greatest fighting machine the world has ever seen.

### BATTLE-READY

Over the course of Rome's long history, the equipment an average soldier carried naturally varied. But here's what a typical Roman legionary would have in his kit at the peak of the Pax Romana:

- Woollen/cloth tunics and undergarments
- *Caligae* – leather boots or sandals, with metal-studded soles
- *Lorica segmentata* – chest armour made from metal, typically constructed from light, flexible hoops
- *Galea* – a metal helmet
- *Gladius* – a short sword for close-up fighting
- *Pilum* – a javelin-like spear
- *Scutum* – a long, curved shield
- Basic tools for use in digging and building fortifications
- Cooking pots for personal use
- A few days' food and water rations

## THE BUILDER-EMPEROR

As well as conquest, there is glory in building too. Trajan's bridge across the Danube is astonishing, but it is not the only great feat of construction he commissions. Across the empire, he signs off on projects to extend roads and build harbours, aqueducts and public buildings. In Rome he erects spectacular new baths, and famously begins work on a new Forum (named after himself, naturally) in honour of the Dacian triumph. Its architect is, once more, the trusted Apollodorus of Damascus, who plans the biggest Forum in the whole city, tucked in between the Capitoline and Quirinal Hills.

### TAKING A DIP

Bathing was a major feature of Roman life, undertaken in both private and public facilities. Here, men and women – usually segregated – of all classes met not only to cleanse but to socialize and gossip. Baths could be small-scale *balnae* or elaborate *thermae*, the latter complexes often expensively decorated. They customarily incorporated a *palaestra* (gymnasium), along with a series of rooms typically including an *apodyterium* (changing room), *frigidarium* (cold room), *tepidarium* (warm room) and *caldarium* (steam room). Slaves were on hand for every service, from guarding belongings to scraping the grime from patrons' skin using an instrument called a strigil. For many Romans, bathing was nothing less than confirmation of their moral superiority over other, less clean races.

It's 113, a year since the Forum was inaugurated, funded by the spoils of the Dacian war. Trajan is passing through but stops to take in progress on the latest addition to the site – a monumental column. He listens to the clang of metal and stone as finishing touches are added to the extraordinary construction. A crane heaves under the strain of lifting into place one of twenty huge cylinders of Carrara marble – each 12 feet in diameter and weighing over 30 tons. The marble is raised by a system of ropes, pulleys and capstans contained within a specially constructed wooden frame. The plan is that the column will eventually stand around 100 feet tall, with a mighty statue of Trajan looking down from its peak. The emperor wanders over to inspect some of the cylinders already in place. He runs his finger over the engraved frieze that will eventually depict over 150 scenes telling the story of his victory over Dacia. With monuments such as this, who can doubt that Trajan's name now ranks alongside the greats of Rome's illustrious past?

Yet even now his hunger for greater glories is not sated. Around the time of the victory over Dacia, Rome also annexed the Nabataean kingdom, which had until then been a client-state, independent but loyal to Rome. It marked an incursion into the Middle East, taking in modern-day southern Jordan and northern Saudi Arabia. The territory is administered as a new Roman province: Arabia Petraea. Now, in 113, Trajan finds himself at odds with Parthia, located in what is modern-day north-eastern Iran. One of the few other global superpowers able to rival Rome, it has locked horns with Trajan over what has in effect been their shared rule over Armenia, which serves as a buffer between them.

Whether driven by desire for more territorial conquest or

greater control over east–west trade routes, Trajan decides the time has come to strike against Parthia, whose lands had once fallen to Alexander the Great, that icon of ancient power. Trajan launches his invasion from his new Arabian province, and by 115 he has succeeded in annexing swathes of Parthian territory. A year later he captures the Parthian capital, Ctesiphon, near today's Baghdad, on the banks of the Tigris. Having installed a client-king to do Rome's bidding, Trajan progresses all the way to the Persian Gulf. Looking across its glassy waters, it is said he weeps as he realizes he is running out of time to replicate Alexander's encroachments into India further east. Even as his body ages, his ambition endures.

## RETREAT

The Roman Empire has never been bigger, covering some 2 million square miles across Europe, Africa and Asia, but almost as soon as it reaches its greatest extent, it goes into retreat as Trajan faces uprisings in both Armenia and Mesopotamia. At the same time, discontent among Jews in several of the eastern provinces ignites in what becomes known as the Diaspora Revolt. With too many fires to fight, Trajan accepts that there is no choice but to turn his back on many of his Parthian gains.

By 117 Trajan is making his way back to Rome. He's in his sixties now and the years are catching up with him. His health has taken a hit, and the long voyage home is not agreeing with him. On a hot August day, his ship arrives at the port town of Selinus, in modern-day Turkey. Weaker than ever, he takes to his bed, but he is beyond help, and soon the 'best emperor' is dead. With Trajan's passing, perhaps Rome's greatest moments are also beginning to move into the past.

Trajan's reign has brought undoubted glories, exceptional even by the standards of Rome. But it also contains warnings. He has expanded the imperial frontiers further than anyone, but the difficulty in maintaining them seems to prove Augustus's warning about pushing too far. Moreover, despite the great riches the Dacian campaign in particular has brought, Trajan's largesse has strained the imperial economy. For all the gold and silver of old King Decebalus, Trajan has been forced to devalue Rome's currency. The good times will roll for a few more years yet, but the fractures that come from trying to rule such a huge expanse are already weakening the whole.

# 14

# THE COLOSSEUM: SPIRIT AND SOUL OF ROME

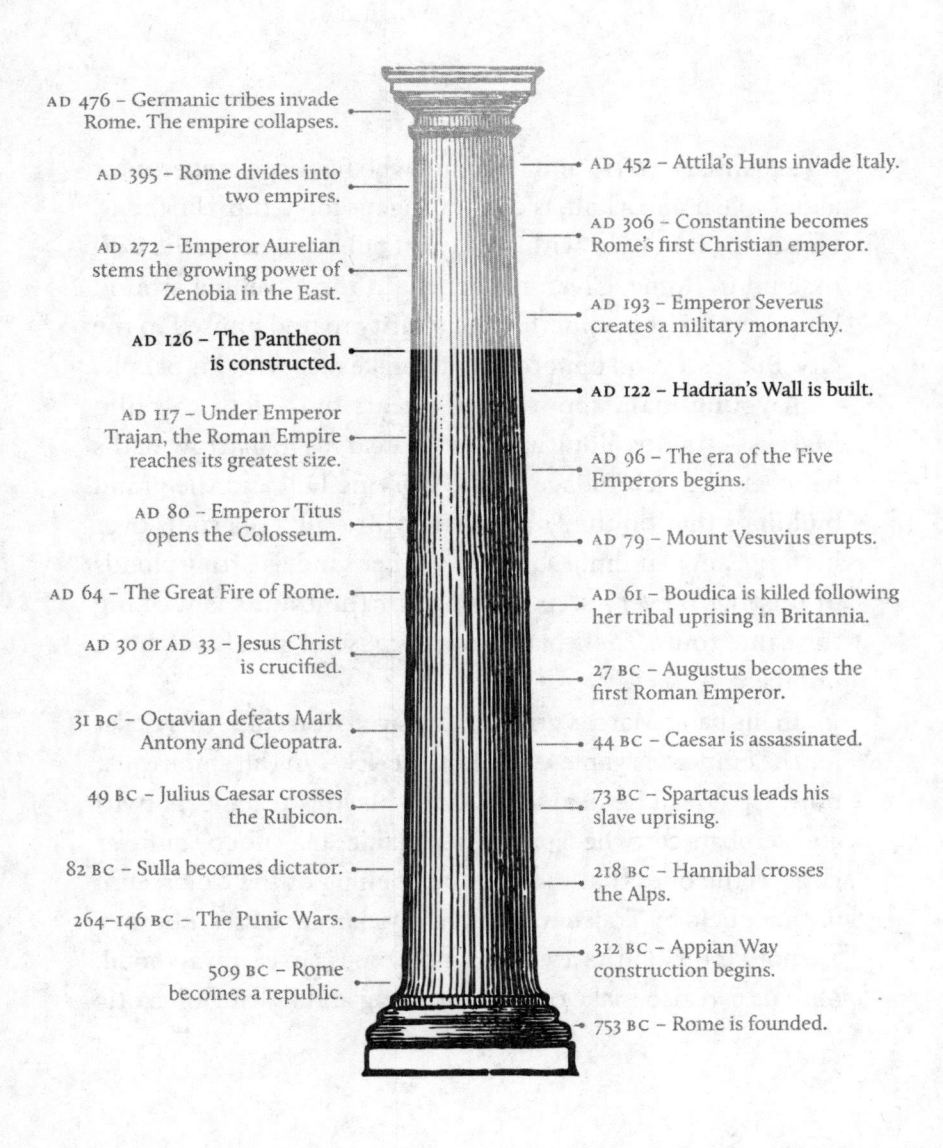

AD 476 – Germanic tribes invade Rome. The empire collapses.

AD 395 – Rome divides into two empires.

AD 272 – Emperor Aurelian stems the growing power of Zenobia in the East.

**AD 126 – The Pantheon is constructed.**

AD 117 – Under Emperor Trajan, the Roman Empire reaches its greatest size.

AD 80 – Emperor Titus opens the Colosseum.

AD 64 – The Great Fire of Rome.

AD 30 or AD 33 – Jesus Christ is crucified.

31 BC – Octavian defeats Mark Antony and Cleopatra.

49 BC – Julius Caesar crosses the Rubicon.

82 BC – Sulla becomes dictator.

264–146 BC – The Punic Wars.

509 BC – Rome becomes a republic.

AD 452 – Attila's Huns invade Italy.

AD 306 – Constantine becomes Rome's first Christian emperor.

AD 193 – Emperor Severus creates a military monarchy.

**AD 122 – Hadrian's Wall is built.**

AD 96 – The era of the Five Emperors begins.

AD 79 – Mount Vesuvius erupts.

AD 61 – Boudica is killed following her tribal uprising in Britannia.

27 BC – Augustus becomes the first Roman Emperor.

44 BC – Caesar is assassinated.

73 BC – Spartacus leads his slave uprising.

218 BC – Hannibal crosses the Alps.

312 BC – Appian Way construction begins.

753 BC – Rome is founded.

It's 24 January AD 119 and Hadrian, who has been emperor for about a year and a half, is celebrating his forty-third birthday. He's doing it in style, with six days of public games at the Colosseum in Rome. Given his penchant for travelling around his provinces, it is something of a rarity to find himself in the city. But it's a good opportunity to make nice with his people.

A young man, about twenty years old – let's call him Marcus – tramps along a street that carves its narrow paths between the rich foliage of the Palatine Hill and the grand buildings that fill the Forum. His white silk toga spills over his long, angular limbs, his thin leather sandals lifting clouds of dust with every step. A crowd of thousands is walking the same route, their pace slow because of sheer weight of numbers.

In his hand Marcus grips an engraved iron chip – his ticket for the emperor's games. The hottest ticket in the empire just now. Up ahead he hears musicians playing as dancers twirl and acrobats cartwheel past. These games may not be quite as large as the ones that marked the opening of the Colosseum or those held by Trajan to mark his Dacian successes, but they are not far off. Spirits are high, and Rome is in carnival mood. Marcus can also make out the growling and roaring of exotic wild animals, for now caged but shortly to be unleashed into the Colosseum's arena. Suddenly there is a surge of excited shouting and cheering, and he cranes his neck to see what's happening. A burly figure passes through the throng – a gladiator, maybe even the unrivalled Flamma, one of Rome's favourite stars.

After a few minutes more walking, Marcus turns a corner and there it is – the vast, oval Colosseum, its spectacular white walls seeming to sparkle in the morning sunlight. Putting his hand across his brow to shade his eyes, he takes in its splendid architecture, its many arches supported by columns – simple Doric, then above these the more slender Ionic topped with their distinctive scroll shapes or volutes, and on the uppermost levels the narrowest, most elaborate Corinthian – rising 150 feet into the sky.

The crowd is more tightly packed than ever here, and the rest of the walk to his designated entrance is little more than a shuffle. After a quick check of his ticket by an official, he is sent off to find his seat. But as he scans the rows upon rows of seating stretching into the heavens, he realizes this is no simple matter. There is room in here for well over 50,000 spectators. Alas, he is not sitting in the lower marble-hewn levels among the great and the good, close to the large, gilded box adorned with feathers and frills where Hadrian will soon claim his seat of honour. But nor is he stuck at the top where men and women are packed like sardines on wooden benches. His family is not one of Rome's old powerful ones, but they have done all right for themselves these last few years and this has bought Marcus a decent spot among the middle echelons with a good view of the sand-covered arena (the word itself derived from the Latin for sand).

He begins his climb, pausing halfway to take a drink from one of the hundred or so drinking fountains spread across the many levels. Should he need them later, he knows there are rudimentary toilets too – seats with holes carved in them and a drain flowing underneath.

As he approaches his spot, Marcus sees that several friends and family members have beaten him to it. Someone offers him wine and a handful of salted peas they have just bought from a snack vendor. Greetings are exchanged, and the rowdy group soon fall into a rhythm of bawdy jokes and speculation about what is to come in the day ahead. The gladiators won't be on until this afternoon, after the execution of some unlucky convicts and the grand animal hunt that will play out below for the delight of the crowd in just a few moments.

*The Colosseum was but one building in a magnificent city, but when it was at full capacity, all life was there. It became a microcosm of the city and its culture, its politics, its social stratification, its lighter side and its dark heart – a manifestation of Rome's very soul.*

## A GIFT TO ROME

The story of the Colosseum begins back in the year 72, four years before Hadrian's birth. After the dynastic disruption following the death of Nero, Vespasian has been on the imperial throne these last three years and he is keen to impose himself on the office. The recent suppression of the challenge to Roman hegemony by Jews in the Roman province of Judaea culminated with the siege of Jerusalem, which has filled

Rome's coffers with looted treasures. Now the emperor has a plan to gift the Romans something spectacular to raise their spirits after the recent years of disruption – a new amphitheatre bigger and better than any seen before. Every Roman politician worth his salt knows that there is power to be leveraged in putting on games and entertainments for the public. To build them a wonderful new home for such activities is an extension of the gesture. Moreover, he plans to build the edifice on land reclaimed from Nero's palace and grounds which was constructed, to the disgust of some, in the aftermath of the Great Fire. Where Nero built for himself, Vespasian plans to build for the people. It's a powerful statement.

It's an early summer day in 72, and those who can are seeking shade wherever they can find it. But on a vast building site in central Rome measuring some 24,000 square metres, hundreds of labourers toil. Dressed only in simple loin cloths, their exposed skin dries and burns beneath the blazing sun. No one complains to the foremen, however. Everyone knows there is no let-up when you're turning the emperor's dream into a reality.

One worker, a young Jewish man enslaved by the Romans in the recent war, leans against his spade. Sighing with exhaustion, he looks around at the work he's done. In a matter of weeks, he and his fellow labourers have drained every inch of the great lake that once stood here. Soon, they'll fill it with a thick ring of mortar that will provide the foundations for the amphitheatre.

His throat is beyond parched and thinking about the lake only makes it worse. He makes for a nearby water fountain. But as he clambers from the trench he's been digging, he's almost decapitated by an enormous slab of travertine – a heavy limestone rock – being heaved into place in the 3-metre-thick walls. Somehow he just about dodges the danger, then heads past gangs of men hammering sheets of iron, and others sawing up thick tree trunks into planks.

He locates the fountain and drinks, but as he does so his eye is drawn by a strange machine nearby – a treadwheel crane, hoisting up heavy bricks to where they're needed, powered by an unlucky worker running endlessly inside a large wheel. Wiping his mouth, our worker recalls the horror stories he's heard of workers being crushed to death while turning the cumbersome wheel. In fact, rumour has it that blind men are being picked to work the crane, so that they won't see the bricks about to fall.

The Colosseum may be Vespasian's gift to the people, but some people pay a hefty price for it. Only in the year 80 is the construction phase completed, one of the world's great buildings soaked through with the blood, sweat and tears of tens of thousands of labourers. It falls to Vespasian's successor, Titus, to finally inaugurate it, and contribute a fourth tier. His younger brother Domitian, who replaces him a year later, adds more gallery seating, and also a network of underground tunnels (*hypogea*) where animals and people destined to be used in public games can be kept out of view until the last moment, when they are released to make spectacular entrances.

### HOW THE MIGHTY ARE FALLEN

One of the great architectural achievements of the ancient world, the Colosseum nonetheless suffered severe damage on numerous occasions, including as the result of several fires and earthquakes. One of the worst blazes came in 217, when much of the wooden seating in the upper levels perished after a lightning bolt seemingly caused a conflagration. Repairs took several decades. The institution also suffered a devastating setback when Emperor Honorius (r. 393–423) outlawed gladiatorial combat, with the Colosseum hosting its last known fights around 435. However, other games, including hunts, continued into the sixth century.

## BLOODLUST

Learning from his predecessors, Hadrian takes advantage of the 'soft power' the games provide him. When people are having a good time, they tend to be far more forgiving of things going wrong and spend less time scrutinizing their leaders. A quick survey of the crowd crammed in today suggests he is quite right. Everything stops for the games: many businesses close, markets shut and the courts and other political institutions take a break. If an emperor gets his games right, he doesn't merely free himself from public scrutiny, he buys popularity too.

As Marcus settles in to enjoy Hadrian's entertainments,

he joins the roar of acclaim that greets the emperor as he takes his seat far below in the imperial box. Marcus now uses his youthful agility to fight for one of the wooden balls the emperor has launched into the crowd. Those lucky enough to claim possession of one can swap it for a designated prize in a kind of lottery. Perhaps he might win a vase or a free meal or, if he's really lucky, some expensive jewellery or even a house.

Unsuccessful in his quest for one of the balls this time, Marcus turns his attention to the arena. Some 250 feet long by 150 feet wide, its glittering sand has been specially selected for its ability to soak up blood. And there will be blood. The truth is, Rome's hunger for its spillage is rarely sated. Given that gladiators have traditionally been gathered from the ranks of prisoners of war and criminals, there is a sense that those who risk their lives for the public's entertainment are not worthy of sympathy. They are merely getting their just deserts. You might even say those trained as gladiators have got lucky, having been given the chance to go out in a blaze of glory. Although the argument is perhaps less strong for those convicts destined for the lunchtime entertainment of public executions.

Hadrian is a man of culture, determined to imbue imperial life with the great Hellenic traditions. But he does not enquire too deeply into what it is in the Roman soul that so loves the brutality of games such as these. Nor do those in the crowd. When Marcus feels the buzz, the pounding adrenalin as he watches another human being on the cusp of life and death, it is a visceral experience, a mingling of sensation, instinct and perhaps inherited memory. Rome, after all, is a civilization that has embraced violence from the moment Romulus slew Remus.

But Marcus cares little about any of that, now that the fanfare of trumpets signals the beginning of the day's first event – the *venatio*, or wild beast hunt. With rocks and trees now adorning the arena floor, the crowd leap to their feet to see the trapdoors and gates leading into it start to open. Unseen, a small army of slaves are working a complex system of ropes and pulleys in the darkness of the underground tunnel complex below.

First come the men – gladiators with spears, bows and whips, rushing across the sand to secure the safest place from which to begin the hunt. Soon, the place is a cacophony of fearsome sounds as exotic creatures imported from distant corners of the empire emerge. Marcus feels the hairs on the back of his neck rise as bears said to have come from Caledonia thunder from the black mouth of one tunnel, followed by lions and trumpeting elephants from Africa. And they keep coming. Soon, the menagerie has expanded to include tigers, wild boar with fearsome tusks, leopards, even rhinos. Time is already ticking for the hunters charged with killing as many of the creatures as they can before they themselves become prey. But as they begin the onslaught, their odds do not seem good. Marcus, though, wills the hunters towards victory, knowing that if the emperor is feeling generous, he might share the meat from the slain animals with the crowd at the event's end.

## THE FIGHT FOR LIFE

It's coming up for midday when the hunt draws to a close. After the gore-fest, Marcus is hungry. He goes for a wander, a chance to stretch his legs but also to intercept one of the stewards as he goes among the spectators with his snacks – fruit and sweets, cakes and pastries. Marcus also purchases a wooden figure of a gladiator as a souvenir. Tickets are distributed for free so he doesn't mind splashing the cash a little now.

He's back at his seat and stuffing dates into his mouth when the execution phase of the day begins. The crowd cheers as a succession of condemned men are paraded into the arena, from thieves and rebellious slaves to army deserters. One by one they are dispatched, the crowd cheering their approval with every new, gruesome method. Some are beheaded, others are tied to stakes and set alight, some are left to face more wild animals unarmed. Marcus shifts in his seat to get a better view of a skinny boy about his own age, ineffectually gouging at the face of a lion. No one is in any doubt about how that particular mismatch is going to play out. And when that's all over and the dead are cleared away, it's time for the highlight of his day – the gladiatorial contests.

Hadrian loves these battles too and is said to be adept himself at handling gladiatorial weapons. The combatants may traditionally have been drawn from what the Romans regard as the dregs of society, but these days the most successful are cultural icons. Every day, Marcus passes traders in the market selling bronze miniatures of them; their faces are even graffitied on the city's walls. No wonder that there are now some free citizens who actively choose to try their luck in the arena, hopeful that their skills will carry them to eventual fame and fortune. There is also currently a trend for female fighters – the *gladiatrix*.

As the afternoon draws on, it is at last time for the confrontation Marcus has been waiting for. To the deafening cheers of the crowd, a hulking man strides out on to the sand, his enormous muscled arms clutching a short sword and a large rectangular shield to cover his bare torso. Many of those in the arena today have been anonymous, but even with the glistening bronze helmet obscuring this man's face, every man, woman and child here knows this fighter's name: he is the one and only Flamma. A slave, part of his legend is that he has been offered his freedom on several occasions but continues to risk his life in conflict. The arena is his home, and the chanting of his name that now rings out in the stands confirms him as one of the greatest of the age.

His opponent now appears, brandishing a trident and a net but wearing no helmet and carrying no shield. This fighter sacrifices protection for speed. He is a *retiarius*, literally a 'net man', whose menace lies in his ability to move fast. Flamma knows he must demonstrate his own nimbleness in his heavy armour if he is to score another victory. Marcus cheers every jab Flamma makes at his opponent, who is forced to shimmy this way and that to stay out of harm's way.

The bout is overseen by an umpire and his assistant, with punishments ranging from a prod with a stick to whipping and branding for infringements of the rules. In the Colosseum, even the adjudication is brutal. That is not to say, however, that all contests end in the death of a competitor. Fatalities only occur in about one in five battles. The simple truth is that gladiators are too valuable a commodity to kill too regularly. Sometimes matches are called as draws. More commonly, one or other of the antagonists raises a finger to indicate they are ready to surrender, either through injury or exhaustion. Today Flamma presses home his advantage, knocking the net man's trident from his grasp and sending him tumbling to the ground.

The referee steps in, and the opportunity arises for some audience participation around the fate of the vanquished fighter. Staring out from his podium, the emperor holds out his closed hand, palm downwards. If the thumb remains wrapped in the fist, the gladiator will be allowed to fight another day. But if the emperor extends his thumb, he must face his fate. Though the decision, of course, is his alone, Hadrian listens to the crowd for an indicator of what he should do. There is a rising tide of booing, and Marcus joins a chorus of 'Lugula!' – 'Slit his throat!' – in the direction of the net man, whom he considers has not put up much of a fight. Waiting for the peak of the tension, Hadrian points his thumb outwards. The audience cheers, and Flamma raises his sword to see off yet another opponent. A broad grin spreads across Marcus's mouth as he drinks in the spectacle. Flamma is presented with a palm leaf to recognize his success and now takes a lap of honour as his opponent's body is unceremoniously dragged from the arena.

Before long it is time for Marcus and the rest of the crowd to wend their way home to refuel and recharge before doing it all again tomorrow. Hadrian has excelled himself, they all agree. He's turning out to be an emperor they can look up to.

For Hadrian, there can be no better result. This latest version of a public relations assault favoured by Rome's leaders going far back has hit its mark, and he will reap the political benefits for a good while to come.

As for the people, they go home content with their lot and proud to call themselves Roman. The day's events have brought together a complex cocktail of ideas of brutality, glory and reward ingrained within the Roman psyche. The tens of thousands of spectators have shared something inimitable in the stadium: all classes, from slaves to the elite, sitting shoulder to shoulder at an event that highlights both the cohesion of their society but also its great inequalities. And the Colosseum itself serves as an awesome symbol of Rome's ambition, not to mention its resources and engineering capabilities. Starting with all those moments of destiny decided out on the sand, nothing about today has been trivial. Rather, the Colosseum and the events it hosts over the centuries reflect a great tapestry of the themes that drive Roman life and make its civilization so awe-inspiring, for better and worse.

# 15

# SEVERUS:
## THE BATTLE FOR STABILITY

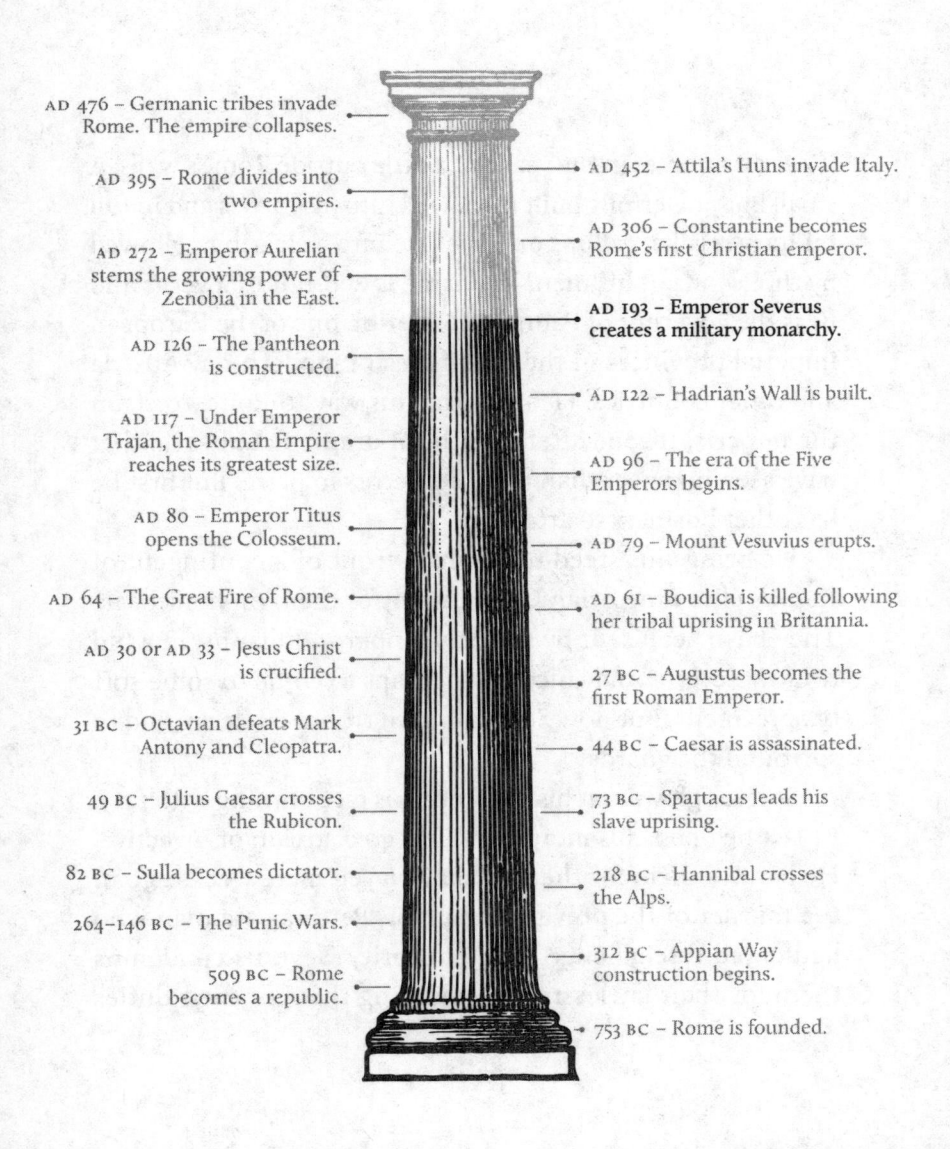

AD 476 – Germanic tribes invade Rome. The empire collapses.

AD 395 – Rome divides into two empires.

AD 272 – Emperor Aurelian stems the growing power of Zenobia in the East.

AD 126 – The Pantheon is constructed.

AD 117 – Under Emperor Trajan, the Roman Empire reaches its greatest size.

AD 80 – Emperor Titus opens the Colosseum.

AD 64 – The Great Fire of Rome.

AD 30 or AD 33 – Jesus Christ is crucified.

31 BC – Octavian defeats Mark Antony and Cleopatra.

49 BC – Julius Caesar crosses the Rubicon.

82 BC – Sulla becomes dictator.

264–146 BC – The Punic Wars.

509 BC – Rome becomes a republic.

AD 452 – Attila's Huns invade Italy.

AD 306 – Constantine becomes Rome's first Christian emperor.

**AD 193 – Emperor Severus creates a military monarchy.**

AD 122 – Hadrian's Wall is built.

AD 96 – The era of the Five Emperors begins.

AD 79 – Mount Vesuvius erupts.

AD 61 – Boudica is killed following her tribal uprising in Britannia.

27 BC – Augustus becomes the first Roman Emperor.

44 BC – Caesar is assassinated.

73 BC – Spartacus leads his slave uprising.

218 BC – Hannibal crosses the Alps.

312 BC – Appian Way construction begins.

753 BC – Rome is founded.

It's early summer in the year 193, a little outside Rome's walls. A small but powerfully built man, well into his forties and in full military regalia, gallops on his horse into a clearing, followed by thousands of his men. His name is Septimius Severus and he is the governor of Pannonia Superior, one of the European imperial provinces in the rough area of modern-day Austria and other countries. He is making his way to Rome to claim the imperial throne after months of dramatic upheaval that have seen no fewer than three emperors in place. But first he has other business to attend to.

He brings his steed to a halt in front of a contingent of Rome's elite Praetorian Guard, many of them on horseback. They have been sent by the new emperor, Julianus, in a bid to slow Severus's advance and perhaps to come to some sort of agreement. But now Severus's own troops circle around to surround the guards.

Severus glowers at his audience, his face burning with fury. At last he opens his mouth and lets go a stream of invective. He berates them for the part they played mere weeks ago in the murder of the previous emperor, Pertinax – a man who had dared to challenge their authority. Severus condemns them for their lawlessness, reminding them of their duties to the state that they have so casually disregarded. Now, he explains, they must face the consequences of their collective action. He orders them to lay down their arms, take off their armour, relinquish their horses and get out of Rome.

The guards, unprepared for such a ferocious encounter, look shaken. Some glance at the line of Severus's men encircling them, quickly calculating their chances in a fight. But they are outnumbered, and they know the odds are stacked against them. Severus watches on with a steely gaze as gradually the guards cast down their weapons and strip down to their simple tunics. Abandoning their horses, they begin to scatter, eager to get away from the scene before trouble escalates. But off to one side, Severus spots some kind of disturbance. One of the guards is being followed by his horse, whinnying its reluctance to abandon him. In desperation, the guard reclaims a discarded sword and drives it first into the animal and then into himself. He is, it seems to Severus, more eager to die than slope off in dishonour.

Once the guards have dissipated and their abandoned arms and beasts have been gathered together, Severus sets off for the city. With the breeze coursing through his hair and luxurious beard, he makes it to the gates but then stops and dismounts. News has reached him that Julianus no longer holds power within. Severus shrugs off his cavalry garb and changes into a toga, walking through the gate not as a military leader but as a civilian – although his men follow close behind. As he makes his way among Rome's streets, his nostrils fill with the aroma of burning incense. Locals rush towards him to express their relief that he is here to restore order, or shout their support from the doorways of buildings garlanded with flowers and bearing blazing torches to mark his arrival.

As he processes, the crowds gather until Severus is ready to address them. People of all classes, from senators down, jostle to hear him. Some climb buildings or are lifted upon shoulders to get a better look. When he speaks, it is to deliver a message of hope but also one of comfort. Despite all the upheaval, he proclaims, he has no intention of executing any senators or taking revenge on their supporters. Rather, he has come to replace discord with peace.

They are bold promises indeed. Only time will tell how true to his word he will be, and how successful his mission to reunite a divided Rome proves.

*It is thirteen years since the passing of Marcus Aurelius, the last of what are sometimes referred to as the 'Five Good Emperors'. His death will, in retrospect, be identified by many as the end of the Pax Romana itself. Moreover, when his son and heir, Commodus, was brutally killed on New Year's Eve 192, it ushered in a period of extreme instability that came to be known as the Year of the Five Emperors (and these five, by general consensus, were far from all being good). But how has it come to this? And will Severus's ascent be enough to save Rome?*

## GROWING UP IN THE GOOD TIMES

Almost fifty years earlier, in the African port city of Leptis Magna (in modern-day Libya), a high-ranking family welcomes a new baby in 145. The child, Lucius Septimius Severus, reflects Rome's multicultural identity, his mother from an Italian background and his father with Punic, or Carthaginian, heritage. Severus can count consuls among his cousins, while his mother's line are the Fulvia, one of Rome's grand patrician families.

In Rome itself, Antoninus Pius is on the throne, having succeeded Hadrian, his adoptive father and uncle-in-law. As the fourth of the so-called Five Good Emperors, his reign is noted for its good order, from advancing the frontier in Caledonia (marked by the eponymous though short-lived Antonine Wall) to extending the provision of drinking water throughout the empire and keeping the treasury in a decent state.

Antoninus Pius dies in 161 and is succeeded by Rome's first joint rulers, his adopted sons Marcus Aurelius and Lucius Verus. Their rule will be marked by war, both in the east against Parthia and against assorted Germanic forces. It is a year later that the still callow Severus arrives in Rome, intent on building a career for himself, making full use of his family connections. Among his first roles, though, is a posting that makes him responsible for aspects of road maintenance in the city – hardly a stellar launch on to the *cursus honorum*.

Gradually, though, his profile rises, and he begins to forge a career in the law. But in the mid-160s disaster strikes Rome in the form of a mysterious but deadly pandemic. It originates with the army on campaign in Parthia but soon makes its way across the empire. All around Severus, and far beyond, swathes of the population come down with high fevers, vomiting, rashes, ulcerations and gastric problems. Around 35 per cent of the afflicted die. It takes a grip that will not loosen for many years, during which time it is estimated that a fifth to a quarter of the population of the empire (somewhere between five and ten million people) succumb. Aside from the myriad personal tragedies, it has devastating impacts on Rome's army, imperial trade and the economy. It's a terrible time to try and forge your way to the top. Severus's career stalls and he goes home to Leptis, hopefully a safe distance from the epicentre of disease. There is talk that he is the accused in a messy divorce case back in Africa, although there are no formal proceedings.

In 169 Lucius Verus dies, possibly another victim of the plague. Marcus Aurelius now rules alone. Old enough at last to hold a quaestorship, Severus makes his way back to Rome at the end of the year and resumes his attempt to climb the greasy pole. In fact, he now starts to benefit from the impact of the epidemic. So many of the senatorial class have died that there are plenty of plum jobs to go round. Severus holds several of them in quick succession, including a stint as quaestor on the island of Sardinia and as a senior official to the proconsul of Africa (who just happens to be his cousin). When he returns to Rome at the end of this posting, he has the emperor's personal backing to become tribune of the plebeians.

When Marcus Aurelius dies in 180 he leaves a Rome battered by war on multiple frontiers and the fallout from the plague. But Severus has at least made his mark.

### THE PHILOSOPHER-EMPEROR

Marcus Aurelius Antoninus has an unequalled status among Rome's rulers as a philosopher-emperor. An adept military leader and administrator, he recorded an extensive collection of his philosophical musings on matters of governance and life in general. He was a disciple of the school of Stoicism, founded by the Greek Zeno of Citium around 300 BC, which promoted a belief that virtue is central to a well-lived life, and that man should live in harmony with nature and foster indifference to the vagaries of everyday existence. Debate remains as to how virtuous Marcus Aurelius's rule really was, but his collected thoughts, known as his *Meditations*, provide a remarkable insight into his psyche. Cassius Dio was a big fan, writing, 'he ruled better than any others who had ever been in any position of power'. An explanation, perhaps, for why many continue to identify him with a Roman 'Golden Age'.

## THE END OF A LINE

Rule in Rome now falls to Marcus Aurelius's son, Commodus, who has already notched up three years of co-rule with his father. Under his solo guidance, Rome's involvement in military conflict reduces. But Commodus doesn't have the patience for the detail of day-to-day rule, so delegates to others the job of putting his will into action. As time passes, he adopts an autocratic style of rule driven by paranoia – not all of it, perhaps, misplaced. He develops a divisive cult of personality, surrounding himself with a gang of sycophants who do his bidding while themselves indulging in a multitude of corrupt practices.

Severus is by now governor of a Gallic province, but though his political career seems on track, his private life takes an unexpected diversion. In 186 his wife of more than a decade dies from natural causes. Now into his forties, Severus is a childless widower – not a good look for anyone who wants to rise to the top in Rome, especially since the Roman people know the danger of dynastic instability. Putting his mind to addressing the problem, a year later he marries again, this time to a Syrian named Julia Domna, fifteen years his junior. A woman of extraordinary talents, a deep thinker with an unrivalled grasp of Rome's political and social idiosyncrasies, to Severus's delight she also births him two sons in quick succession. First comes Lucius Septimius Bassianus (better known as Caracalla for the type of hooded tunic he comes to favour) in 188, and then his brother Geta a year later.

But even as his personal life prospers, Severus's political life, along with that of the rest of the senatorial class, is getting trickier in the face of Commodus's increasing megalomania. After fire ravages the city in 191 the emperor takes the opportunity to rename Rome after himself – Colonia Commodiana, the 'colony of Commodus'. Similarly, he remodels the calendar, retitling the months after his various regnal names. Despite this astonishing level of self-regard he's still desperate for the affections of the public, so he puts on ever more extravagant games to woo them. But by now neither the ordinary Roman citizens nor the city's elite, who are increasingly having to fund his profligacy, are in any mood to be won over.

In November 192 the Colosseum is packed to the rafters, the anticipation palpable as the afternoon sun begins to wane. A figure strides out from beneath the shadow of the towering arches wearing the hide of a lion over his shoulders that snakes down his back to the sand. His armour is styled after no less a figure than Hercules himself. The crowd roars in appreciation, but then, as thousands of eyes squint at the lone warrior walking confidently into the arena, a murmur breaks through the cheers. Yes, there's no doubt about it . . . it's the emperor himself. But these days there is nothing very unusual about that. Commodus has fought hundreds of bouts, despite there being many at all layers of society who consider it unbecoming of one of his standing.

Of course, each one of these contests has been carefully orchestrated to ensure that the emperor wins unscathed. Today his opponent lumbers around the arena after him, occasionally half-heartedly jabbing a wooden sword in his opponent's general direction without ever being in danger of making contact. Commodus soon tames his rival, using a club to secure submission before graciously acceding to his pleas for mercy. The opponent lives to fight another day, which is more than can be said for the warriors the emperor is said to have killed or maimed in the practice ring. He even decapitated an ostrich at this venue not so long ago, before carrying the poor creature's head over to some watching senators as a warning that they might be next.

Rome is awash with rumours that the emperor intends to have some of his political enemies murdered, perhaps even in front of the Colosseum crowds. On 31 December 192 Commodus is lying in his bath, mulling over his plans for the coming year as he drinks a glass of wine. But he feels out of sorts. His brow is moist with sweat and his stomach is cramping. He begins to heave until he brings up the remnants of his recent meal – meat, it turns out, that has been poisoned by his mistress, Marcia, who has been informed she features on his kill list. As he is being violently sick, Commodus begins to suspect the nature of the plan afoot against him.

It is a moment of extreme danger for Marcia and her co-conspirators when word reaches them that he has survived. Perhaps his over-fondness for alcohol has helped him for once, prompting a purge of his system, but in any case they know they must act quickly. They call upon the emperor's wrestling coach – a man hired to prepare him for his bouts in the arena – who bursts in on Commodus and strangles him in his bath. In death, he is decreed a public enemy, and Rome reverts to its customary name, buries the old tyrant quickly and sets about suppressing his memory. So ends almost a century of the Nerva-Antonine dynasty. But what comes next?

## THE YEAR OF THE FIVE EMPERORS

While this drama is playing out, Severus is a safe distance away in Pannonia Superior, the governorship of which he was awarded a couple of years ago. Commodus has died without heir, and as numerous candidates stake their claim to succeed him, Severus finds himself in an ideal geographical position. Nestled between Italy to the west and Dacia to the east, he has easy access to Rome but can stand apart from all the upheaval in the capital as he considers his next steps.

It is the Praetorian Guard that makes the first decisive move. Though the Senate hasn't officially lost its right to theoretically appoint an emperor, this group established by Augustus as his personal bodyguard are, by all accounts, now Rome's emperor-makers. But those whom the guard manoeuvre into power do well to remember who put them there, as it is often the same soldiers who see to their downfall. One of their number is already implicated in the plot that has seen off Commodus. Now they anoint Pertinax, a man in his late sixties but with a long and distinguished career in both the military and political spheres, as the new emperor.

> ### POWER BEHIND THE THRONE
>
> The Praetorian Guard cast a long shadow over imperial Rome. In republican times, bodyguards defended Roman generals, with the first organized unit appearing in the historical record in the third century BC, protecting members of the famous Scipio family. From Augustus onwards, the Praetorian Guard was responsible for the emperor's security and for maintaining order in Rome and Italy. Because of the nature of its work, the guard was populated with elite soldiers, reflected in a higher rate of pay than the average legionary by several fold. It came to be feared by politicians and the public alike, frequently operating as a secret police force, and was implicated in the assassinations of over a dozen emperors – and those are just the ones we can be fairly sure about. It was not until the fourth century AD that Emperor Constantine finally dissolved the organization.

However, the guards soon set aside any hopes that they have a malleable man in place. Pertinax, drawing inspiration from Marcus Aurelius, plans for a cool, considered reign that will get Rome back on a firm footing. This includes bringing the Praetorians into line. He sets out as he means to go on by withholding part of the financial gift emperors have customarily paid to them, and proposing reforms that will tighten up discipline.

On 28 March 193 Pertinax is in his imperial palace when he hears a commotion outside. A detachment of guards, several hundred in number, are bursting through the palace gates – and the emperor's own men are doing nothing to stop them. An adviser pleads with him to flee while he still can, but Pertinax instead seeks to negotiate. He goes outside to meet the guards, laying out his plans for Rome. It actually seems like he is making progress when one of them suddenly breaks ranks, rushes at him and strikes him dead. Rome must find yet another emperor after just three months.

Deaf to criticism of their overreach, the Praetorians announce that the next emperor will be the man who bids the highest for the office. Pertinax's father-in-law, Sulpicianus, arrives at the Praetorians' camp, ostensibly in an attempt to soothe frayed nerves and de-escalate tensions. But instead he becomes embroiled in the auction himself. Outside the camp, a general by the name of Didius Julianus is refused entry but nonetheless continues to bellow his own bids. The fate of Rome rests on who can most efficiently bribe the Praetorian Guard – a grim state of affairs. Sulpicianus offers every soldier 20,000 sesterces. Julianus goes to 25,000. The guards unlock the gates and Julianus is ushered in to be proclaimed the new emperor. It is as simple as that.

Evening is drawing in and Julianus rushes off to the Senate House, escorted by a small army of Praetorians carrying flags as if marching off for war. They make an intimidating sight, which is just what they intend. Among the fearful senators is the writer and historian Cassius Dio, who records his eye-witness account of the night's events. He has been close with

Pertinax and has crossed swords with Julianus in the law courts, which gives him extra reason to be nervous. Cassius Dio listens attentively as Julianus sets out all the reasons why he is the best choice to rule. Wishing to appear a peace-maker, he explains that he came here alone, unattended by soldiers – a claim he makes even as heavily armed troops mill about inside and outside the building. Fearful of what will happen if they oppose him, the Senate rubber-stamps his appointment. The new emperor now proceeds to his palace, where he orders a banquet, gorges himself and then plays dice, even as the body of his predecessor remains in the building.

## MORE CHANGING OF THE GUARD

This coup does not go down well with the populace, and Julianus strikes back at protestors with a heavy hand. News of the turmoil in Rome quickly spreads through the provinces and galvanizes several powerful figures. Among them are the generals Clodius Albinus, based in Britannia, and Pescennius Niger, operating out of Roman Syria. Each is now proclaimed emperor, supported by their respective legions. But there is a third man with a military-backed claim too – Severus, who can call on the Rhine and Danube legions for support. Moreover, he is the one with easiest access to Rome.

Over the coming weeks he strikes a deal with Albinus, offering him the title of Caesar (a designation understood to denote the heir apparent to the imperial crown) and possibly hinting at a power-sharing arrangement if he does not stand in Severus's way. Severus then makes his march on Rome, meeting the Praetorians en route and sending them scuttling. He also takes control of Ravenna, an important base for the

Roman fleet, prompting other Italian cities to join his side. As Severus nears Rome, Julianus's support dissolves away. Even the Senate finds its backbone, declaring a death sentence on Julianus and proclaiming Severus as emperor.

Holed up in his palace, Julianus knows he is running out of options. Today is 2 June 193, sixty-six days since he seized power, and he is alone, wearily reclining and trying to work out his next move, when he spots a member of the palace security approaching him. Before he can react, the soldier charges forward and kills him. When Severus enters the city a short while later, there is no rival to oust. The empire is his, and he immediately sets about reimposing order. He roots out and executes all those responsible for the assassination of Pertinax, then overhauls what remains of the Praetorian Guard. He fills its ranks with men loyal to him and introduces a programme of anti-corruption reforms. But already sections of the Senate are uncomfortable at his emergence, given that he is, after all, just one more in a chain of emperors to grab power through armed force.

Meanwhile, Severus still has Niger and Albinus to deal with. With Albinus for the time being appeased by the granting of his title, Severus goes east to deal with Niger, whose forces are now in Asia Minor, in modern-day Turkey. In 194 Severus conclusively defeats his rival at the battle of Issus. Niger manages to escape the battlefield, retreating to Antioch, but Severus's men apprehend him after just a few days and put him to death.

Next, Severus spends several months travelling further east, to deal with the remnants of Niger's support in Parthia. He also announces that his son, Caracalla, will eventually succeed him as emperor – news that does not go down well with Albinus. The Caesar launches an invasion of Gaul from Britannia, and in mid-February 197 Severus engages him near modern-day Lyon in France. It's estimated that there are upwards of 120,000 men on the battlefield, possibly more than twice that, with Severus commanding the narrowly bigger number. For two brutal days they slug it out in what is by most reckonings the bloodiest battle ever contended by two Roman armies.

Albinus flees the battlefield but it is only a brief reprieve. With the enemy closing in, he is killed, though whether by his own hand or that of another is unclear. What is certain is that indignity is hurled upon him in death. Some report that Severus commands Albinus's naked body be laid on the ground so that he might personally trample it on horseback. Albinus is then beheaded, the head sent to Rome to be displayed on a spike. As for the rest of his body – along with those of his murdered wife and children – Severus casts them into the Rhine. Five men have laid claim to the imperial titles since the death of Commodus; now, only one remains.

Confident in his position at last, Severus imposes himself on his opponents in Rome. He has dozens of senators arrested and executed on charges of corruption and treason, and increasingly relies on the advice of his Praetorian prefect, a man named Plautianus. For those who have worried that Severus is framing up to be another military dictator, this seems to prove the point. Nor does the relationship go down well with Julia Domna, who fears that Plautianus is usurping powers that ought to fall to her and her sons. In early 205 the power-battle comes to a head when she and Caracalla persuade Severus that his prefect is planning to have the emperor and his heir murdered. Plautianus is himself killed as he tries to defend himself of the charges.

By now Severus has already undertaken successful military operations in Parthia and Africa. He has annexed swathes of Mesopotamia, seized important Parthian cities and extended the empire's desert frontier in Arabia to bring back memories of the glory days of Trajan. In Africa, too, he has made significant progress, advancing the southern frontier. Now, in 208, he turns his attention to Britannia.

## ENRICH THE SOLDIERS, SCORN ALL OTHERS

It's a characteristically bleak day in 210 in the central lowlands of Caledonia. Weariness fills Severus's limbs as he leads his men on another day's advance, cutting through dense forest shrouded in fog. Age is catching up with him and he has resorted to being carried in a litter. It is not the look of a proud warrior but he knows he is not up to a route march. Up ahead, a forward party finish work on a bridge to carry the legionaries over a frothing river. It has been a strange expedition so far. Severus has faced no pitched battle against the Caledonians, despite the locals' ferocious reputations. There has been the odd guerrilla attack, but little more than that. The Caledonians don't even seem to have made much effort to herd their sheep and cows to safety. Instead, there is frequently livestock for the Romans to claim, a welcome way to fill their tight bellies. So on and on they go, Severus noticing that his men's greatest enemies are the elements and exhaustion. But when he has made his way virtually unopposed through most of the territory, the Caledonians make their move, attacking the heavily fatigued Romans and claiming, it is said, many thousands of lives. It is as if they have allowed the Romans to march themselves into a position of disadvantage. Yet neither side has sufficiently the upper hand to secure a decisive victory. Instead, Severus agrees a peace, retreating but not without securing some new lands beyond the old frontier.

When some of the Caledonian tribes later rise up in defiance, an incandescent Severus orders nothing less than their complete annihilation, even down to babes in the womb. He hopes this will be the campaign that at last secures all of Britannia for Rome. But as he prepares to set out, he grimaces with the pain of the gout that is overtaking him. He withdraws to Eboracum (modern-day York in northern England), where he hopes for a speedy recovery.

By February 211, however, he is not feeling any better. The reverse, in fact – so much so that his thoughts turn to succession. Though his sons are already nominally co-emperors with him, there is no doubt who has the final say-so. With the cold northern European climate sinking ever further into his bones, he summons the boys to a meeting. He ushers them close, ready to receive his hard-earned wisdom so that they might have its benefit when he is no longer here. 'Be harmonious,' he tells them. 'Enrich the soldiers, scorn all others.' Within days, on 4 February, he is dead. But he has lived by his words, forging the connection between power and the military, while dismissing the importance of the Senate and Rome's other great political institutions.

His sons, with the assistance of their mother, rule jointly for a while, but it is a doomed alliance. Before the year is out, Caracalla murders his brother and embarks on a solo rule noted for its cruel tyranny until his own assassination by a disgruntled soldier in 217. The Severan dynasty, as it is known, will go on to reign until 235. To that extent, Severus may have regarded his attempts to bring stability back to the empire as successful. But what follows is a prolonged phase of extreme instability. His rule has set the standard for increasing imperial reliance on the military for power, and – as Trajan did before him – he seriously devalued the currency in his pursuit of expansion, storing up economic troubles ahead.

Rome is about to embark on what ominously comes to be known as the Crisis of the Third Century.

# 16

# ZENOBIA: ROMAN DIVISION AND DECLINE

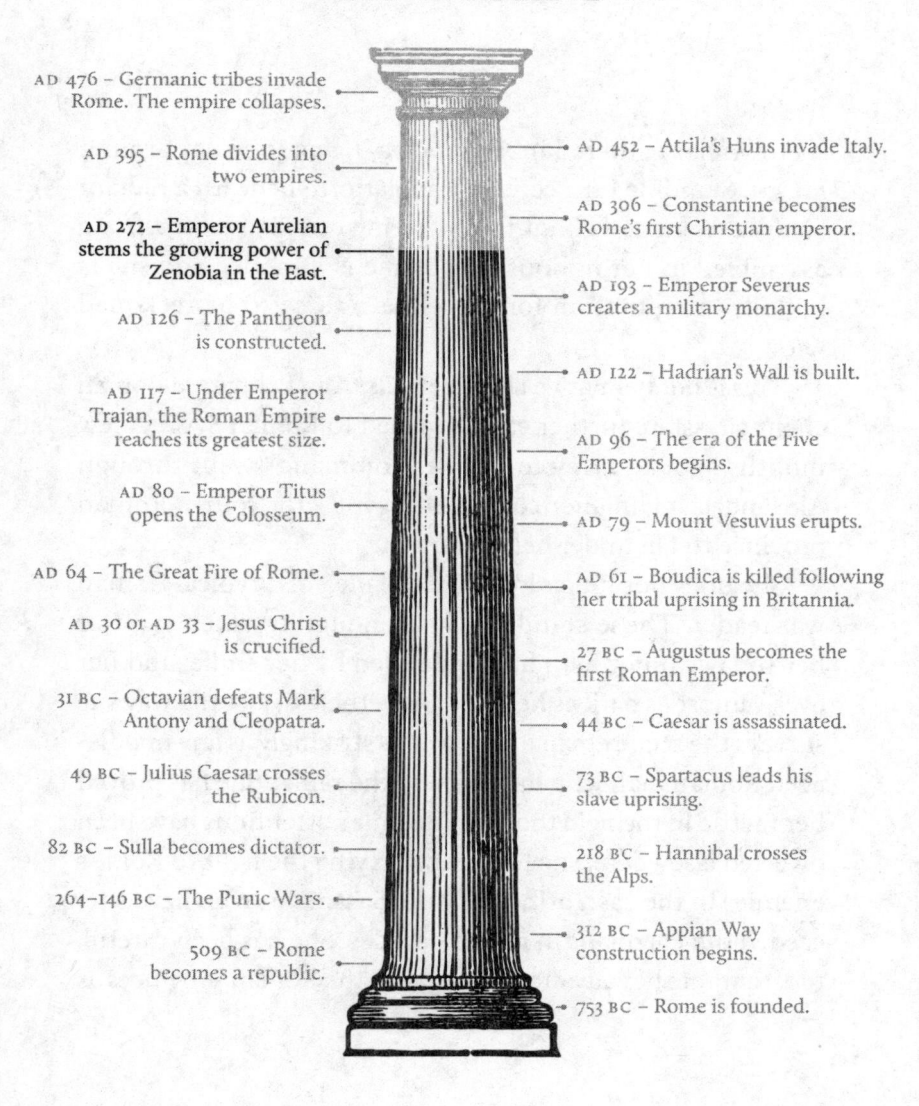

AD 476 – Germanic tribes invade Rome. The empire collapses.

AD 452 – Attila's Huns invade Italy.

AD 395 – Rome divides into two empires.

AD 306 – Constantine becomes Rome's first Christian emperor.

**AD 272 – Emperor Aurelian stems the growing power of Zenobia in the East.**

AD 193 – Emperor Severus creates a military monarchy.

AD 126 – The Pantheon is constructed.

AD 122 – Hadrian's Wall is built.

AD 117 – Under Emperor Trajan, the Roman Empire reaches its greatest size.

AD 96 – The era of the Five Emperors begins.

AD 80 – Emperor Titus opens the Colosseum.

AD 79 – Mount Vesuvius erupts.

AD 64 – The Great Fire of Rome.

AD 61 – Boudica is killed following her tribal uprising in Britannia.

AD 30 or AD 33 – Jesus Christ is crucified.

27 BC – Augustus becomes the first Roman Emperor.

31 BC – Octavian defeats Mark Antony and Cleopatra.

44 BC – Caesar is assassinated.

49 BC – Julius Caesar crosses the Rubicon.

73 BC – Spartacus leads his slave uprising.

82 BC – Sulla becomes dictator.

218 BC – Hannibal crosses the Alps.

264–146 BC – The Punic Wars.

312 BC – Appian Way construction begins.

509 BC – Rome becomes a republic.

753 BC – Rome is founded.

A crowd has gathered in Alexandria, Egypt, one day around AD 271. Standing on a ceremonial platform beneath a radiant sun is a woman of about thirty, gazing out across the throng assembled in her honour. Her name is Zenobia, and she is building a reputation for herself as a force to be reckoned with.

This is not her native city. She hails from Palmyra, a Roman client city-state further east, attached to Roman Syria. A few months ago, an army under her command swept through Alexandria, giving her control of Egypt – the fourth Roman province to fall under her dominion.

She does not much look like the idea of a typical Roman war leader. Those standing close enough to catch sight of her today cannot help but be dazzled by her smile, and her eyes, almost as dark as her hair. Nonetheless, just the way she surveys the scene emanates power as strikingly as any middle-aged Roman man who has risen up the ranks. She has proved her mettle in the field too. While Rome's attentions have been diverted elsewhere, she has been carrying the fight to Rome's enemies in the east, principally the Sasanians, who have succeeded the Parthians in recent decades. She has been careful, too, to frame her advance throughout the Roman provinces as in the interests of Rome itself. She may have all the trappings of a queen, but she has so far made no claim to be anything but subservient to the emperor.

Even so, her actions have raised eyebrows in the imperial court. She has proved too effective at sweeping away the opposition, and word has got to her that the current emperor, Aurelian, considers her a threat. An army is on its way from the west even as she stands here in the glow of the Egyptian sun. She could simply shrink away, escaping – or at least minimizing – whatever wrath is headed her way. But that is not her style.

Instead, she chooses to double-down. If Rome does not want to co-exist with her, she will make an open play to usurp its territories – starting now. Beside her stands her son, Vaballathus, aged about eleven and already three years into his reign as 'King of Kings' – an honorary title that fell to him after the death of his father. Although no one has any doubt that his mother is the one who really wields the power.

Doing his best to emulate her poise, he tries to hide his excitement for the ceremony about to play out. There's a hush among the crowd as an official walks slowly towards him, carrying a laurel wreath. He places it on the child's head, before oaths confirm Vaballathus as Augustus – the title normally reserved for Rome's emperors. Then it is his mother's turn. She exudes an air of tranquillity as she too is crowned, and bestowed with the honorific Augusta, reserved for women of the imperial family. There is no disguising the subtext. Moving from their assumed position of subservience to Rome, Zenobia and her son are now openly challenging the authority of the established imperial masters. She does not want to replace Roman rule in the east so much as to re-centre its power through her. She addresses the crowd, who hang on her every word. The message is clear: it is she and her son, not Aurelian, who are in charge in these parts, and she will defend their right to rule without interference.

Although the sound of Aurelian's legions stampeding their way to Egypt are still far out of anyone's hearing, Zenobia knows it will not be long before she must back up these sentiments with deeds.

*Rome and its empire are at a crossroads, mired in a half-century-long existential crisis. Riven by instability – military, social and economic – rule has fallen to a rapid succession of imperial claimants, some reigning for only a few weeks at a time. Zenobia's move in Alexandria confirms an extraordinary situation in which the empire itself has effectively been divided into three. Rome remains at the heart of one of these divisions, comprising Italy and the surrounding regions. But, for the last decade, the self-proclaimed Gallic Empire has claimed Britannia, Gaul, Germania and, for a while, even Hispania as its own. And now this rival empire in the east is gaining in strength too.*

*The question hovers: is the Roman Empire fractured beyond repair? Does this so-called Crisis of the Third Century signal permanent decline? Or is there somehow a way back?*

## END OF THE SEVERANS

While its root causes have been developing for much longer, the trigger for the crisis comes in March 235, a few years before Zenobia is born. Severus Alexander has enjoyed an impressive thirteen years on the imperial throne, even though he is still not yet twenty-seven. His reign started with the assassination of his cousin and adoptive father Emperor Elagabalus, with whom he shared a grandmother, herself the sister-in-law of Emperor Septimius Severus. Evidence that Rome just cannot shake off its internecine politics.

Severus Alexander's rule, in which he has been heavily influenced by his mother Julia Mamaea, has had its successes, especially in instilling a sense of stability and prosperousness in Rome itself. But there have been challenges too. He has managed to stave off the advances of the emerging Sasanians for the time being, but he has also faced incursions from Germanic tribes. Though he's tried to stem their advance through diplomacy and bribery, the approach has not gone down well with certain figures in the military.

As the story goes, he has just finished lunch on this March afternoon and is preparing to meet several critical generals to discuss strategy in a tent at Moguntiacum (modern-day Mainz). His mother – and eternal adviser – sits close by, her presence doing little to alter opinion that he lacks personal strength of character. Amid the machismo of the Roman army, it doesn't do for an emperor to defer to his mum on military matters. The place simmers with tension as no-holds-barred talks begin. Then, suddenly, a servant appears, signalling an ambush of the emperor. Severus Alexander is set upon, and within moments he is slain – and his mother too.

There are conflicting reports about the exact location and circumstances of his death, but the key facts are not in doubt: Severus Alexander is murdered by mutinous soldiers. Now the army intends to impose its own choice of emperor – the first of several appointed in this way who are collectively referred to as 'barracks emperors'.

## RISE OF THE BARRACKS EMPERORS

The first of these appointees is a man-mountain and a career soldier, Maximinus Thrax, so named for his Thracian heritage. He is the first emperor to hail neither from the senatorial nor the equestrian class, and he manages to cling to power for a little over three years. But just as he took the throne in the aftermath of a military-masterminded assassination, so too he exits the scene, murdered by a group of disgruntled soldiers in 238. In his wake, chaos reigns in what comes to be called the Year of the Six Emperors. Multiple claimants for the imperial throne arise in both Africa (where there is a major uprising in protest at Rome's tax demands) and in Rome itself.

The man who emerges from the infighting in possession of the purple toga is . . . not a man at all, but the thirteen-year-old Gordian III, whose youth sees him begin his rule as a puppet of the Senate. But any belief that together they can wrestle back control from the military and secure long-term stability is illusory. The volatility that threatens Rome's power and prosperity has many deep-rooted causes, and they're all about to hit at the same time.

## CRISIS? WHAT CRISIS?

In Rome's long history, transfers of power have rarely been smooth. Intrigue and murder have been regular features of accession, both within and between dynasties. Nor has the army always made an effort to keep itself distant from civil affairs, frequently dethroning those it has not liked and installing replacements more palatable to the military frame of mind. Nonetheless, army interference has been growing in frequency and intensity – as Severus's warning of nearly thirty years ago to 'enrich the soldiers' and 'scorn all others' seems to prove. Its meddling goes into overdrive in the Year of the Six Emperors, during which it becomes clear that personal loyalty to individual generals now outstrips loyalty to the office of the emperor itself. It is as if history, with the huge personal armies of the generals who dominated the dying days of the republic, is repeating itself.

But trust between Rome's military and civilian spheres is straining. Even as the army demands its say in politics, there is a feeling that it is becoming less effective at its primary job of protecting the empire. Where it has previously been an unstoppable force, driving Roman expansion and consequently raising the quality of life for its citizens, as guardian of a now vast dominion it is dangerously overstretched. The Germanic tribes, for example, are a perpetual thorn in Rome's side, testing the strength of its northern frontiers. Climate change, including rising sea levels, has seriously impacted the ability to farm successfully in the northern reaches of the continent, prompting large-scale tribal migrations that are exacerbating territorial rivalries. Meanwhile, in the east, the Sasanian Empire has taken over and is intent on reclaiming territory long ago lost to the Romans by its Parthian predecessors.

The economic impact of all this upheaval runs deep. It costs a vast amount to police the empire and protect these frontiers. And since anyone who wants to stay in power realizes they need to keep the troops happy, it has been necessary to dig ever deeper to do so. Far too many emperors have looked to lessen the pain of paying out all that money by minting more coins containing a smaller proportion of precious metals – in other words, by devaluing the currency. But with each sesterce now worth less than before, businesses put their prices up, leading to rampant inflation. With prices rocketing, the soldiers – and everyone else, for that matter – want to be paid more. It is a painful cycle made worse still by the collapse in trade resulting from the activities of the Sasanians and the Germanic tribes, not to mention sporadic uprisings within the empire too, like the one that has overcome Africa. On top of all this, the class aspect to the economic downturn means that the poor and the administrative middle class feel the pinch far more than rich landowners, who insulate themselves from some of the pain by raising the prices on whatever their landholdings produce.

None of these various challenges dogging the 230s are new to Rome. Indeed, for a great many who live their lives untouched by civil infighting and far away from threatened frontiers, life goes on much as it ever did. Some regions – Britannia, North Africa and Egypt among them – are positively thriving. Besides, over its fabled past, Rome has dealt with enough formidable enemies, social turbulence, economic boom-and-busts, dynastic conflicts, over-mighty military commanders and all manner of natural disasters. But it is difficult to remember a perfect storm such as the one that seems to be enveloping the empire just now. No wonder unity in the imperial capital is in short supply. It would be a miracle if there weren't a crisis.

### FIRST LADY OF PALMYRA

Fast forward to the year 255, where in Palmyra, just over 130 miles north-east of Damascus, a girl of about fifteen – well educated and from a well-to-do family – is wandering through her hometown. She makes her way down a colonnaded street, hardly noticing the grand buildings – a spectacular theatre here, a magnificent temple there – in all directions. So familiar are these landmarks that their opulence washes over her. But to any visitor, this evidence of Palmyra's prosperity is breathtaking. Perched on the edge of the Syrian Desert, it's an important staging post for the caravans that wend their way along the Silk Road, laden with exotic goods to transport between east and west. Palmyra has grown fat on the profits of this international trade.

But the girl, Zenobia, is unconcerned with global economics. Instead, her mind is focused on an upcoming event of far greater personal importance: her marriage. Her betrothed, Odaenathus, is some twenty years older than her, and this is his second marriage. He is an important figure in the city. In fact, the most important – the *ras*, or lord, of Palmyra – in charge of the day-to-day running and defence of the city, although he ultimately reports to Rome.

Rome, however, seems very far off to Zenobia. The ever-changing cast of emperors means little to her. In position these last two years are joint emperors, both of the senatorial class: Valerian, in his fifties, and the son he appointed himself, Gallienus, in his thirties. Valerian has a plan to restore equilibrium to the empire, and to him, success in that task is all about decentralization. Rather than have everything fall on the shoulders of a single emperor, the two men will now share the work. He entrusts the job of securing Rome's western provinces against Germanic raiders to Gallienus, while he heads east to take on the Sasanians. But what does any of that matter to Zenobia as she looks ahead to her nuptials?

## ROME DIVIDED BY THREE

The year 260, by which time Zenobia has been married for five years, sends shockwaves through the Roman Empire. In the spring Valerian leads his army into battle against the Sasanians, led by their 'King of Kings' (a title in use in the region for well over a millennium, and equivalent to Rome's 'emperor') Shapur I, at Edessa in modern-day Turkey. An already stern military challenge is made harder for Rome because its army is suffering the long-term impacts of an extended and deadly outbreak of disease (known as the Plague of Cyprian) that has severely reduced manpower. Valerian is himself now in his sixties, his energies not what they once were. When the two sides clash, the Romans are routed, losing some 10,000 men in a day. Valerian himself is taken prisoner – the first Roman emperor to suffer such indignity – and stories abound about the treatment he receives in captivity. Some say that Shapur uses him as a human footstool when he mounts his horse, and that he is eventually killed, perhaps by having molten gold poured down his throat when he attempts to negotiate a ransom, or possibly by being flayed alive, his skin stuffed and kept as a trophy. Others suggest he is treated much more graciously, and perhaps even ultimately released. Though the truth is elusive amid the many stories, all of which have propaganda value of one kind or another, what is certain is that at this point he disappears from history, and his son now rules alone.

> ### PLAGUE OF CYPRIAN
>
> Even among the many challenges Rome faced in its century of crisis, the Plague of Cyprian was horribly grim and recalled the devastation wrought by the Antonine Plague the previous century. Breaking out in the late 240s and running through to the 260s, its modern identity is uncertain, with measles, smallpox and assorted viruses all considered contenders. Its name references St Cyprian, the Bishop of Carthage, who documented the progress of the pandemic. While there are no accurate figures as to its death toll, it is said to have killed 5,000 a day in Rome alone at its peak, and has been identified as the likely cause of death for at least two emperors. It was also responsible for structural problems within the empire, gutting the army of soldiers and prompting a rush of exposed rural populations into the cities, leading to a collapse in agricultural production. Although not heralding the end of days, at times it felt close – and the Christian Church was one of the few institutions to benefit, winning many new followers for its role in caring for the living and the dead.

Gallienus is now in an unenviable position. With his energies fully consumed in Europe – right now, he is dealing with local uprisings in Pannonia – he can do nothing about events further east. And then he is hit by another hammer bolt. The governor of Germania Superior and Inferior, a man named Postumus, decisively defeats the forces of the dangerous Franks (one of the Germanic tribes), establishing himself as the de jure Roman strongman. While Valerian is incarcerated and Gallienus is tied up with fire-fighting, Postumus is declared emperor by his legions of a new Gallic Empire, a fluid entity comprising the Roman provinces of Gaul, Germania, Britannia and (temporarily) Hispania. Although Postumus never challenges for control of Rome itself, he has effectively annexed a vast swathe of its European territories as his own.

Meanwhile, for Zenobia's Palmyra, Rome's defeat by Shapur has potentially devastating consequences. Shapur builds on his victory to consolidate his power in Syria, disrupting trade and threatening the stability that underpins Palmyrene success. But Roman ill fortune also brings opportunity for Odaenathus and his wife. The lord of Palmyra now rebrands himself as its king and sets about increasing his armies. Before long he recaptures Edessa from the Sasanians, along with several other Persian garrisons established in Roman Mesopotamia. By 263 he makes it to the Sasanian capital, Ctesiphon, and completes the job of driving the enemy out of Roman lands. It's great news: for Gallienus, who basks in the reflected glory of a victory entirely not of his making; and for Odaenathus himself, who assumes the title 'King of Kings'. Except, this does rather imply that Odaenathus considers himself ruler of all these officially Roman lands in the east, especially when he extends the title to his son – Zenobia's step-son. For now, Gallienus seems at peace with this arrangement. As long as Odaenathus does not directly challenge Roman sovereignty, he may operate as a client-king. Even so, however much Gallienus convinces himself that this is a state of happy co-existence, it looks a lot like his empire has divided into three distinct chunks, with the section he controls sitting sandwiched uncomfortably between the Gallic Empire to the west and Odaenathus's domains in the east.

## OUT OF THE SHADOWS

The change comes in around 267, when Odaenathus is assassinated, along with the son he'd named as heir. Exactly where, when, by whom and why is heavily disputed. Some point the finger at Gallienus, or Sasanian agents, or maybe even Palmyrene traitors. Others look closer to home, to someone in Odaenathus's family bearing a grudge – maybe even Zenobia, in a bid to have power pass to her own son, Vaballathus. The truth remains elusive. What is certain is that the slaying of the reigning King of Kings and his son leaves a power vacuum.

It is Zenobia, previously the dutiful queen at her husband's shoulder, who steps into the void. She ensures that Vaballathus, still but a child, assumes his father's royal titles without opposition, while she seamlessly inhabits the role of regent. Launching a programme of fortification and strangling any pockets of resistance, she establishes herself as the de facto authority in Roman Syria, Mesopotamia and Arabia. Maintaining, for now, the appearance of subservience to Rome, she has new currency minted with the image of Vaballathus alongside the Roman emperor to demonstrate the point. And until now she's only been fighting the Sasanians to protect Rome's borders. The enemy of her friend is *her* enemy, after all.

But then, in 270 she advances into new territory, leading her army into Roman Egypt and taking Alexandria for herself – or at least for her son, who will be crowned Augustus in the city. In Antioch, capital of Roman Syria, the mint starts issuing coins not featuring the emperor in Rome, but Vaballathus and Zenobia instead. Zenobia is effectively empress of four vast provinces, unchallenged in her power in the Roman east. No longer a client of Rome, but a usurper.

Until now, Rome has seemed powerless to stem her rise, and its endless crises show no sign of letting up. In the three years since she took up her husband's mantle there have been four different Roman emperors on the throne. First came Gallienus's assassination by, predictably, a discontented army officer, after which Gallienus's son inherited the imperial title for barely a month before he too was murdered. Claudius Gothicus (named after an earlier victory over the Goths) was next to claim the throne, but managed just short of two years before illness – likely the dreaded plague – saw him off. His brother succeeded him, but he lasted less than a month before dying in mysterious circumstances.

Now, in August 270, comes Aurelian. A decorated cavalry commander, he is determined to start digging Rome out of its deep hole. And he has Zenobia in his sights.

### THE DOCTOR WILL SEE YOU NOW

Roman medicine was a combination of superstition and science. The true causes of disease were often little understood, so that many people considered phenomena like the Plague of Cyprian to be expressions of divine displeasure. Religious rituals were thus one popular response to the onset of disease. However, the gradual assimilation of Greek and Egyptian medical knowledge greatly informed the development of Roman medicine. Herbal remedies were widely used, with differing levels of efficacy, and army physicians developed new surgical methods – unsurprisingly given the large number of patients they had to practise on – although in an age of ineffectual anaesthesia, the cure was often worse than the ailment. A need to treat troops also prompted the establishment of the first Roman hospitals. While the exact causes of disease and its transmission were often misunderstood (miasma, or 'bad air', was often held to blame) the Romans at least grasped the importance of hygiene for good public health – a fact attested to by their commitment to regular bathing, their attempts to provide clean drinking water, and their practice of burying the dead beyond city walls. Moreover, the link between good diet and good health was clearly understood. Medical science has come a long way in the millennia since, but many of our modern practices have their roots deep in the ancient world.

## A FIGHT TOO FAR

In the early summer of 272 Aurelian begins his reclamation of Roman dominions in the east. His troops flood through Asia Minor and into Egypt, winning back control of Alexandria within a matter of weeks. Next, it is to Syria, where Zenobia is encamped in Antioch. His troops claim a battlefield victory about 25 miles north of the city, but she refuses to yield. She plans to withdraw, inducing the Romans further south for a showdown. To calm her people's fears, she even claims Aurelian has been killed. A lookalike is hired to be paraded around Antioch's streets as evidence. Not long after that she leaves at the head of an army 70,000-strong. Behind her, Antioch is besieged and soon falls.

The two armies eventually meet on a plain close to Emesa (modern-day Homs in Syria). To begin with, it seems like Zenobia has the upper hand, the heavy Palmyrene cavalry pummelling their counterparts. Zenobia is at the heart of the action, roaring orders to her generals from horseback. But the tide begins to turn. The Romans rally and start to gain the upper hand. Likely victory turns into inevitable defeat, but not before Zenobia has extracted herself from the fighting, leading a team of her closest advisers to Palmyra to regroup. She is running out of options, and she knows it.

With the Romans bearing down on the city, so the story goes, she mounts a racing camel and makes a run for the Euphrates to try to escape. However, she is recognized and handed over to the Romans. When Aurelian receives the warrior queen, clamped in chains, he puts her and most of her surviving court on trial. It's reported that she tries to shed herself of responsibility for her actions, arguing that she has been acting on the counsel of her male advisers. This, however, may well be a story the Roman authorities put about to discredit her and make her look weak and cowardly.

She is, at least, spared her life, along with her son. Most of the others on trial are executed. Again, legend begins to attach itself to her as her name becomes weaponized in the battle for Rome's reputation. Some say she is humiliatingly paraded on the back of a camel through various of the cities once under her command. Another report has it that she spends three whole days on public display in her manacles in Antioch's hippodrome. More reliably, it's reported that she and Vaballathus are paraded through Rome as part of Aurelian's triumph to mark his success in reclaiming Rome's territories. Then the stories diverge again. Zenobia may have been executed, or alternatively granted the freedom to live out the rest of her natural life discreetly and comfortably. Palmyra itself is granted no such mercy, instead being razed to the ground, and erased from the historical record.

Zenobia has defied the social expectations of her age to rule over a huge chunk of the Roman Empire in her own name for more than a year. But in the end, Rome's might has proved too great. Nonetheless, and albeit briefly, she has arguably been the woman to hold the most direct power in all of ancient Roman history. And despite her defeat, in bringing the fight so decisively to the Romans she has highlighted its desperate fragility during a half-century of crisis that still has several years to run.

## REBALANCE

As for Aurelian, he backs up his reclamation of the Roman east by also defeating the forces of the Gallic Empire in 274. He has pulled the empire back from the precipice, reunited its breakaway wings and earned himself the title *restitutor orbis* ('restorer of the world'). His reward, just a year later, is assassination by a group of Praetorian Guards, who have been tricked by a notary's lie into believing the notoriously strict emperor planned to execute them. Further civil war ensues until Diocletian asserts his claim to be emperor in 284.

Though Diocletian becomes synonymous with the ruthless persecution of Christians, he also puts into action plans to ensure that the crises that have dogged Rome for five perilous decades are not repeated. Accepting that responsibility for the entire empire is too much for any one man, he introduces a system known as the Tetrarchy. The empire is divided into two halves (Eastern and Western), each under the rule of an Augustus, supported by a Caesar who is expected eventually to succeed the Augustus. It's a new approach designed for stability and greater dynastic clarity, so that the revolving door to the imperial throne will not spin so wildly again. And given that between the murder of Severus Alexander in 235 and the accession of Diocletian forty-nine years later there have been no fewer than twenty-seven emperors, the move doesn't come a moment too soon.

In addition, he introduces a raft of other administrative, economic and military reforms. He divides the existing provinces to create almost twice as many, and establishes four major regional capitals at Trier (in modern-day Germany), Milan (Italy), Sirmium (Serbia) and Nicomedia (Turkey). Local administration is streamlined, and he directs an overhaul of the taxation system so that there are better accounting practices, a greater sense of equity in how taxes are levied, and an upturn in revenues too. Amid incessant inflationary pressures, he also attempts to cap the price of essential goods and services. As for the army, he bolsters the military infrastructure, introduces systems to optimize use of his most mobile units and increases troop numbers by 25 per cent.

The Crisis of the Third Century, with Zenobia an iconic figure at its heart, seemed destined to break the empire once and for all. But when it most mattered, a series of leaders – competent and inspired, by degree – have mined Rome for the attributes that see it reborn.

# 17

## EMPRESS HELENA:
## THE RISE OF CHRISTIANITY

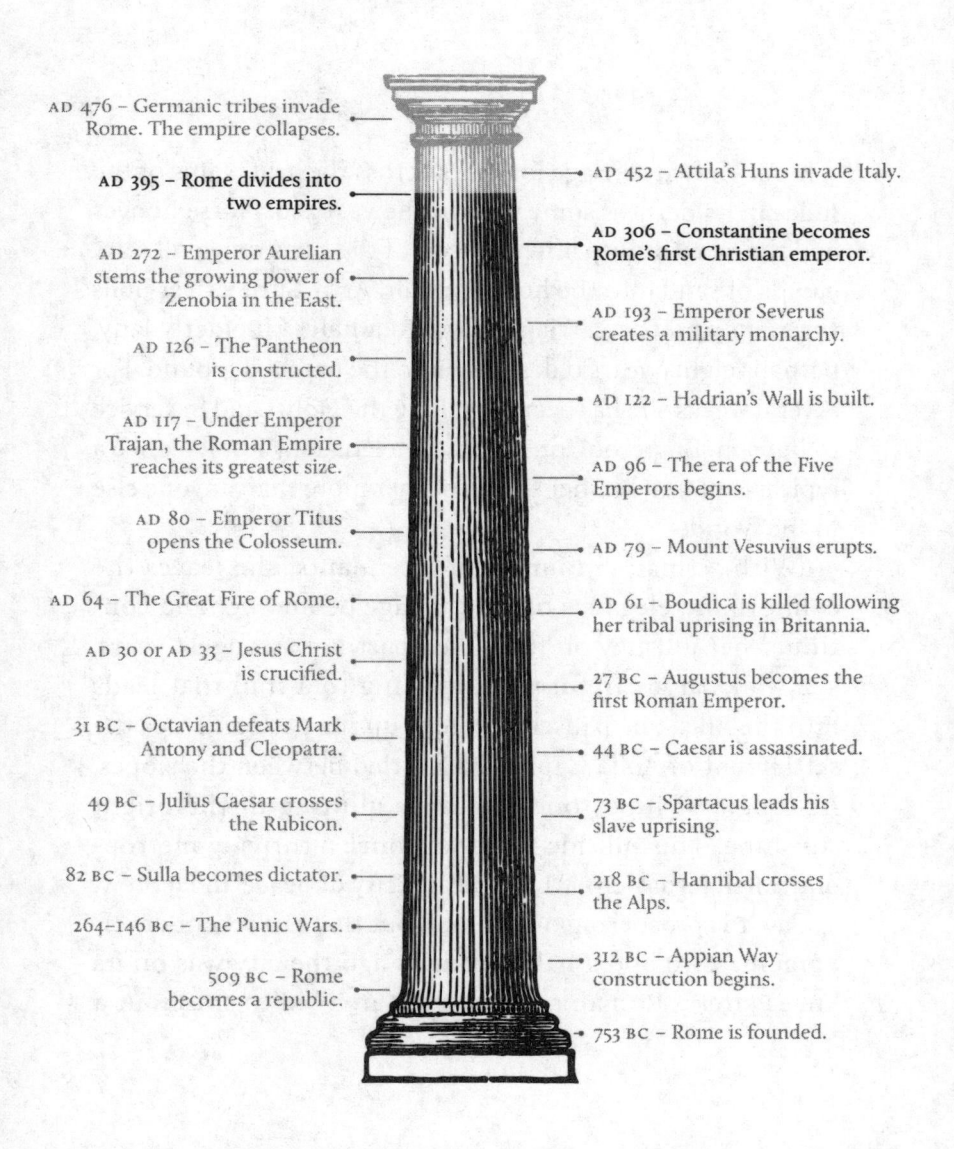

AD 476 – Germanic tribes invade Rome. The empire collapses.

AD 395 – **Rome divides into two empires.**

AD 272 – Emperor Aurelian stems the growing power of Zenobia in the East.

AD 126 – The Pantheon is constructed.

AD 117 – Under Emperor Trajan, the Roman Empire reaches its greatest size.

AD 80 – Emperor Titus opens the Colosseum.

AD 64 – The Great Fire of Rome.

AD 30 or AD 33 – Jesus Christ is crucified.

31 BC – Octavian defeats Mark Antony and Cleopatra.

49 BC – Julius Caesar crosses the Rubicon.

82 BC – Sulla becomes dictator.

264–146 BC – The Punic Wars.

509 BC – Rome becomes a republic.

AD 452 – Attila's Huns invade Italy.

AD 306 – **Constantine becomes Rome's first Christian emperor.**

AD 193 – Emperor Severus creates a military monarchy.

AD 122 – Hadrian's Wall is built.

AD 96 – The era of the Five Emperors begins.

AD 79 – Mount Vesuvius erupts.

AD 61 – Boudica is killed following her tribal uprising in Britannia.

27 BC – Augustus becomes the first Roman Emperor.

44 BC – Caesar is assassinated.

73 BC – Spartacus leads his slave uprising.

218 BC – Hannibal crosses the Alps.

312 BC – Appian Way construction begins.

753 BC – Rome is founded.

A horse-drawn carriage journeys across the arid plains of the Judaean wilderness some time in the year 326. Horse hooves and the beautifully painted wheels of the carts they pull send clouds of sand into the hot desert air. At last, the driver pulls the reins and the carriage slows to a halt. An elderly lady, perhaps eighty years old, steps on to the parched ground. For several weeks she has been travelling the Holy Land in service to her son, Emperor Constantine. Helena may not look like a typical explorer, but her son trusts her more than anyone else in the world.

With a small entourage of attendants, she leaves the comfort and elegance of the carriage behind her and continues her journey on foot. Well past her strongest years, she walks at a careful pace, heading to a trail that leads into the hills. She pauses to squint up the path and sees the settlement of Aelia Capitolina nestled between the slopes, its tangle of limestone buildings glinting in the bright sunshine. This hillside town was once a thriving metropolis called Jerusalem, which means 'city of peace' in Hebrew. Today it is prospering once more, but that is a recent development. Two and a half centuries ago the city was on its knees after a Roman army razed it in a bid to snuff out a dangerous Jewish revolt. When the city's Jewish inhabitants again refused to worship Rome's pagan gods some decades later, they once more experienced the empire's wrath firsthand. To add insult to injury, once the Romans were finished they renamed what was left of the city after themselves – Aelia, after Emperor Hadrian's family name Aelius, and Capitolina, denoting the so-called Capitoline Triad of Roman gods, Jupiter, Juno and Minerva.

Yet as Helena comes into the centre of the city, its inhabitants greet her with reverence and not a little surprise, unused as they are to visitors of her rank. But though Helena is a regal woman, an empress no less, she is here today not on a diplomatic mission or a stately visit but with a higher purpose altogether. Because to her, this is a pilgrimage to the land once walked by Jesus of Nazareth and his followers. If the Christian texts are to be believed, she will be able to visit the sites Christ himself inhabited around 300 years ago – his home, the places from which he preached, even the site of his execution. And in travelling to the region to locate the holy places of Christianity, she hopes to help reshape the faith of the Roman Empire.

*Despite playing a crucial role in the final days of the Roman Empire, the woman who will one day become Empress Helena didn't begin life with any expectation of such status. Likely born in Greece to uncertain parentage, her connection to one of the most powerful men in Rome began as little more than a glance across a crowded room – a matter of being in the right place at the right time. But out of this moment of serendipity was born one of the most pivotal leaders in the history of Rome – Constantine I, 'the Great'. How did this unknown woman from a remote corner of the empire find her way to the centre of its power? And once she'd* got there, what was her influence on this next, critical chapter in its story?

## CONSTANTINE'S BIRTH

In 272, over fifty years before Helena's trip to the Holy Land, the world she inhabits looks very different. In her mid-twenties, she walks through the near-pitch darkness of the legionary camp in Naissus (modern-day Niš in Serbia), dressed in little more than rags. Her path is occasionally illuminated by flaming torches made from scraps of cloth soaked in sulphur and lime. The good-natured shouts and laughter of men off-duty rise in the air as she strolls past rows of barracks, training areas and latrines before entering the tavern where she works as a barmaid.

Inside are dozens of soldiers. Weary after their long journey along the Via Militaris, the main road through the Balkan Mountains that loom over the camp, they're drinking local wine and playing dice, making the most of a little downtime. In recent days, more soldiers have arrived from the far-flung corners of the empire, stopping off here before preparing to head east where they will battle the armies of Queen Zenobia, the powerful ruler of the Palmyrene Empire.

As Helena begins her barmaid duties, she senses someone watching her – a lavishly dressed officer seated in the corner of the room. Her colleague spots it too, and when she comes over with a wry smile, they quietly identify him as Flavius Constantius. Helena's eyes widen. She knows the name, of course, because everyone knows the name: he's one of six tribunes in the legion camped at Naissus, a commanding officer who oversees around 800 soldiers. Now he approaches her, and strikes up a conversation. Everyone else in the place seems to melt away as they talk, and before she knows it the tavern is closing up for the night. It's not long before the two are talking about making things official.

With Roman officers allowed to reside with their wives and concubines in camp, Helena begins living with Constantius, and a little while later she gives birth to a son. He's named officially as Flavius Valerius Constantinus, but he's known as Constantine.

During the child's early life his father is largely absent on military campaigns, leaving Helena to raise Constantine alone. In 293, under the Tetrarchy system, Emperor Diocletian names Constantius Caesar of the Western Empire. In return for this new role he is forced to abandon the low-born Helena in favour of a more politically advantageous marriage.

## THE ROMAN GODS VERSUS CHRISTIANITY

The society in which Helena lives is deeply superstitious. There are numerous Roman deities, including Mars (god of war), Cupid (god of love), Pluto (god of the underworld), Bacchus (god of wine and fertility) and the king of the gods, Jupiter (god of the sky and thunder). They are accompanied by a wide array of demigods – humans who have attained semi-divine status, such as Hercules and Romulus – and countless nature spirits, like Faunus (god of the forest and fields), nymphs such as the Oreads of the mountains and Dryads of the trees, and the Lares, who are household spirits. When people are ill, they might call upon Hygeia, the spirit of health; when they're struggling with advancing years, they may make sacrifices to Geras, the spirit of old age. With no harmonizing sacred text that defines the vast array of beliefs and practices, nor a single central godhead, one worshipper may, for instance, choose to make sacrifices to a god associated with their city or type of work, while their neighbour might revere a physical object or natural place, such as a river or a tree.

### THE PANTHEON

There was no more famous temple in ancient Rome than the Pantheon. A vast circular-shaped building, its concrete dome, 142 feet in diameter and 71 feet high, was one of the great engineering feats of the age and the largest in the world until the fifteenth century. In fact, the Pantheon we see today is not the original. That was a much simpler construction erected on the same site by the consul Marcus Vipsanius Agrippa during the reign of Augustus. This first temple burned down in AD 80. The current version was finished in the reign of Hadrian, although it may have been started by his predecessor, Trajan. Although the name 'Pantheon' suggests a temple to all the gods, its exact purpose remains a mystery. It became a symbol of the spread of Christianity when the Byzantine emperor Phocas gifted the building to Pope Boniface IV, who had it reconsecrated as the Church of St Mary and the Martyrs in 609.

Christians and Jews, on the other hand, believe in one God as the creator of all things, and view any form of worship directed towards other deities as idolatry.

The number of Christians living in the Roman Empire has grown for over 200 years, initially spurred by what was likely intended to be a routine execution on the outskirts of Jerusalem. When a Roman prefect named Pontius Pilate ordered a Judaean holy man to be crucified, he could not have known that this macabre administrative task would set the Roman world on a new path. Exactly when Jesus of Nazareth, also known as Jesus Christ, was put to death is disputed, although it was likely either 7 April AD 30 or 3 April AD 33. What stands his execution apart from countless others is that, several days after his death, his disciples said they saw him alive, resurrected from the dead. Whether one believes that story or not, his disciples certainly did, and they set out to tell the Roman world what they claimed to have witnessed. These followers came to be known as 'Christians', and they proved particularly effective in their mission, with women and slaves among the most likely adopters of their faith. Key tenets of Christian belief – equality, loving one's neighbour, humility, serving others and forgiveness – seemed to stand in stark contrast to Roman values of military power and conquest, and the new faith's emergence was viewed with suspicion by Rome's elites.

Exactly how to deal with Christians has always been a difficult question. Around 110, for instance, Pliny the Younger – then a provincial governor in what is now Turkey – wrote to Emperor Trajan for advice on just that matter. Trajan suggested that if an accused was found guilty of being Christian, they must be punished, but advised that they should not be hunted for trial in the first place – a sort of 'don't ask, don't tell' policy. Nonetheless, despite there being no empire-wide attack on Christians before 251, localized outbreaks of persecution do occur. Followers of the faith who refuse to renounce their beliefs are recorded as being thrown to wild animals, burned alive or beheaded. The *Annals*, written by Tacitus less than a century after Jesus's death, state that all who admit to being Christian are variously covered with the skins of animals and torn apart by dogs, nailed to crosses or burned alive as human candles – that gruesome alleged favourite torment of the infamous Nero.

In times of persecution, many Christians go into hiding and adopt coded communication – for instance, the symbolic use of the image of a fish. The Greek letters that spell the word for fish – *ichthys* – are used as an acronym representing the phrase *Jesus Christ, God's Son, Saviour*. It's said that if a Christian meets another person whom they suspect is a fellow follower of their outlawed religion, they might draw half an oval in the dirt with their toe. If the other person mirrors the arc, forming a fish shape, it confirms their shared faith. Many believers also discreetly wear the fish symbol on rings and pendants, or carve it into the walls of their hiding places.

But by 300, Christians have benefited from around forty years of relative freedom, with some estimates putting as many as six million people (10 per cent of the empire's population) as followers of the religion. It is evidence of the authorities' long-term decision to hold back from a large-scale clampdown, with adherents particularly numerous in the east and in urban areas.

However, in 303, Christian communities face a significant threat. After nearly twenty years of rule, Diocletian suddenly ramps up the victimization of Christians in an era later known as the Great Persecution. He demands that every Roman offer sacrifices to the gods in exchange for a document acknowledging their compliance. But with their belief in one God, Christians refuse, even under threat of torture and execution. While many Christians continue to live openly and relatively unaffected, some communities feel compelled to go into hiding, fleeing to wilderness areas where the Romans have less presence or control, or living underground in catacombs.

An unexpected result of this mistreatment is that the Christians' stoic resistance actually encourages many newcomers to explore Christianity themselves. As one Christian chronicler, Tertullian, had earlier noted, 'the blood of the martyrs is the seed of the Church'.

## CONSTANTINE BECOMES EMPEROR

Though little is written about Helena in this period, there is much speculation among historians that she herself may have been inspired by these martyrs. Even so, when Diocletian and his co-emperor Maximian abdicate in 305 and Constantius becomes Augustus of the West, there is not yet any evidence to suggest that Helena has adopted Christianity.

As he settles into his new role, Constantius invites his son Constantine to accompany him to Britannia. It's the first time in twelve years the father and son have seen each other. While in Britannia, the young man gains popularity among his father's soldiers, so much so that when his father dies the following year, his soldiers switch their allegiance to him personally. In 306 his newly acquired army proclaim him emperor. According to the nascent rules of the Tetrarchy it's an unlawful claim, and soon four rival generals are fighting for absolute control over the empire.

Helena returns to the history books of Rome in late 306 as Constantine formally names her *nobilissima femina* ('most noble woman'). And with the Tetrarchy system now in tatters, and the empire spiralling into another civil war, within a few years change will come to Rome in the most unlikely of forms.

## THE BATTLE OF THE MILVIAN BRIDGE

It's 28 October 312, and Constantine's forces are assembled on the banks of the Tiber near Rome. Constantine mounts his horse and begins to canter towards the water's edge. Ahead of him lies the Milvian Bridge, a chokepoint across a wide, fast-flowing section of the river. If his forces are to launch their attack on Rome, there's no option but to cross this bridge. But it's not as simple as that. Maxentius, who also seeks to become the sole emperor of Rome, has packed the bridge so tightly with troops that it resembles a fortress rather than a river crossing.

Constantine looks back at his soldiers, each bearing a Christian symbol known as a chi-rho, a monogram comprising the first two letters of the Greek word for 'Christ', freshly painted on to their shields. Constantine has not been a long-time follower of the faith. But, as the story goes, at some point prior to this critical battle he saw a heavenly vision of a burning cross in the sky. Moved by the experience, he ordered each of his soldiers to paint the Christian symbol on their shields. Now, with a roar from his men, the battle commences. Constantine lifts his sword as a volley of arrows fills the sky, and his cavalry thunders into the frontline of men attempting to hold the bridge for Maxentius. Screams and the clang of metal reverberate as soldiers chaotically slash at each other in a desperate bid to advance, or hold their lines, or simply save their own lives. Amid the stampede, Maxentius falls into the swollen river and is swept downstream. Weighed down by his armour, his lifeless body will be fished out of the water hours later, by which time his troops are decisively routed.

Constantine now seizes Rome, becoming the uncontested leader of the Western Roman Empire. And though the veracity of his alleged vision of the blazing cross has been the subject of much speculation, the battle of the Milvian Bridge marks a turning point in Rome's history. Constantine attributes his victory to the Christian God, and it's around now that the Roman Empire begins to soften its response to that emerging religion.

## IMPERIAL FAVOUR

Shortly after his victory, Constantine issues the Edict of Milan, an agreement between himself, the ruler of the West, and Licinius, the ruler of the East, that promotes religious tolerance, especially for Christians. The accord marks a rapid decline in persecutions throughout the empire, and with Christians once more able to openly proselytize and benefitting from Constantine's patronage, the number of adherents grows exponentially.

In 324 Constantine defeats and kills Licinius, bringing the whole empire under his rule, including the more numerous eastern Christians. In the same year, Helena is formally given the title Augusta ('Empress'), making her the first imperial mother to receive this honour. By this time she has converted to Christianity, and now becomes a significant influence on Constantine's religious policy throughout the empire. Though its followers remain very much a minority, the faith now has a major supporter at the heart of government.

New churches begin appearing all over Europe. Where the Circus of Nero once served as a killing ground for early Christians, and the suspected burial place of Peter the Apostle, Constantine builds a church dedicated to the martyr that will one day become the centre of the Christian world.

## HELENA IN THE HOLY LAND

By the time Helena arrives in Jerusalem in 326, Christianity is rapidly growing and establishing itself across the empire. Constantine is eager to identify, authenticate and preserve significant objects relating to the life of Jesus Christ. His mother's journey to the region is a personal religious pilgrimage, but also a highly symbolic gesture of Rome's new espousal of the faith it has persecuted for centuries.

She finds evidence of that persecution at every turn, but ironically it is Emperor Hadrian's prior mistreatment of Christians in the region that helps her locate the place where Jesus was said to have been resurrected. Pilgrims had been travelling to venerate the exact spot throughout much of the first century, but had Hadrian not erected the Temple of Venus over the location in an attempt to deter them, the site may have been lost to time. Now, with the authority of Rome at her disposal, Helena orders that the temple be destroyed and the Church of the Holy Sepulchre be built in its place.

Helena also directs the construction of a church over a cave in Bethlehem, where early Christians claim Jesus was born, and builds another church on the Mount of Olives, from which it's said that Jesus ascended into heaven. The fifth-century Roman historian Socrates Scholasticus notes that she arranges for large quantities of earth from Jerusalem to be shipped to Rome to be used in the foundations of the Basilica of the Holy Cross. In later Christian legend, Helena will be remembered as the discoverer of the True Cross itself, the sacred relic of Christ's crucifixion.

Helena's work helps locate some of the most notable finds in the Holy Land. And although she does not discover all of these sites herself, her careful documentation of their locations helps centralize the Christian faith around a specific geographical area – a region that will be venerated for millennia to come.

## CHRISTIANITY'S LEGACY

Back in Rome, the adoption of Christianity incrementally leads to the city's pagan temples being abandoned or repurposed into Christian churches. Throughout the fourth century, effigies of Roman gods that once dotted the city are gradually replaced with crosses. It's a time of far-reaching social change too. The enthusiasm for gladiatorial combat goes into decline, for example, while the early Church establishes orphanages, hospitals and food banks for the poor. Sundays are instituted as days of rest, and the Church also imposes strict codes around sex and marriage, banning polygamy, divorce and sexual relationships outside monogamous heterosexual marriage. Just as importantly, Christians are promoted to positions of power in the military and civilian administrations.

In 330, four years after Helena's journey to the Holy Land, Constantine declares Constantinople (modern-day Istanbul) the new capital of the Roman Empire. It's a perfect spot on a natural peninsula from which to defend the whole empire, and he devotes enormous energy and resources into developing it not only as the imperial capital but as the centre of Christendom. Christian symbolism is etched everywhere in its buildings and artworks.

Around the same time as he founds his new power base, Constantine faces the grief of losing his mother. He may console himself, however, with the knowledge that she has witnessed the first signs of an extraordinary blossoming of the faith she worked so hard to cultivate. Christianity is no longer the marginalized faith of a persecuted minority, and in the years to come it will emerge as the dominant religion of the Roman elite, crucial in moulding imperial policy. Indeed, all but one future Roman emperor will profess to be Christian. When, in the 360s, Emperor Julian attempts to mitigate the impact of Christianity by reviving pagan practices and restoring pagan temples, he makes little long-term headway. In contrast, the Catholic Church, which develops in this era, will one day become the longest-established institution in the western world, able to trace its history back two millennia.

Rome may have taken over the western world, but now Christianity appears to have taken over Rome.

# 18

# ATTILA: HARBINGER OF DOOM

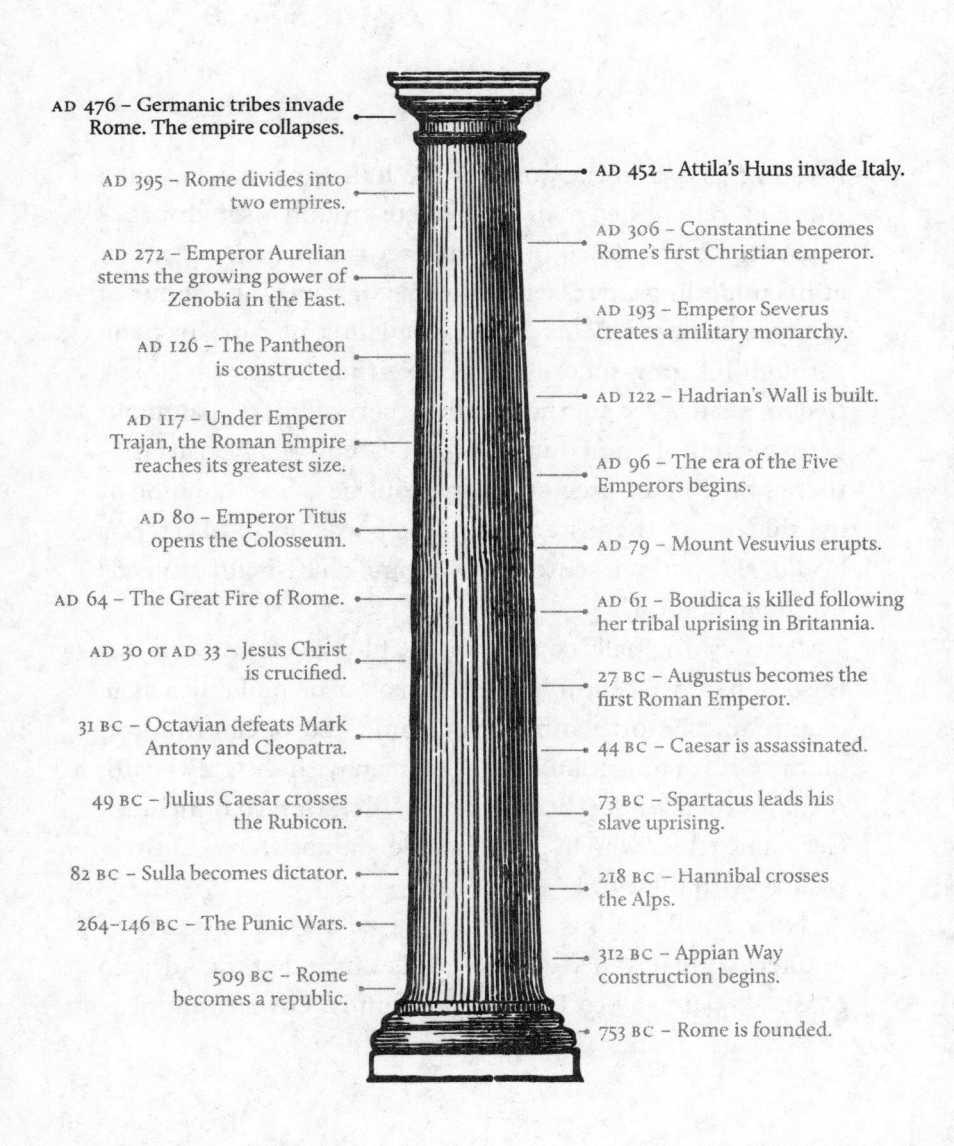

AD 476 – Germanic tribes invade Rome. The empire collapses.

AD 395 – Rome divides into two empires.

AD 272 – Emperor Aurelian stems the growing power of Zenobia in the East.

AD 126 – The Pantheon is constructed.

AD 117 – Under Emperor Trajan, the Roman Empire reaches its greatest size.

AD 80 – Emperor Titus opens the Colosseum.

AD 64 – The Great Fire of Rome.

AD 30 or AD 33 – Jesus Christ is crucified.

31 BC – Octavian defeats Mark Antony and Cleopatra.

49 BC – Julius Caesar crosses the Rubicon.

82 BC – Sulla becomes dictator.

264-146 BC – The Punic Wars.

509 BC – Rome becomes a republic.

AD 452 – Attila's Huns invade Italy.

AD 306 – Constantine becomes Rome's first Christian emperor.

AD 193 – Emperor Severus creates a military monarchy.

AD 122 – Hadrian's Wall is built.

AD 96 – The era of the Five Emperors begins.

AD 79 – Mount Vesuvius erupts.

AD 61 – Boudica is killed following her tribal uprising in Britannia.

27 BC – Augustus becomes the first Roman Emperor.

44 BC – Caesar is assassinated.

73 BC – Spartacus leads his slave uprising.

218 BC – Hannibal crosses the Alps.

312 BC – Appian Way construction begins.

753 BC – Rome is founded.

It's summer 452 in the north of the Italian peninsula, and a short, barrel-chested man somewhere around his mid-forties is pacing up and down in his military camp, barking orders at his underlings. Dressed in flexible lightweight armour of the type favoured by his people, the Huns, he runs his hand through his grey-specked beard. Neither he nor his horse, tied up nearby, are adorned with the sort of finery that might be expected of someone of his elevated social position – there's no gold or precious stones on the sword hanging at his side, or on the fastenings of his boots or on his steed's bridle. He exudes a sense of power and charisma that needs no augmentation.

Possibly originally coming from China or central Asia, for the best part of a century the Huns have been building a huge empire to the north and east of Rome's European frontier, on the Great Hungarian Plain. The man with the grey beard, Attila, is their leader, head of a confederation that includes Germanic tribes who live side by side – if not always entirely easily – with the Huns.

Now, Attila and his army are poised on the outskirts of Aquileia, a great walled city a few miles inland of the Adriatic coast – a gateway to Rome's heartlands. For two months now Attila's forces have had Aquileia under siege but so far its fortifications have held strong. When the inhabitants first heard word of the imminent arrival of the Huns they evacuated children, the old and infirm. Those left behind are demonstrating impressive resilience. But what else should Attila expect of a town whose womenfolk once, long ago, cut off their hair to make ropes for the defensive catapults that saw off an earlier invader? Every time the Hunnic forces attempt to advance, they are met by barrages of arrows, hot tar and burning oil. And at night, the inhabitants sneak beyond their defensive walls to ambush their attackers, setting fire to their siege weapons, raiding their camps and poisoning their water supplies.

But today Attila seems buoyed. As he gives his commands, he spots a bird rising in the cloudless sky, taking flight from its nest high up on the city battlements. This, he is sure, is a good sign – the equivalent of a rat fleeing a sinking ship. It is only a matter of time, he tells his men. The troops prepare their siege engines with renewed energy. They prime their catapults with great boulders, ready machines that can fire off metre-long bolts, and check the battering rams they intend to use to smash through the city gates.

A few hours later, after weeks of toil by the Huns, Aquileia's walls begin to buckle. At Attila's signal, his men spill into the city. The locals, weak from deprivation, do their best to fight back, but it's a lost cause. Attila looks on with satisfaction as he sees a posse of enemy fighters struck down one after another. He revels in the sound of sharpened blades slicing through flesh, the artistic spray of blood.

Attila and his Huns have a reputation as barbarians among the Romans. But what does that even mean? A conventionally nomadic people, they do not have a grand tradition of producing cultural and political institutions like the Romans. Their rise is thanks to their skill as warriors, their mastery of the bow striking fear into their enemies. So Rome condemns them as a barbarian 'other', never mind its own ruthless martial history.

Yet the word does Attila an injustice. Even as he revels in his victory here, he is nothing if not sophisticated. He is a master strategist and a charming and skilful negotiator when necessary, who sees violence as a means to achieve his broader aims. What is clear to him is that Rome is vulnerable, and by exerting just the right pressure he can enrich his own people at their expense. The razing of Aquileia is a blood bath, but it's also a study in the art of controlled brutality.

And a warning to Rome that its enemies are getting the upper hand.

*The Roman Empire in the fourth century underwent profound changes, particularly with the rise of Christianity. Yet no one alive in that century could possibly have foreseen Rome's calamitous demise in the next. By the time of Attila's attack on Italy in 452, the empire's Western and Eastern halves are on different trajectories. It is the Eastern realm that is doing much better. The Western Empire is on its knees – its frontiers under constant threat of invasion, its interior populated by an array of hostile tribal groups and its old institutions tearing apart at the seams. The city of Rome itself is a shell of what it once was, its status more symbolic than anything else. But where did it all go wrong? And where will it all end?*

## A GATHERING STORM

When Emperor Constantine dies way back in 337, he leaves an empire newly unified around Christianity and not obviously in a state of decay. Its Eastern and Western wings largely seek to cooperate with one another, and when Constantine's sons share the empire between themselves, in effect they are following a tradition going back to Marcus Aurelius in the second century. But though one of them, Constantius, eventually claims dominion over both halves, it will soon become clear that this is only a temporary arrangement. Over the next decades, the empire will oscillate between division and unification. Yet for now, it seems to be business as usual in terms of defending the imperial frontiers and administering its territories. Even when, in 363, the pagan Emperor Julian suffers a disastrous loss on campaign against the Sasanians that costs him his life, the empire is able to regroup remarkably effectively. Rome is nothing if not durable, or so it appears.

With the second half of the fourth century underway, the so-called barbarians are increasing in might and ambition – groups such as the Alemanni, Burgundians, Franks, Vandals and Goths. As the Huns make ground west of the Volga river, they prompt a westward migration of many of these Germanic peoples whose lands they swallow up. Rome's frontiers are under constant pressure. On top of that, its long-standing problems of economic decline and manpower shortages mean it simply doesn't have the resources to take on all comers.

In some instances, the new inhabitants agree to become Roman allies. But even then, friendly relations cannot be relied upon. Take, for example, the Goths. Perhaps 100,000 of them – men, women and children – have been displaced by the Huns, so in the 370s they ask to be allowed to settle in Roman territory. It's a migration crisis of epic proportions, which the Romans struggle to handle (and, at times, clumsily attempt to exploit). Within a few years diplomacy has collapsed and the newcomers are fighting the Romans of the Eastern Empire at the battle of Adrianople (in Thrace, in modern-day Turkey), killing at least 10,000 (around two-thirds) of their men in a single afternoon. Among the victims is the Eastern emperor, Valens. They then remain locked in a bloody six-year-long war, only settled when Theodosius, for now the sole ruler of both wings of the empire, agrees major concessions to the enemy.

But when Theodosius himself dies in 395, he will go down in history as the last emperor to rule the entire Roman Empire. His sons, aged seventeen and just ten, become rulers of one half each, and the two parts will never again be unified.

The sporadic rivalry between the Eastern and Western divisions of the empire leads to both sides calling into service fighters from various of the Germanic tribes when necessary. This continuation of Rome's tendency to civil war both drains Roman power and increases the military expertise of potential Germanic enemies, embedding these tribes further into Roman territory, culture and society. A recipe for disaster.

## THE SACKING OF ROME

By the early years of the fifth century – when Attila is still a child, growing up as a nephew of the joint kings of the Hunnic people – Rome is a pitiful shadow of its former self, no longer even the first city of the Western Empire. Theodosius's successor in the West, Honorius, established his court at Mediolanum (modern-day Milan), but these past few years it has relocated to Ravenna, where Julius Caesar once based himself ahead of crossing the Rubicon. A port on the Adriatic coast ideal for trade, Ravenna is surrounded by swamps and lagoons that promise defensive strength. It is considered a safer choice than Rome, which bears the scars of long years of corruption and political instability, as well as economic hardship. Once the world's greatest metropolis, Rome is today symptomatic of the malaise overtaking the Western Empire, which has fallen behind its Eastern counterpart in terms of prosperity. The Eastern Empire benefits from being plugged into the rich trade routes that bring produce to and from the lands beyond its borders. Militarily it is harder for potential invaders to penetrate, its food supplies are more secure, even its administration is more stable. The Western Empire wants what the Eastern Empire can offer, but has little that the East wants, creating a serious imbalance between the two. An imbalance that increasingly manifests as war.

In August 410 an army of one of the Germanic tribal groups, the Visigoths, makes its way from the Adriatic along the Via Salaria (or 'salt road') towards Rome. Their leader, aged somewhere around forty, is Alaric, one of those 'barbarians' born outside the empire but who has lived most of his life within its boundaries. He speaks Latin and has fought for the Eastern Empire against the Western Empire on two previous campaigns. Having spent years caught up in the crossfire of imperial politics, what he really wants is land where his people might settle and some sort of recognition within the empire. As such, he has prodded at Italy for the past several years, hopeful of winning some sort of deal. But currently the Western Empire's politics are dominated by a party with a distinctly anti-barbarian stance. It seems like it's now or never for the Visigoth leader.

Although Ravenna is the real centre of power these days, Rome still possesses symbolic value – and a weak underbelly. When Alaric arrives at its walls, its defenders initially repel his army. But late in the night, disgruntled slaves within Rome open the gates to the Visigoths. The attackers immediately set fire to buildings and loot its great palaces, and – with the help of the rebellious slaves – slaughter anyone who dares resist them.

Amid the violence, however, there is some restraint. It is said, for instance, that the Visigoths' Christian faith compels them to protect sacred objects which they deposit at the Church of St Peter, and they spare the lives of those who have managed to take sanctuary there too. But the assault goes on for three days, at the end of which they leave laden with plunder and captives, including the emperor's own half-sister. For the first time in 800 years, Rome has been sacked.

Taking the Via Appia southwards, the Visigoths raid settlements as they go, enriching themselves before a planned crossing to North Africa. But then Alaric falls ill and dies, so instead his successor negotiates with Ravenna for territory in Gaul – a province that has seen a surge in Germanic settlers displaced by the Huns further east.

## AUGUSTINE AND *THE CITY OF GOD*

The sacking of Rome in 410 brings questions of religious faith to the fore. Those who still believe in Rome's traditional deities consider the attack as evidence that Christianity has weakened the empire, breaking the bond with the old gods who had seen it prosper. The fact that the Visigoths themselves are Christians (although not Roman Catholics) confirms the suspicion many have of Christianity's negative impact. Meanwhile, Rome's Christians are left pondering why they, the righteous, have suffered such trauma.

Augustine of Hippo, a bishop in Roman Africa, sets about trying to address some of these questions in his landmark work of Christian philosophy *The City of God*, published in the 420s. Emphasizing the spiritual over the political and temporal, he argues that the history of the world is one of continuous conflict between good and evil. The sacking is a symptom, then, of the moral collapse that has long overtaken Roman society and which Christianity can help reset. Besides, he points out, hasn't Rome suffered plenty of setbacks long prior to the arrival of Christianity? For Augustine, the real point is that the true rewards of faith will come in the next life; the trials faced in this one must thus be endured and faith maintained in God's great plan. His work nonetheless attests to the deep damage the attack of 410 has done to Romans' sense of themselves, and their place in the universe.

## ENEMIES EVERYWHERE

By the 430s the Hunnic Empire beyond the Eastern Roman Empire's frontiers is huge and thoroughly immersed in Roman imperial affairs, sometimes raiding, at other times providing mercenary forces for either its Western or Eastern wings. A complex relationship develops so that they routinely expect and receive payment from the Romans, either for services rendered (as the Romans typically think of it) or as tribute (as the Huns themselves consider it). They are, it is sometimes said, at once slaves and masters of the Romans.

By the middle of the decade, both of Attila's ruler-uncles are dead and control of the Hun realms falls to both him and his brother, Bleda. The pair meet with a delegation from the Eastern Roman Empire at Roman-held Margus (modern-day Požarevac in Serbia) and, while seated on horseback in the Hunnic tradition, attempt to reach agreement on their future relationship. In reality, they want to see what they can extort from the Romans in return for leaving them alone. At the end of the talks, the Romans agree to pay Attila and his brother a hefty quantity of gold each year – about 700lb of the stuff (worth about £3.5 million today). The siblings also secure the hand-over of two Hun princes who opposed them and have been claiming refuge with the Romans. Once these political prisoners are in their custody, Attila and Bleda have them impaled on 9-foot-long wooden stakes. Thus satisfied, they retreat back to their own territory, financially richer and their authority stronger than ever.

The Western Empire, meanwhile, is less concerned with the Huns right now than the Vandals. After crossing the Rhine frontier in 406, this Germanic group have raided across Gaul and Spain, and in 429 they invaded Roman North Africa. For a while this latter territory has been the empire's most prosperous province and increasingly its bread basket, but the Vandals are strangling the supply of grain from there and diverting it to other regions. With Rome unable to muster a sufficient military response, the Vandals establish a kingdom consuming large chunks of Rome's African territory.

While the Western Empire has been at war with the Vandals, Attila has been working in partnership with one of its leading generals, Aetius. The pair go back a long way. Amid all the upheaval in the Roman Empire, Aetius – who comes from an important political family – was once a child-hostage in the Hunnic lands, forging a friendship with his close contemporary, Attila, that has endured. When Roman has been set against Roman in more recent years, Aetius has sometimes turned to his old Hunnic comrades to provide mercenary muscle. As commander-in-chief of the Western Roman army, in 436 he calls on Attila to help carry out a devastating raid on Borbetomagus (modern-day Worms in Germany), which has fallen under the control of the Burgundians. A combined force under Aetius and Attila razes the city to the ground, with as many as 20,000 of its inhabitants reckoned killed in a single day. The Burgundians take many years to recover from the assault. The episode also illustrates Attila's fluid relationship with the Romans – making deals with the Eastern Empire one year, allies with the Western Empire the next.

## HUNS ON THE MARCH

Into the early 440s Attila's focus shifts once more to aggression against the Romans, and specifically the Eastern Empire. The truth is, Attila and Bleda's power relies on feeding the Hun military machine. Theirs is not a settled dominion that thrives in peacetime; war and plunder are essential to their economic model. Therefore, when spies from Constantinople report that the current emperor, Theodosius II, is set to deploy his forces in support of a planned assault by the Western Empire on the Vandals (evidence that the Eastern and Western Empires are not always at loggerheads) – and having seemingly defaulted on some of the gold payment due to the Huns – Attila senses opportunity.

Claiming a Roman bishop has strayed into Hun territory, Attila demands still more gold from the Romans. When Theodosius refuses, Attila has his grounds for attack. It's around 442 when he and Bleda target the fortress city of Naissus (in modern-day Serbia), a location steeped in symbolic value as the birthplace of Constantine the Great. It is strategically important too, located on a *via militaris* – a 24-foot-wide superhighway – that leads directly to Constantinople. But it is a mighty garrison, protected on one side by a river and its great walls unbreached for at least 200 years. The Huns will need all their ingenuity to break through. They build a pontoon bridge to manoeuvre siege towers, on top of which stand their elite archers. Behind are iron-pointed battering rams, and in the rear, scaling ladders for a final assault. The defenders put up an impressive fight, raining down wagon-sized boulders on the Hunnic ranks, but in the end they cannot hold out against this plethora of military technology.

With Naissus still smouldering, a rumour sweeps the Huns that the fabled Sword of God – or, as the Romans will call it, the Sword of Mars – has been found by an itinerant Hun herdsman and presented to Attila. As it is told, when Attila clasps the hilt, he receives a divine revelation that he will become ruler of the entire world. There can be no greater spur to Hunnic ambitions, but the prophecy raises a conundrum too. If power resides in Attila, what is to become of his co-ruler, Bleda? The question is resolved around the middle of the decade, when Bleda is apparently killed on a hunting trip. There are those who assume Attila is behind the death, despite the absence of direct evidence. But with Bleda now gone, and armed with a prophecy of greatness to come, Attila begins to plot the capture of Constantinople.

## THE DESTINY OF NEW ROME

Constantinople, or the New Rome as some call it, is an enormous and magnificent city of some 300,000 to 400,000 people, serving as a bridge between two continents. It far outshines Rome these days, surrounded by the sparkling waters of the Bosporus and defended by miles of walls – three layers of them in total. Some say that it is impregnable, and the claim is given greater credence when it withstands a massive earthquake in 447. But it sustains damage nonetheless, so now, its walls vulnerable and the Sword of God at his side, Attila fancies his chances.

This same year, he begins his advance, first through the territory of modern-day Bulgaria and on to the fortress city of Ratiaria – headquarters of the Roman fleet patrolling the Danube – which his army razes. Then it's a race down the *via militaris* until he meets a Roman army somewhere along the 120-mile length of the Utus river. He dispatches the enemy and proceeds to claim city after city, the cumulative death toll unrecorded but catastrophic, and the number taken captive in six figures. In Constantinople, a large part of the terrified population decides that flight is the best, if not only, option.

Now, with the grand prize beckoning, something remarkable happens. Attila orders his men to turn back before they reach Constantinople's gates. It is true that Theodosius has agreed to pay him still more gold in tribute, and Attila now rules swathes of former Roman territory in the Balkans, so perhaps this is enough to satisfy him. Divine sword or not, maybe he recognizes that the imperial capital might be a step too far even for him. Better to retreat unscathed with the Romans schooled in just what a threat he poses, his fearsome reputation standing him in good stead for the future. Whatever the reason, Constantinople endures. But Attila still needs to keep the war-wheel turning to satisfy his warrior people. Having taken perhaps as much as he can from the Eastern Empire, now he targets the weaker Western Empire. But how will he justify an assault?

## MARRYING INTO THE FAMILY

Ravenna in 450 is a city on the up. New churches, official buildings and even a circus are rising from the mud. The empire's finest artists and craftsmen are slogging away to turn this place into one worthy of the title of imperial capital.

But in its palace, tempers are frayed. The Western emperor, Valentinian III, is having a ferocious showdown with his sister, Honoria. They're clashing over the question of who she is going to marry. Valentinian wants her to choose someone suitably unambitious who will not pose a threat to his rule. But with her hair pulled tightly back, Honoria has a determined look about her. She is not about to allow herself to be strongarmed into a match against her will. Instead, she agrees to swear an oath of chastity until a fitting husband can be found.

She does not keep to the agreement for long. But when she starts an affair with her business manager, Valentinian has the man executed. Devastated by the loss and furious at her brother, Honoria strikes upon a plan. When her mother was young, she'd run off and married a barbarian. Perhaps Honoria will do the same. Though she's likely never met the man, she writes to Attila for his help in finding her a suitable match, enclosing a signet ring as proof of her serious intent.

When Attila receives the message, he hits on what he thinks might be the perfect solution. *He* will marry Honoria – and he accepts her ring as proof of their betrothal. Furthermore, he sends a delegation to Ravenna to demand Honoria is given the title of joint ruler of the Western Roman Empire, which will make him emperor by marriage.

It's fair to say that Attila does not represent the safe option Valentinian has been angling for. Though he knows that by blocking the union he can expect the Hun to use it as grounds for an attack, he strenuously refuses the demands, and sets about preparing for the repercussions.

At about the same time, Attila also sends representatives to the new ruler of the Eastern Empire, Emperor Marcian, to complain about missed tribute payments. Deep down, he surely knows that both his marriage proposal and his demand for more gold will be turned down. But that will give him the right, as he sees it, to wage war on either of the empires, which will in turn leave both to wonder which will be first in his sights. He is sowing uncertainty among his enemies.

In 451 he makes his decision. It is the Western Empire, more vulnerable than its Eastern counterpart, that he will hit first. He begins by moving into Gaul, which is already destabilized by the presence of so many Germanic peoples with limited loyalty to the Roman cause of unity. The invasion has an intriguing subplot. Attila is pitting himself directly against Aetius, supreme head of the Western Empire's armies. The old brothers-in-arms are about to become battlefield enemies.

## GO WEST!

Attila heads west with an army perhaps 50,000 to 70,000 strong – an amalgam of Huns, various Germanic tribesmen absorbed into his territories and, as time goes by, prisoners picked up en route. They swarm through the European countryside, ransacking farms and villages whenever their supplies run low. They have no concern for winning hearts and minds, staying in no place long enough to elicit anything but fear and resentment.

They advance into Gaul, Attila in the vanguard with his elite horsemen. They take several great cities before heading to Durocortorum (now Reims), where it will be reported that the local bishop is decapitated as he recites a psalm. But moves are afoot to counter the Hun surge. In Tolosa (now Toulouse), which the Visigoths have adopted as their capital, King Theodoric is determined to resist, as is Aetius. The two agree to unite their forces, an uneasy alliance built on common enmity. More barbarian groups with their own axes to grind against the Huns join the coalition.

Soon, at a site known as the Catalaunian Plains around 80 miles south-east of Paris, Attila draws his enemies out for what promises to be a decisive battle. As the sun rises on 20 June 451 Attila sits in his saddle, directing his men to their positions. Hun warriors – including himself – will keep to the centre, while mercenaries and those who have been forcibly conscripted are ranged around them, fodder for the Roman legionaries. Using a classic Hun gameplan, he expects his horse-archers to fire off volleys to pin back the Roman infantry until they can be encircled. But when the two sides at last hurtle towards each other, it is the Romans and Visigoths who secure the vital high ground. Even Attila's brilliantly drilled ranks cannot win while battling uphill. Then, as defeat seems inevitable, it's reported that Attila delivers a blockbuster speech to inspire his men. Once more they race up the hill, and this time Aetius is separated from his men and Theodoric is felled by an arrow. This promises to be an extraordinary victory, even by the standards of the Huns.

It's now, however, that the pendulum swings again. Theodoric's son rallies his cavalry, who charge at the oncoming Hun forces, scattering them. Those who are able to flee do so, but soon the earth is awash with blood as the bodies pile up. Attila still stands, but as he takes in the carnage around him, the odds of him surviving a reversal like this seem slim. And then . . . nothing. The final assault by Aetius and his men never happens. Is it possible that Aetius has spared his old buddy? Or have the Visigoths forced his hand, opting to head home to lick their wounds with victory secured rather than pursue complete annihilation of the Huns?

Attila leads his forces away. He is thousands of men down and their caravan of plunder gained on campaign has been pillaged. He realizes that if he has any chance of maintaining his position at the head of his people, he needs to avenge this defeat, and quickly. But first, it's back to the Great Hungarian Plain to regroup.

## MISSION ITALY

Less than a year later, in the spring and summer of 452, Attila launches a lightning strike against Italy, pouring through the Alps on the way to bringing Aquileia to its knees. Next it is fast across the Po Plain, that great verdant gateway to the Alps upon which Hannibal descended all those centuries before. Soon he is battering down the doors of the imperial palace in Mediolanum. Inside, his eye alights on a painting. It depicts a selection of Roman emperors seated on golden thrones, dead Hun warriors lying at their feet. Attila now commissions an artwork of his own. This new piece has him on the throne, with the Roman emperors heaving sacks of gold that they pour at his feet.

From here, it might seem logical to head to Ravenna, where his 'fiancée' Honoria still resides. Instead, Attila turns to Rome. By the autumn he is around 300 miles north of the city, but his forces are getting bogged down, caught up in a succession of lengthy and draining sieges. Disease is taking its toll too, and he lacks the kind of supply network that once served Rome's own armies so well for so many centuries. His men close to dead on their feet, he now hears reports that the East's emperor, Marcian, is launching attacks on the Hunnic homelands. Like a jewel, Rome sits tantalizingly before him, but there are too many demands on his resources. So he turns round and heads for home.

In early 453 Attila takes a new wife, and celebrates the event by drinking too much wine before heading for the marital bed. Next morning, his bride cannot wake him. His bodyguards batter down the door to find that he has suffered a haemorrhage and choked to death on his own blood. A suitably gruesome death for a man who will go down in history for his bloodlust and barbarism.

Without their great leader, the Huns quickly go into decline and never again threaten Rome. But the Western Empire cannot escape the long-term impact of Attila's rule. He has cost them a fortune in tribute, defensive costs and war damage. Yet perhaps even more damagingly, the rise of the Huns has changed Europe's demographics, forcing inside the Western and Eastern Empires Germanic groups that once harboured hostility to the Romans from beyond the imperial frontiers. It's a development with which it never gets to grips.

## ENDGAME

Rome, of course, can be its own worst enemy too. Valentinian and Aetius descend into bickering, with the emperor eventually accused of killing his finest military leader with his bare hands, before Aetius's bodyguards dispatch the emperor in revenge.

In 455 the Vandals who have established themselves in North Africa make the quick dash across the sea to launch their own attack on the city of Rome, and this time there is no escape. The new Western emperor, Maximus, is slaughtered and the city plundered for fully two weeks. After the intervention of Pope Leo I, at least most of its people are spared and its buildings left largely undamaged, but Rome is spent as a stronghold. Then, in 476 it falls to Odovacer, a Roman general of Germanic descent whose army comprises a disparate array of soldiers, including Germanic mercenaries unhappy with what they have hitherto been granted as reward for fighting for Rome. Together, they complete the job that Attila and his Huns never saw through. After the city is seized and the last Western emperor, Romulus Augustulus, is deposed, the Western Empire at last collapses in on itself. A story that began well over a thousand years ago with one Romulus ends ignobly with another of the same name.

Even so, to say that 476 marks the end of the Roman Empire is to do what remains a disservice. The Eastern Empire will continue for another thousand years, known as the Byzantine Empire, before itself being subsumed into the Ottoman Empire for centuries more to come. But the fall of the Western Empire brings down the curtain on arguably the greatest polity of classical antiquity. The glorious – and frequently inglorious – era of ancient Rome is finished.

# POSTSCRIPT:
# THAT WHICH IS LEFT BEHIND

'A great civilization is not conquered from without until it has destroyed itself from within.'

– *The Story of Civilization*, Will and Ariel Durant

The decline of the Western Roman Empire marks a gear change in global history, in which the age of classical antiquity gives way to the Middle Ages. But even as 476 provides a convenient cut-off point, it does not signify a 'light-switch' moment when everything suddenly changes.

Just as Rome's ascent took centuries, so too will its decline. No single event causes the collapse of the Western Empire. To what extent the above quotation points us in the right direction is ripe for debate. A maelstrom of reasons have been suggested over the years. Economic downturn. Dynastic rivalries and political instability. Over-reliance on an increasingly overstretched military. The impossibility of maintaining an empire so vast. The emergence of powerful enemies, both outside and within its frontiers. Moral degeneracy. Religious upheaval. Natural disasters and environmental change . . . The list can seem endless.

But whatever you may choose to identify as the major causes of its decline, the Roman Empire does not simply disappear in the fifth century. In the west it is replaced by myriad new kingdoms whose rivalries recalibrate western Europe, ushering in the often decried medieval period. True, life in these times can be nasty, brutish and short, but so too was it for most who were not part of a privileged, educated elite in the classical era. Indeed, the medieval age likely offers a better experience for many of those who might otherwise have been slaves had Rome maintained its control of the lands in which they live. For most, like the subsistence peasants working the land, the change in day-to-day living standards is perhaps not as noticeable as you may think. This is a time of transformation, certainly, but without necessarily being immediately transformative. Evolution rather than revolution.

And of course the Eastern Empire continues to thrive for centuries to come. Indeed, under Justinian in the sixth century it hits new heights and produces iconic cultural achievements like the Hagia Sophia that stands to this day as a mesmerizing presence in Istanbul (as Constantinople will become). Even the city of Rome, seemingly brought low beyond revival, bounces back. By the time Michelangelo is precariously perched on scaffolding in the early sixteenth century painting the ceiling of the Sistine Chapel, he is working in a city that is not merely the beating heart of Italy but of the entire Christian western world.

As we look around us today, in the twenty-first century, we cannot fail to see the legacy of this extraordinary civilization, built out of the dust to become a world power, its rise and decline a subject of eternal fascination and instruction. Its shadow remains everywhere we look – in language and culture, technology and architecture, religion, politics and the law. An ancient civilization that has never stopped informing the present.

Mighty, sophisticated, cultured, brutal, magnificent Rome.

# ACKNOWLEDGEMENTS

This book is dedicated to the talented team behind the *Short History of...* podcast. Co-author Dan Smith and I would particularly like to thank the show's producer, Kate Simants, for her assistance with editing this book, as well as Jo Furniss, Nicole Edmunds and Jeff Dawson, whose podcast episodes about Boudica, the Colosseum and Julius Caesar have aided our research on these topics. We are also grateful to Dr David Gwynn from Royal Holloway University for providing invaluable academic insights throughout the writing process. Thank you to Chris McDonald for helping shape the book and Ned Merz for his research assistance.

It has been a pleasure collaborating with Henry Vines and his talented team at Penguin Random House, and thanks to my publishing agent, Emily Barrett, for working closely and diligently at each step of this journey.

Thank you to Martin Hargreaves for his impressive cover artwork.

# ABOUT THE AUTHOR

Pascal Hughes is the founder and CEO of Noiser, a podcast production company creating qualitative podcasts for history lovers. Noiser is the home of eleven history-related podcasts, with a total of over 300 million downloads to date across its network. Pascal writes material for some of the podcasts.